Seeking Inalienable Rights

NUMBER 112
Centennial Series of the Association of Former Students
Texas A&M University

Seeking Inalienable Rights

TEXANS AND THEIR QUESTS FOR JUSTICE

Edited by Debra A. Reid

TEXAS A&M UNIVERSITY PRESS
College Station

First edition

This paper meets the requirements of ANSI/NISO Z39.48-1992 (Permanence of Paper).
Binding materials have been chosen for durability.

Library of Congress Cataloging-in-Publication Data

Seeking inalienable rights : Texans and their quests for
justice / edited by Debra A. Reid.—1st ed.
p. cm. — (Centennial series of the Association of Former
Students, Texas A&M University ; no. 112)
Includes bibliographical references and index.
ISBN-13: 978-1-60344-118-6 (cloth : alk. paper)
ISBN-10: 1-60344-118-2 (cloth : alk. paper)
ISBN-13: 978-1-60344-123-0 (pbk. : alk. paper)
ISBN-10: 1-60344-123-9 (pbk. : alk. paper)
1. Civil rights movements—Texas—History—19th century. 2. Civil rights movements—Texas—History—20th century. 3. Civil rights—Texas—History—19th century. 4. Civil rights—Texas—History—20th century. 5. Minorities—Civil rights—Texas—History—19th century. 6. Minorities—Civil rights—Texas—History—20th century. 7. Texas—Race relations—History—19th century. 8. Texas—Race relations—History—20th century. 9. Citizenship—Texas—History—19th century. 10. Citizenship—Texas—History—20th century. I. Reid, Debra Ann, 1960– II. Series: Centennial series of the Association of Former Students, Texas A&M University ; no. 112.
F395.A1S44 2009
323.0973—dc22
2008051135

The photo on the title page is courtesy of the North Texas History Center, McKinney.

In memoriam,
Robert A. Calvert

To Donna Hannah-Calvert
and
To Robert A. "Bob" Calvert's Extended Family

Contents

Acknowledgments

The contributors owe a tremendous debt to their dissertation advisor, mentor, former colleague, and friend, Robert A. "Bob" Calvert (1933–2000). He held strong opinions about the road to equal rights and justice, and his convictions proved inspirational. Through his teaching, writing, advising, and personal friendship, he helped steer contributors Patricia Gower, David Chrisman, James Seymour, and Debra Reid through coursework at Texas A&M University and toward careers in academia. Bob's friendship and intellectual sparring sustained Alwyn Barr and George Green. Steve Wilson and Brian Behnken address topics that Bob lived through and fought for—the civil rights movement of the 1960s. In Bob Calvert's memory, and to his wife, Donna Hannah-Calvert, and to Bob's extended family, we dedicate this anthology.

Bob was born in Stephenville, Texas, on October 18, 1933, and he pursued higher education with conviction. Bob attended Southern Methodist University and North Texas State University before he entered the U.S. Army in 1954. After discharge, he completed his BA (1957) and MA (1960) in history at North Texas, and then he taught in Denton, Texas, public schools and at Nicholls State College in Thibodaux, Louisiana, before earning a PhD in history at the University of Texas at Austin. He taught at Texas A&M University in 1965 and 1966 then accepted a tenure-track position at North Texas State University in 1967, where he attained the rank of associate professor. He rejoined the history faculty at Texas A&M University in 1975. At the time of his death on November 30, 2000, Bob coordinated graduate studies in the Department of History at Texas A&M and served the Texas State Historical Association, the Texas A&M University Press, and his colleagues and students tirelessly.[1]

During his nearly forty-year teaching career, Bob Calvert worked to put scholarly treatment of minorities in the hands of university students. His earliest efforts gathered writings on Mexican Americans from a variety of disciplines. He edited, along with Renato Rosaldo and Gustav L. Seligmann Jr., *Chicano: The Beginnings of Bronze Power,* originally published in 1973, because "never have the Mexican Americans been included as an integral part of the American past. Seldom have scholars viewed Mexican Americans as an active force in the socio-historical picture." Robert E. Kreiger Publishing issued a second edition, titled *Chicano: The Evolution of a People,* in 1982.[2]

Bob then strove to make Texas history more accessible to college students. He and coeditor Robert Wooster selected eighteen articles from the *Southwestern Historical Quarterly* that addressed a "broad range of Texas history from the earliest Spanish exploration to the present." *Texas Vistas* first appeared in 1980 and remains in print, and the third edition was issued in 2006. Minority Texas history likewise benefited from his efforts. In 1981, Bob and his friend Alwyn Barr coedited *Black Leaders: Texans for Their Times,* a collection of nine essays that focused on individuals not otherwise treated in full biographical studies. The essays, written by scholars at various stages of their careers, addressed black Texans' contributions from the Spanish-Mexican era through slavery and Reconstruction and during the century between the First and Second Reconstructions. Then in 1988, in an effort to influence the writing of Texas history even more, Calvert, with the support of his colleagues at Texas A&M University and other noted Texas historians, met to discuss Texas historiography. Calvert and Walter Buenger, a friend and colleague, coedited the anthology that resulted, *Texas through Time: Evolving Interpretations,* in 1991. The essays helped graduate students recognize the avenues open to them for new research in Texas history. Most contributors to this volume benefited from these publications and have taken this opportunity to return the favor.[3]

Seeking Inalienable Rights evolved out of conference papers delivered by several of Bob Calvert's former PhD students at the 2007 conference of the Texas State Historical Association. All the speakers studied with Calvert, and he either served on their committees or advised their dissertations: David K. Chrisman, Ricky Floyd Dobbs, Patricia E. Gower, Debra A. Reid, and James B. Seymour. Two of Calvert's friends and colleagues, Randolph "Mike" Campbell and Walter Buenger, chaired and commented on the papers. Mary Lenn Dixon, editor-in-chief at Texas A&M University Press, expressed interest in the project at that time, and without her enthusiasm this anthology would not have materialized.

Practical assistance came from across the nation. Nancy Lurkins, a graduate student at Eastern Illinois University, read through the anthology at an early stage and identified some photographs. Martin J. Hardeman of Eastern Illinois University, and Lynnea Magnuson of Soldier's Memorial Museum in St. Louis, Missouri, helped hone Reid's contributions. Three anonymous reviewers likewise offered comments on the anthology that strengthened individual submissions and improved the overall quality. Several helped secure quality images, including Daniel Alonzo and Grace McEvoy of the Austin History Center; Bev Cruse of Eastern Illinois University; Joel Draut of Houston Metropolitan Research Center; Stephanie Elmquist, Ashley Kempenski, and Laura Ramos of Cushing Memorial Library and Archives, Texas A&M University; Taffey Hall of Southern Baptist Historical Library and Archives, Nashville, Tennessee; Kathey K. Hunt of The Kaufman County TXGenWeb Project Site; Bryan Lean of North Texas History Center, McKinney; Patrick Lemelle of the Institute of Texan Cultures, San Antonio; Naomi Taplin of Texas Baptist Historical Collection, Dallas; and Kristin Welzenbach of the National Agricultural Library, Beltsville, Maryland.

Bob advocated for more study of the history of underrepresented Texans, and his enthusiasm for this cause proved infectious. We hope this collection about diverse Texans and their quests for rights and justice inspires future students as Bob inspired us.

NOTES

1. Robert Arnold Calvert, "Vita," in "The Southern Grange: The Farmer's Search for Identity in the Gilded Age" (PhD diss., University of Texas at Austin, 1969), n.p.; Robert A. Calvert, "Curriculum Vitae," Personnel Files, Department of History, Texas A&M University. "Biographical Note," Robert Calvert Papers, 1970–1995, Southwestern Writers Collection, The Wittliff Collections at the Alkek Library, Texas State University–San Marcos, http://alkek.library.txstate.edu/swwc/archives/writers/calvert.html (accessed July 14, 2008). Larry Hill, "Memory of former TSHA President Robert A. Calvert," *Southwestern Historical Quarterly* 104, no. 4 (April 2001): 590–95.

2. Renato Rosaldo, Robert A. Calvert, and G. L. Seligmann Jr., "Preface [to the Original Edition]," *Chicano: The Evolution of a People,* 2nd ed. (Malabar, Fla.: Krieger, 1982), n.p.

3. Ralph A. Wooster and Robert A. Calvert, *Texas Vistas: Selections from the Southwestern Historical Quarterly* (Austin: Texas State Historical Association, 1980), vi. Alwyn Barr and Robert A. Calvert, eds. *Black Leaders: Texans for Their Times* (Austin: Texas State Historical Association, 1981).

Introduction

Debra A. Reid

When John Brooks Porter, a farmer and businessman in Terrell, Texas, died in 1917, his obituary described him as "liberal, broad minded, his leadership was always desired." He earned such accolades for his service in the Confederate army, the fortune he amassed as a Texas farmer and businessman, his regular attendance at the Methodist church, and his financial investments as a stockholder in the First National Bank of Terrell. Yet, others may not have agreed that Porter "commanded the unstinted respect of everyone who knew him," as the obituary claimed. In fact, many resented white male authority and the political and economic influence often associated with it, and not all Texans accepted the inequality that resulted from it. After the Civil War, Texans increased their efforts to ensure government protection of their personal liberty as well as their "class," defined by their economic situation, race, sex, or ethnicity. Porter, for example, enjoyed personal liberty as a white male head of an elite household in the New South. Ironically, others often suffered an individual or collective loss in the wake of such success. *Seeking Inalienable Rights* explores how selected Texans pursued their rights by contrasting the ideal of personal liberty in a capitalist society with the reality of the price that others paid for rights expansion.[1]

Texas historians Robert A. "Bob" Calvert and Arnoldo De León believed that "the state's two most prominent ethnic minorities: African Americans and Mexican Americans," began the civil rights movement but that "organized campaigns . . . were not launched until the early twentieth century." *Seeking Inalienable Rights* pushes the start of rights campaigns earlier, into the post–Civil War time period, and broadens the concept of "organized" campaigns to include efforts of men and women who allied within classes and sought political and professional influence and economic opportunity, in addition to government protection of defined rights.[2]

Texans conceptualized their rights broadly to include natural or inalienable rights (life, liberty, property, and happiness) as well as civil rights (government-protected rights including but not limited to speech, assembly, and justice). Contributors to this volume explore how personal interest in inalienable rights coalesced into quests undertaken by socioeconomic, racial, ethnic, or gender-defined groups, or classes. These studies indicate that in Texas, a multiethnic southern state, classes most frequently found their potential for rights attainment defined more by racial and ethnic distinctions than by economics or gender. Only under certain circumstances could cross-race or cross-ethnic efforts emerge to challenge the dominant white male culture for political control and therefore influence rights acquisition and ultimately justice.[3]

Historically, Texans seeking to expand rights found support through liberal or loose interpretation of the U.S. Constitution and the Texas Constitution. In general, liberal constitutionalists advocated legislation that increased protection of rights for groups as well as individuals. Such liberal thinking, when combined with persistent, broad-based activism, helped a greater number of Texans enjoy full citizenship. Yet, expansion of civil rights at any given time did not guarantee protection of rights in perpetuity. Conservative constitutionalists believed that expansion of civil rights had the direct consequence of infringing upon and compromising the conservative's perceived rights. This resulted in counter movements undertaken by special interest groups, partisan organizations, and even religious denominations, each of which sought to preserve authority in the face of legislation and practices that jeopardized its status.

Bob Calvert claimed that the civil rights movement had, in fact, died by 1982, when Americans lost faith "that the national government could play a positive role in erasing social and economic injustice." In response to the civil rights movement, conservative constitutionalists rationalized that individuals, not the national government, bore responsibility for securing liberty. Calvert saw this as a dismal failure, and he argued that "the Second Reconstruction ended with the least expensive price paid by whites—equal protection before the law—and denied the most difficult sacrifice—the granting of social justice and equal economic opportunities."[4]

The goals that Texans pursued in their quests for justice emerged predominately from English common law. At least four centuries of court decisions established Englishmen's legal rights, including the right to trial before a neutral judge and jury; the guarantee that one's life, liberty, and property could not be seized without proper legal processes; the right of the accused to be informed of charges levied; the understanding that the accused was innocent until proven guilty; and the right of the accused to legal counsel and the right to present witnesses. Immigrants to the British North American colonies brought these ideas

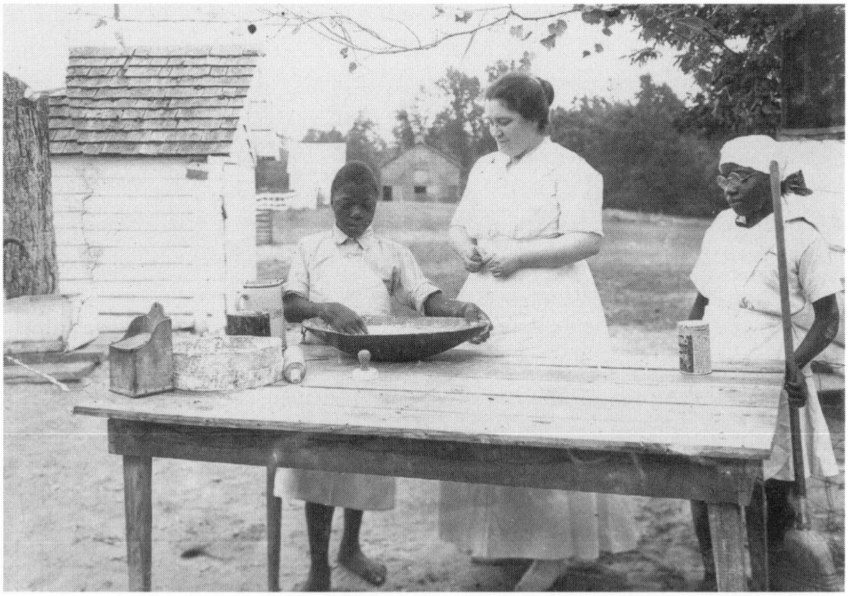

Fig. 1. African American girls being instructed in biscuit making near McKinney, Texas (Collin County). A USDA photographer documented these activities of Mrs. McGee's Home Demonstration Club in 1917. Credit: North Texas History Center, McKinney.

with them and used them to justify revolution and independence. In 1776, the Declaration of Independence expanded civil rights within the United States to include natural or inalienable rights: "We hold these truths to be self-evident, that all men are created equal, that they are endowed by their Creator with certain unalienable Rights, that among these are Life, Liberty, and the pursuit of Happiness." In 1791, ratification of the Bill of Rights made explicit specific rights that the U.S. government had to protect. Any Texan of British origin, as well as immigrants from other states within the United States, comprehended common law ideas and believed the government bore responsibility for protecting their inalienable as well as civil rights.[5]

The constitution adopted by the Republic of Texas in 1836 during the heyday of the "common man" included the U.S. Constitution's preamble verbatim, and it outlined seventeen rights, including two that clearly defined the relationship of citizen to government. First, "all men, when they form a social compact, have equal rights, and no man or set of men are entitled to exclusive public privileges or emoluments from the community." Second, "all political power is inherent in the people, and all free governments are founded on their authority, and instituted for their benefit; and they have at all times the inalienable right to alter their government in such manner as they might think proper." The remaining declarations defined freedom of expression, worship, protection of property, and security of justice in keeping with British common law and U.S. ideals of justice and rights.[6]

The Texas Constitution of 1836 made clear the discrepancy between the ideal of equal rights under the law as articulated by enlightened political philosophers and that held by many Texans. Section 9 under General Provisions defined the institution of slavery, declaring that "all persons of color who were slaves for life previous to their emigration to Texas, and who are now held in bondage, shall remain in the like state of servitude; provided, the said slave shall be the bona fide property of the person so holding said slave as aforesaid." Obviously, "persons" of color were not part of the "mankind" that law was created to protect. Furthermore, government in Texas existed to protect the property rights of free white Texans because section 9 prohibited free persons of African descent from migrating into the state without consent of Congress. The Texas Constitution also prohibited Texans from freeing their slaves without consent of Congress, so the property rights of Texans who wanted to manumit their slaves were restricted because the interests of committed slaveholders took precedence. This race and class bias continued into the twentieth century, and it existed in the spirit of the law, even though the actual law, particularly the Fourteenth Amendment to the U.S. Constitution, included statements about equality and protection for all, because these were not enforced.[7]

The tension between idealized concepts of personal liberty and the reality throughout the South precipitated a constitutional crisis as the Union dissolved. Texans joined the Confederate States of America on March 5, 1861. After the war, Texans convened a constitutional convention, revised the state constitution, and ratified it during November 1869. The 1869 Texas Constitution accepted the U.S. Constitution as the supreme law of the land, prohibited slavery, and recognized that all people should have equal rights under the law. Subsequently, the Texas legislature completed additional requirements for readmission by ratifying the Fourteenth and Fifteenth Amendments to the U.S. Constitution, and Texas rejoined the United States officially on March 30, 1870.

Texans chafed under national authority until 1875, when they convened another constitutional convention. Delegates proposed a total rewrite of the 1869 Constitution. Texans adopted it during February 1876. This constitution, though amended, still defines the form and function of Texas government. The 1876 Constitution began with a long bill of rights. But section 1 of the bill of rights protected the "general, great and essential principles of liberty and free government," rather than the rights of the people. Section 2 of the bill of rights vested political power in the people, pledged them to preserve a republican form of government, and protected their "inalienable right to alter, reform or abolish their government in such manner as they may think expedient." Section 19 included oft-repeated inalienable rights: "No citizen of this State shall be deprived of life, liberty, property, privileges or immunities, or in any manner disfranchised, except by the due course of the law of the land." Of course, the 1876 Texas Constitution set up a system of government based on state sovereignty, ruled by the white majority with the authority to deny rights if they followed legal means.[8]

Conservative Texans had to devise new strategies after the Civil War to respond to efforts to expand civil rights during the First Reconstruction. They believed that all were not equal, that some were dependent, and that government could justifiably "harm" another's life, liberty, or possessions in the interest of the collective good. Legislators responded by systematically restricting others' access, largely by making others subordinate on the basis of their race, ethnicity, sex, or economic situation. The legalized discrimination that resulted from such legislation compromised humanitarian principles.

Texas as a multiethnic state provides an important case study to explore the ways that competing definitions of rights and special interest legislation have affected rights. "We the people," as expressed in the U.S. and Texas constitutions, held great promise, but strict interpretations of who belonged to "the people" undermined minority quests for justice. The federal system of government that vested some powers in the U.S. government and some in state governments created situations where neither government assumed responsibility to protect rights. Furthermore, even if courts ruled legislation unconstitutional, government often ignored or defied the courts' interpretations. The philosophy of federalism combined with conservative constitutionalism made it possible for southern states to legislate racial discrimination and for the national government to sanction it. Not until the Second Reconstruction did liberal constitutionalists ally with minorities, but even then they often disagreed among themselves over the best course to follow to secure liberty and justice.

Essays in *Seeking Inalienable Rights* all explore how Texans tried to protect their rights under the state's constitution. Their efforts precipitated intense legal, personal, and societal battles because the individuals involved often believed that they would have to surrender their rights if others' rights expanded. The struggles varied depending on the personal relationships of those involved, but friendship or patronage did not protect everyone because self-interest often undermined efforts to share goals. Thus, the securing of rights became a contest that often yielded mixed results. Sometimes the protagonists realized justice, sometimes they failed and even lost ground as their efforts stimulated counter movements.

Alwyn Barr addresses the strategies that African American men pursued between the 1860s and 1890s to realize some influence in local economic development. They followed their dreams by organizing and attending self-segregated conventions that welcomed participants regardless of class. The convention platform allowed black Texans to express their concern over restricted political influence, decreasing opportunities for economic advancement, and increased racial oppression. The proceedings of the conventions indicate that attendees did not agree on solutions to abuses of their rights, but they exercised their freedom of expression in their quest to secure liberty and protection of their property interests.

George Green's study of organized labor shows how both laborers and railroad corporations believed they deserved protection of their rights. During an era of laissez-faire constitutionalism, laborers had little hope as they challenged railroad corporations to offer higher wages, ensure safer working conditions, and provide more benefits to workers injured on the job. Without governmental regulation, individuals as well as classes of workers were denied full protection of their rights to life, liberty, and property. Ironically, corporations likewise believed in their rights to liberty and to accumulate property. Law theorists had applied concepts of rights to corporations as well as individuals, and court decisions protected corporation's rights as a result. Green explores how laborers tested laissez-faire constitutionalism in Texas during the 1880s.

Debra A. Reid analyzes a clash that pivots around societal perceptions of race and gender in rural Texas. White men sought to keep cheap black labor on Texas farms and women in the farm home. Yet, black men sought economic independence and landownership, while women, both white and black, sought education and influence. In the face of change in rural Texas, white male Democrats preserved their control by defining competent Texas farmers as white men and instituting government programs to meet their needs while marginalizing women and blacks. The contest played out among individuals and special interest groups—and within state and national government agencies. By 1915, Texans codified both race and gender segregation by creating the Negro division and the home demonstration program of the Texas Agricultural Extension Service.

James Seymour focuses on the efforts of white Texas women to secure the vote during the Progressive Era. They based their quest, in part, on the effort to offset the votes of ethnic Texans, specifically Texans of German descent, during a time of war. The white Texas women believed that if their vote could not be counted, the votes of German Texans would threaten the security of the United States. Seymour's essay indicates how well-heeled white women believed the vote could be used to help them secure their power in the struggle against arbitrary power (in favor of control over their life, liberty, and property) and against enemies.

Patricia Gower studied the actions of white Texans during the Progressive Era, as well, and has documented the ways they implemented efficient city government in Dallas and San Antonio. They did so to protect their self-interest and economic investments. White progressives legislated and zoned cities in ways that limited other residents' access to municipal services, all in the name of ensuring that those who lived in better neighborhoods and ran the cities' businesses could benefit. As a result, the whites with power secured protection at the expense of those without power, or with less power. Gower documents those who put up barriers rather than those isolated by the barriers. The commission form of government effectively silenced minority voices in both Dallas and San Antonio. Yet, ethnic and cultural relationships affected the degree of isolation and marginalization. White elite control triumphed in Dallas because all black and poor voices lost influence. Zoning isolated poor and minority residents to neighborhoods outside the city limits. Dallasites therefore did not have to devote expensive services to the poor minority community. In San Antonio, however, blacks and Hispanics found that they could participate in elections but only when politicians needed their votes and paid accordingly. Yet, no area of San Antonio emerged as privileged.

David Chrisman analyzes the contest that played out among members of the Southern Baptist Convention and the General Convention of Texas over inclusion of African Americans during the 1950s and 1960s. More conservative members defended their systematic denial of access to minorities on the basis that their equal inclusion would weaken society as white Texans knew it. Many white ministers refused to embrace the spirit of integration and allied with their parishioners in the fight to maintain their tradition of race-based discrimination and segregation. These ministers and parishioners sought liberty (authority over their own church's and convention's rules). Obviously the goals of those who sought to exclude some people, in the interest of protecting their right to worship without blacks, proved unpalatable to those who sought more inclusive policies. Perhaps neither blacks nor whites wanted to integrate their congregations, but the traditional racial exclusion was outdated, and many sought more inclusive policies. The contest that played out, mostly between white Texans because they held the decision-making authority, reflects the ageless conflict over which rights should be protected— those of the greater public good, which might be better served by inclusive policies, or individual liberties, which could protect a member's right to not share his church pew with a person of color. Chrisman makes clear that the moral justification of slavery remained an undercurrent of the debate in southern and Texas Baptist churches in the 1950s and 1960s.

Brian Behnken explores how minorities failed to ally in a mutual quest to overcome race bias in Houston during the 1960s. Instead, tension over who should be guaranteed their inalienable rights divided Hispanic Americans and African Americans. Hispanic leaders believed their rights, because they qualified as "white," would be compromised if blacks also gained access. In 1964, Felix Tijerina grudgingly integrated his restaurant in Houston and, as a former national president of League of United Latin American Citizens

(LULAC), continued his discourse about race and rights that helped keep the black and Mexican American civil rights movements separate. Then, legislation to integrate Houston's public schools passed in 1970, and Mexican Americans perceived this as a new assault on Mexican American rights. Mexican Americans used the courts to protect their rights to go to school with people like them (whites), and not to integrate with blacks, but other Mexican Americans wanted to force integration on "whites." The lack of unity among Mexican Americans eventually led to the failure of self-segregated Huelga schools. In contrast, African Americans felt threatened by the "brown" movement that seemed determined to further isolate black quests for equal access. Fundamentally each group—white, black, and brown—believed that the other thwarted their efforts to secure life, liberty, and property.

Steven Wilson focuses on two court cases that developed from Mexican and Mexican American attempts to expand student rights during the immediate post–civil rights years (1965–1969) in Hidalgo County, Texas. He argues that well-publicized civil rights marches in the South energized a generation that founded the *Chicano* movement in Texas and other Southwestern states. Yet, the civil rights struggles of black college students did not inspire them; rather, the efforts of migrant laborers and César Chávez motivated *Chicano* activists. Mexican Americans launched their race-conscious challenge to segregation and rights restriction in two rural school districts (Edcouch-Elsa Independent School District and La Feria Independent School District) in South Texas. Ultimately, the *Chicano* movement's contribution to civil rights history was not in achieving a separate sphere for themselves, but in bringing about a meeting of the minds with the Mexican American generation. This allowed a "brown" quest for rights to triumph, but did the victory come at the price of a quest for color-blind rights and justice?

Black and brown as well as white Texans participated in the conservative backlash that resulted from rights expansion. During late 1968, as the conservative backlash to the civil rights movement exacerbated racial tensions and compromised opportunities for citizens to enjoy increased rights, historian Bob Calvert thought about the failure of rights struggles. He introduced his history of the southern Grange by noting its failure: "the organization expected to correct the evils that led the farmer to the Grange, [but] it could not do so." The words seem even more poignant when contextualized in light of Dr. Martin Luther King's assassination, the rise of militant black power, and increasingly violent civil rights and anti–Vietnam War protests. Yet, liberal-minded Texans were not willing to revert to inequity given the century of struggle that had consumed their energies between the First and Second Reconstructions.[9]

In 1969, Texans ratified amendments to the Texas Bill of Rights. The preamble, in one brief sentence, linked protection of rights to the "general, great and essential principles of liberty and free government." Then the first section indicated that Texas, while "a free and independent State," still had to recognize the authority of the Constitution of the United States. This proved a major departure from earlier versions of the Texas Constitution, and it reflected the culmination of goals at the heart of the civil rights movement, namely, the requirement that southern states comply with the Fourteenth Amendment. The amended Texas Bill of Rights moved equal rights from section 19 to section 3. But the text did not change: "All free men, when they form a social compact, have equal rights, and no man, or set of men, is entitled to exclusive separate public emoluments, or privileges, but in consideration of public services." Regardless, it conveyed that the state of Texas would be more committed to enforce the concept. Yet, not until 1972 did Texans further amend section 3 to read: "Equality under the law shall not be denied or abridged because of sex, race, color, creed or national origin."

During the early 1970s, Bob Calvert helped tell the history of rights struggles undertaken by Mexican Americans, the nation's second largest minority, in *Chicano: The Beginnings of Bronze Power,* much as C. Vann Woodward had done for African Americans with *The Strange Career of Jim Crow.* Calvert and coeditors Renato Rosaldo and Gustave L. Seligmann Jr. explained that the collection did "not offer solace to those who supported the *status quo,* nor succor to those who want[ed] to upend it, rather it is intended to help explain to Chicanos and to scholars how and why change came." They selected essays that showed "Chicanos in the act of fomenting their own revolution." And the editors "hope[d] to encourage other students to investigate and write a multi-ethnic history of what is in fact a multi-ethnic nation."[10]

Historians heeded the call and remain busy in Texas archives ferreting out stories of rights expansion and retrenchment. Increased focus on racial and ethnic groups, and women and gay rights have significantly expanded understanding of the ways that a triracial population distributed in rural as well as urban locations affected rights expansion and contraction. Historically, racism, sexism, and class bias blinded conservative Texans to the cost that their own self-interest exacted on the public good. Yet, the Texas Constitution pledges that "equality under the law shall not be denied or abridged because of sex, race, color, creed, or national origin." These high expectations remain just within reach but just beyond a firm grasp.[11]

NOTES

1. "Mortuary: Captain J. B. Porter," *Kaufman Herald,* October 19, 1917, http://www.txgenweb5.org/txkaufman/obituary/porterjb.htm (accessed March 22, 2007).

2. *Handbook of Texas Online,* s.v. "Civil Rights Movement," http://www.tsha.utexas.edu/handbook/online/articles/CC/pkcfl.html (accessed August 7, 2007).

3. Political philosopher John Locke conceived of natural rights as "that being all equal and independent, no one ought to harm another in his Life, Health, Liberty, or Possessions." "Mankind" shared one "Community of Nature," and in that community "there cannot be supposed any such *Subordination* among us, that may Authorize us to destroy one another." Locke went on to explain the mutual responsibility to protect the rights to which every man was entitled: "When [Man's] own Preservation comes not in competition, ought he, as much as he can, *to preserve the rest of Mankind,* and may not unless it be to do Justice on an Offender, take away, or impair the life, or what tends to the Preservation of the Life, Liberty, Health, Limb or Goods of another." Locke, section 6 of chapter 2: Of the State of Nature, *Second Treatise on Government,* 1690, http://libertyonline.hypermall.com/Locke/second/second-frame.html (accessed July 31, 2007).

4. Robert Calvert, "The Second Reconstruction," in *Conflict & Change: America, 1939 to Present,* eds. William W. MacDonald, Walter A. Sutton, John M. Carroll, and Frank W. Abbott (St. Louis, Mo.: River City, 1983), 87, 97. C. Vann Woodward, in 1955, used the term "Second Reconstruction" to define the emerging civil rights movement. Woodward, *The Strange Career of Jim Crow,* 3rd rev. ed. (New York: Oxford University Press, 1974), 6–7, xv–xvi.

5. English Bill of Rights, 1689, http://www.yale.edu/lawweb/avalon/england.htm (accessed July 31, 2007).

6. The Constitution of the Republic of Texas, March 17, 1836, http://www.republic-of-texas.net/archives/founding/cons1836.shtml (accessed July 31, 2007).

7. Section 9, under General Provisions, The Constitution of the Republic of Texas.

8. Article I, Bill of Rights, Constitution of the State of Texas, 1876, http://tarlton.law.utexas.edu/constitutions/text/IART01.html (accessed July 31, 2007).

9. Robert Calvert, "The Southern Grange: The Farmer's Search for Identity in the Gilded Age" (PhD diss., University of Texas at Austin, 1969), iv. Calvert published several articles on civil rights issues including "The Second Reconstruction," in *Conflict & Change: America, 1939–Present,* ed. William W. MacDonald (St. Louis, Mo.: River City, 1983), 87–99; "The Civil Rights Movement in Texas," in *The Texas Heritage,* ed. Ben Procter and Archie P. McDonald (St. Louis, Mo.: Forum Press, 1980), 147–64; "Protest Movements," in *Encyclopedia of Southern Cultures,* ed. Charles Reagan Wilson and William Ferris (Chapel Hill: University of North Carolina Press, 1989); 1173–76. Calvert, along with Alwyn Barr, also edited *Black Leaders: Texans for Their Times* (Austin: Texas State Historical Association, 1987).

10. Renato Rosaldo, Robert A. Calvert, and Gustav L. Seligmann Jr., "Preface" [to the original edition] in *Chicano: The Evolution of a People,* 2nd ed. (Malabar, Fla.: Robert E. Krieger, 1982), v, vi. For an abridged version, including only three sections of the six-section anthology, see Renato Rosaldo, Robert A. Calvert, and Gustav L. Seligmann Jr., *Chicago: The Beginnings of Bronze Power,* abridged ed. (New York: William Morrow, 1974). Woodward wanted to educate college students about the government conspiracy against U.S. citizens' rights, and he recounted the history of segregationist legislation, which had "effectively disfranchised [the Negro] throughout the South, firmly relegated [him] to the lower rungs of the economic ladder, and that [allowed

him] neither equality nor aspirations for equality in any department of life." Woodward, *The Strange Career of Jim Crow,* 6–7.

11. Steven A. Reich, "Soldiers of Democracy: Black Texans and the Fight for Citizenship, 1917–1921," *Journal of American History* 82, no. 4 (March 1996): 1490–92. Yvonne Davis Frear, "Generation Versus Generation: African Americans in Texas Remember the Civil Rights Movement," in *Lone Star Pasts: Memory and History in Texas,* edited by Gregg Cantrell and Elizabeth Hayes Turner (College Station: Texas A&M University Press, 2007): 203–19. Bibliographic essays by Arnoldo De León, "Texas Mexicans: Twentieth-Century Interpretations," 20–49, and Alwyn Barr, "African Americans in Texas: From Stereotypes to Diverse Roles," 50–80, and Fane Downs, "Texas Women: History at the Edges," 81–101, appear in *Texas Through Time: Evolving Interpretations,* ed. Walter L. Buenger and Robert A. Calvert (College Station: Texas A&M University Press, 1991). Subsequent essays include Arnoldo De León, "*Estudios Tejanos:* A List of Historical Literature on Mexican Americans in Texas," *Southwestern Historical Quarterly* 98, no. 3 (January 1995): 457–70, De León, "Whither Tejano History: Origins, Development, and Status," *Southwestern Historical Quarterly* 106, no. 3 (January 2003): 349–66. *Hopwood v. Texas,* decided by the Fifth U.S. Circuit Court in 1996, is considered the first successful legal challenge to racial preference in university admissions requirements since the *Regents of the University of California v. Bakke* decision in 1978. For materials on *Hopwood v. Texas* see the Tarleton Law Library at the University of Texas at Austin, http://tarlton.law.utexas.edu/hopwood/ (accessed August 2, 2007). The decision in *Grutter v. Bollinger* (2003) annulled the *Hopwood* decision. The U.S. Supreme Court expanded rights of same-sex couples in the *Texas v. Lawrence* decision (2003).

Seeking Inalienable Rights

CHAPTER ONE

Early Organizing in the Search for Equality

AFRICAN AMERICAN CONVENTIONS IN LATE NINETEENTH-CENTURY TEXAS

Alwyn Barr

African American leaders in Texas began to hold conventions during the Reconstruction period, thus joining a movement that originated in the North during the 1830s. These conventions continued every three or four years at the state and national levels until the 1890s. Before the Civil War, these meetings provided a place for black leaders to discuss the issues that concerned the African American community, such as slavery in the South and discrimination in the North. Although delegates generally agreed on the issues, solutions ranged widely. Moral arguments aimed at persuasion appeared to be dominant in the 1830s, while political action became more attractive in the 1840s. Self-help and emigration emerged to broaden the possibilities during the 1850s.[1]

After the Union defeated the Confederacy, freed African Americans in the South, including Texas, embraced the convention movement and it spread rapidly, resulting in larger national meetings and more numerous state gatherings. Black Texans alone held ten meetings in the late nineteenth century—more than historians generally have recognized. In a broader study of black thought during the postwar period, historian August Meier suggested trends in ideas and goals. He believed Reconstruction meetings focused primarily on civil and political rights, though concerns shifted in the late 1870s to a greater concentration on economic issues. By the 1880s, problems of violence and segregation came to dominate discussions.[2]

Texas conventions put forward even broader agendas than Meier proposed and reveal sustained discussion of reform that focused on economic and social goals as well as political and civil rights. The variety evident in Texas conventions raises many questions. Did organization and issues at the state level vary from the suggested pattern because of prewar variations in the size and composition of black population or the nature of economic development in a state? Did the delegates represent an African American elite, an emerging middle class, or the large working class? How did class shape their concerns? Since men filled all of the delegate positions, did they reflect gender bias or express concern for some issues that focused on women? Finally, since the climate of race relations could vary in subtle ways from state to state, how did white southerners respond to the black conventions? The following overview of African American meetings in Texas indicates a high level of awareness across class lines in the black community and a willingness on the part of African Americans to form their own organizations to seek and protect not only their civil rights but also their basic rights as citizens to social and economic opportunity.

Free blacks from the United States had entered Mexican Texas primarily during the period between Mexico's independence from Spain in 1821 and establishment of the Texas Republic in 1836, seeking the greater flexibility of a less settled region where racial discrimination seemed less pronounced. The white-dominated Republic of Texas instituted strict laws protecting the growth of slavery while limiting the expansion of the free black population. In 1860, the United States census counted over 180,000 slaves in Texas compared to only 355 free African Americans, although the number of free blacks may have been double that figure.[3]

The few free blacks scattered across the rural antebellum state had little opportunity to develop leadership skills. Nevertheless, potential leaders began to emerge after emancipation in towns such as Galveston, Houston, and Austin, that would result in the calling of conventions in these towns. Thus, black Texans entered the convention scene later than residents in some older states where larger free black communities had been expanding since the colonial period or the revolutionary era. The growth of towns that included concentrations of free African Americans facilitated leadership development in older states and led to black conventions in 1865. The first meeting of black leaders in Texas did not occur until early 1866.[4]

African Americans met for the first time to express black community views on public issues at Austin, the state capital, in March 1866. Ten black men gathered to discuss specific questions regarding which white leader and organization would be the most sympathetic and committed to aiding African Americans while allowing them opportunities for advancement. These black spokesmen titled their group the Texas State Central Committee of Colored Men, "whose business it is to see to the general welfare and interests of their race in this state."[5]

This group issued a statement in response to "An Appeal" by Episcopal Bishop Alexander Gregg of Texas, who lived in Austin. The bishop sought northern funding for missionary efforts, especially "the promotion of the best interests of the freedmen." Gregg then listed his goals as construction of churches and a hospital as well as salaries for school instructors and ministers. The Central Committee of Colored Men explained that Gregg "has no authority" to issue the appeal "from the class he proposes to benefit and if we desired funds for any purpose, we should never appoint Bishop Gregg to submit them." The black leaders clarified their concern by stating that the bishop had supported secession and "as a slaveholder, he was known to be a cruel and hard master."[6]

Instead the African American leaders endorsed the Freedmen's Bureau and hoped it would continue to protect "the Free Labor system." They described Gen. Edgar M. Gregory, assistant commissioner of the bureau for Texas, as "our friend and protector" and expressed faith that he would offer any assistance needed by the elderly or ill among the freed people. The black committee members closed their comments by explaining the new Texas Constitution written in 1866 denied African Americans any public funds for education. They might need northern aid to establish schools, but they would send a more sympathetic representative to speak for them.[7]

Public criticism of a white leader and public expression of black views required some courage only a few months after emancipation on the southern frontier where violence and intimidation occurred frequently. Most former slaves still worked on farms and plantations as wage laborers. The committee members, however, resided in Austin or small towns nearby, such as Bastrop. Austin in 1860 contained a population of only 3,494, which grew to 4,428 by 1870. Yet it ranked as the fourth largest town in Texas, with better law enforcement than rural areas and the presence of some Unionists in its population as well as federal troops. Living in town did not shield African Americans from retaliation by white employers, and black laborers in Austin probably would have feared losing their jobs if they challenged the social order.[8]

Members of the Central Committee of Colored Men held more independent economic status, which allowed them to speak. Jacob Fontaine, president of the committee, had been a preacher under slavery and continued as a Baptist minister after the war. Jeremiah J. Hamilton and Stephen Hopkins worked as skilled carpenters. Henry Madison and Henry B. Willis used their talents as shoemakers. Samuel Scott had acquired the skills of a stone mason. Madison and Willis owned property by 1870. Five of these six ranged in age from mid-twenties to late thirties, while Fontaine had reached his mid-fifties.[9] They represented the potential early emergence of a black middle class. Yet the absence of any free blacks from the prewar period may have been important in keeping the focus of the committee on economic and social issues, support for the free labor system, the creation of public schools, and continued protection by the Freedmen's Bureau. The leaders made no mention of political rights, although such hopes probably existed. In those ways the early African American leaders in Central Texas differed to some extent from their counterparts in older southern states.

Committee members expressed real concerns made all too immediate when the director of the Freedmen's Bureau in Texas, Gregory, was replaced in April 1866 for being too critical of manipulations or refusals by planters to abide by labor contracts. Yet African American leaders probably found reason to be encouraged by the cooperative efforts of the bureau and northern churches to establish schools and provide teachers in Texas. Those efforts quickly led to 90 schools and almost 4,600 students in 1866, although a variety of problems resulted in fluctuating numbers of schools and students thereafter.[10]

Congressional concern about violence and discriminatory black codes under former Confederate leaders led to the Civil Rights Act in 1866 and the Reconstruction Acts of 1867. These new laws provided protection of basic civil rights, extended voting rights to African American men, and required new state constitutions in southern states, including Texas, that had rejected the Fourteenth Amendment. Black voters joined white Unionists to form the new Republican Party in Texas, which elected E. J. Davis as governor and a majority in the Twelfth Legislature that included fourteen black members. Three members of the 1866 Committee of Colored Men played roles in the new political developments. Anderson Scroggins urged organization of the Republican Party in Austin and rejected appeals from Democrats. In Bastrop County, Jeremiah Hamilton served as a voter registrar in 1867 and later won election to the Twelfth Legislature, which established a public school system that included black children for the first time. Further measures created a state police force, with some African American members, which sought to limit violence in the state. The 1872 Republican State Convention selected Henry Willis to represent Travis County on the State Executive Committee.[11]

In support of these new political developments at the national and state levels, a National Convention of Colored Men met in January 1869. Because there appears to have been no state convention in Texas to select representatives, no Texans appeared in the list of delegates. Yet the National Executive Committee included George T. Ruby, a free African American who had come to Texas with the Freedmen's Bureau, later joined the Republican Party, won election to the state constitutional convention in 1868–69, and served as a state senator in the Twelfth Legislature. Texas sent two delegates to the National Colored Labor Convention in Washington, D.C., in December 1869—William T. Clarke and Thomas Powell, a farmer from Robertson County. Their presence reflected a continued concern for economic issues that among black Texans ranked as high as political or civil rights.[12]

African Americans seem to have found no need for a black convention in Texas to address their concerns as long as Republicans held some power in

Fig. 1.1. Lithograph depicting men and women at the January 1869 National Colored Convention, Washington, D.C. George T. Ruby, a Republican who first came to Texas to work with the Freedman's Bureau attended. Credit: *Harpers' Weekly* (Feb. 6, 1869), 85.

state government. After Democrats won a majority of seats in the legislature by the beginning of 1873, the need for a convention to discuss the changing political climate and consequences of the transition began to emerge among African Americans. In early June, Texas newspapers published the call for a convention issued by thirty black leaders from fourteen counties across East and Central Texas, ranging from Harrison County in the northeast to Bexar County in the southwest. From the Central Committee of 1866, Jacob Fontaine joined in the invitation. The core of support, twelve signers, came from Galveston on the coast. Nine members or former members of the legislature participated in the call. Community leaders held local meetings to select delegates in late June—in Houston at a Baptist Church. The statement urged discussion of issues ranging from politics, economics, and education to social and religious concerns.[13]

Delegates to the meeting arrived in Brenham, between Austin and Houston, on July 3 by railroad, horseback, or in buggies and wagons. One hundred twenty-six men gathered from sixteen counties in Central and East Texas. About one-fourth of the delegates came from Galveston, Houston, and Austin, with each town sending ten representatives. That number appears to have been greater, for state senator George Ruby and his brother, both of Galveston, represented neighboring Brazoria County. Among those who can be clearly identified, five supported their families as skilled craftsmen, while even more engaged in farming, at least half of them with property. One was employed as a teamster, while another sought to organize workers into a union. Two men operated their own small businesses. Professionals included three teachers, five ministers, and a newspaper editor. The 1873 meeting reflected the peak involvement of political leaders in any convention of black Texans, with nine present or past legislators, four local officeholders, and four men employed by the federal government in offices such as customs inspector. Half of the convention officers had government experience including its president, Norris Wright Cuney of Galveston, a federal customs inspector and leader in the Galveston Union League. The delegates also included at least seven African Americans who had been free before the Civil War, three of them sons of white fathers and slave mothers in Texas. Yet the number of prewar free black delegates in Texas ranked well below the figures for black conventions in older southern states.[14]

The public address adopted by the delegates sought "good feelings between ourselves and our white fellow citizens of the State." Black leaders reminded white Texans that slavery had kept them uneducated. Delegates then sought to explain that African American desire for civil rights did not mean "social privilege" or "social relations" with whites. The address urged open meetings by black Texans to allay white fears of black hostility. In turn delegates requested "that all acts of violence toward" African Americans "be condemned" so "law and order shall be enforced." African Americans received encouragement to seek ownership of land, while the leaders accepted the need for black Texans to pay their share of taxes to eliminate the state debt. In a move to reduce tension between African Americans and German Americans within the Republican Party, the delegates denounced any opposition to immigrants. Finally, the leaders asserted their commitment to the Republican Party and thanked its national leaders for their efforts on behalf of African Americans.[15]

Democrats elected most leaders of the state government in Texas during the 1870s, Reconstruction came to an end, the nation struggled through a depression, and African Americans encountered growing problems with violence, discrimination, segregation, and limitations on economic opportunity. A new approach to these issues emerged in the black "exodus" movement from southern states to Kansas. Historian Nell Painter, in her study of that migration, which attracted the rural working class, concluded that middle-class black leaders in the South had mixed reactions to the movement and offered only cautious support. Texas delegates to a national black convention in Nashville, Tennessee, also held diverse views about the exodus movement.[16]

In 1879 and 1880, Texas leaders held two conventions that debated the exodus idea. The 1879 meeting in Houston listed a range of problems that stimulated interest in migration, but it focused primarily on economic concerns. Delegates expressed support for the exodus if conditions in Texas did not improve—perhaps an effort to pressure large landowners for better treatment of sharecroppers. The leaders urged organization at the county level to coordinate preparations for migration, while regional leaders gathered information about possible places to relocate. Discussion focused on Kansas, but it also praised the work of S. A. Hackworth, a white Texan of Washington County, "in colonizing and encouraging the colored people in procuring homes of their own."[17]

Convention delegates in 1879 represented at least thirty-two counties across East and Central Texas, from Harrison in the north to Goliad in the south and from Galveston on the coast to Travis and Bexar in the west. Richard Allen, a contractor and former legislator from Houston, presided, but only four other delegates came from larger towns. Most of the leaders represented rural areas. Five church leaders and three teachers joined three craftsmen, three local officials, an editor, and two farmers—among the delegates who can be identified. As a group they seemed less political in their experience and closer to the black working class, which helped keep their focus on hopes for land in less settled areas.[18]

The second exodus convention met at Dallas in 1880 with a completely different group of delegates representing ten North Texas counties. Preachers and teachers provided the leadership, along with farmers and a small business owner. William R. Carson, a Methodist minister, and Allen R. Griggs, a Baptist minister, presided at the sessions. Discussion noted problems of discrimination, opposition to black voting, and the need for more schools. The delegates focused primarily on organizing "to settle in a colony in northwestern Texas." G. W. Veal came from Fort Worth with a proposal to sell the group "700,000 acres of land in Tom Green county," at one dollar an acre with "one-third down" and three years to pay the other two-thirds at 8 percent interest.[19]

On the second day, delegates formed a Texas Farmers Association that would sell 400 shares for $25 each to raise $10,000. They elected a board of directors led by Carson. He and S. H. Smothers, a teacher and secretary of the board, also received the title of agents to locate land for settlement. Veal's "land on the Pecos River" received a positive committee report. A new proposal arrived by mail from A. Ary in Tennessee, who claimed to own "sixty thousand acres of land" in Texas that he hoped to settle with African Americans including some from his home state. Some white observers feared a political goal of increasing the number of Republican voters in Texas.[20]

Despite efforts by Kansas government officials to discourage the exodus, a total of 15,000 to 25,000 African Americans migrated to the plains state, with about 20 percent coming from Texas. Several returned to their home states when they found less opportunity than expected. Plans for migration to West Texas appear to have failed for lack of funds or because less land was available than had been claimed. Yet the conventions of 1879 and 1880 brought together mostly new groups of leaders, with less political experience and more focus on economic and social concerns and goals. Their willingness to support migration separated them from some delegates in other states or at national conventions.[21]

The 1880s brought new problems in race relations as well as social and economic conditions. African Texans held four conventions from 1883 to 1889 as they expressed a high level of concern about shrinking political clout, decreased economic opportunity, and increased racial violence and discrimination. Abraham Grant, an African Methodist Episcopal Church minister, presided over delegates to the 1883 convention in Austin that criticized the United States Supreme Court decision that declared the Civil Rights Act of 1875 unconstitutional. Yet they also invited Gov. John Ireland, a Democrat, to speak to the delegates who met in the House of Representatives hall at the state capitol. Ireland advised them to avoid politics and public accommodations issues, which reflected the dominant white racial ideas of the period. A lively debate followed among the black leaders over whether to focus on civil rights or social and economic issues of the community such as temperance and homesteads. Committees considered a wide range of issues including education. Some delegates called for federal funds for schools, while others supported a petition to the legislature for an appropriation to expand Prairie View, the new state college for African Americans.[22]

The following year, black leaders met again at Travis Street Colored Methodist Episcopal Church in Houston with many of the same social issues on the agenda—education, homesteads, and gambling. New interests in 1884 included widows and orphans, mercantile associations, training in trades, and the formation of unions. Some delegates expressed criticism over black legislators endorsing the administration of Gov. John Ireland, who they considered "hostile" toward African Americans. Others focused on specific concerns such as white fears of "Negro uprisings" because additional black units had been organized for the state militia. That led to the dismissal of the organizer and some of the units. Yet at the same time there had been several acts of violence toward African Americans without any arrests. Denial of jury service and mistreatment of state and county convicts also received attention, with a proposal to place juvenile offenders in separate reform schools.[23]

In 1886, a third "Colored Men's State Convention" within four years brought delegates together in St. John's A.M.E. church at Brenham with the Reverend J. Harvey Jones of Bryan presiding. Leaders proclaimed the meeting "nonpolitical" with a focus on "the moral, intellectual and industrial condition" of black Texans. Delegates emphasized education, including craft skills, and sent a memorial to the legislature urging creation of "an industrial school for colored youth."[24]

Delegates to a fourth convention in seven years met at Waco in 1889 with a minister, B. W. Roberts of Austin, as chairman. Although they again proclaimed their discussions to be nonpolitical, they protested the surge of violence aimed at eliminating African Americans as voters in some counties with large black populations. Delegates also expressed concern that qualified African Americans faced rejection as potential jurors in a growing number of counties. Furthermore, they complained about exclusion from "first-class cars" on passenger trains. These black leaders then sought to make a positive case for African Texans by outlining their progress in the postemancipation period. The ownership of land and the emergence of black businessmen, inventors, and attorneys, as well as skilled workers, farmers, and ranchers received mention. Delegates cited the number of churches, charitable groups, schools, instructors, and students. Finally, they expressed appreciation to the state and to several larger towns for funding public education, including "Prairie View state normal school."[25]

These conventions of the mid- to late 1880s appear to represent a transitional period in both membership and issues. Delegates continued to include significant numbers of farmers and craftsmen as well as church leaders and teachers, with a scattering of political figures. Austin, Galveston, and Houston sent several delegates but did not dominate the meetings in which the majority came from small towns and rural counties of East and Central Texas. In recognition of the statewide Democratic majority among Texas voters, black leaders often described their meetings as "nonpolitical" and focused much of their time on education, economic issues, and social concerns. Nevertheless, they spoke clearly against segregation, discrimination, and lawlessness when court decisions and mob violence demanded responses.[26]

National black conventions ended in 1890, with the exception of an 1893 meeting called by Bishop Henry Turner to consider emigration. African American leaders in Texas continued to employ conventions through 1895 as forums to discuss black community concerns. The conventions of 1891 and 1895 proved to be larger than any earlier meeting, with more delegates from South and North Texas joining those from the East and Central regions. Larger numbers of businessmen and teachers as delegates reflected the growth of those groups within the African American middle class, especially in the emerging cities of the state. The 1891 meeting at Market Hall in Houston, with Methodist minister and educator Isaiah B. Scott presiding, expressed concerns over issues ranging from land, labor, and migration, to education and families, as well as political and legal rights. By 1895, delegates met again in Houston at the United Brothers of Friendship Hall in response to a call from political, religious, and business leaders. Their focus had narrowed to politics, violence, and segregation, in reaction to a new state law for separate coaches on railroads and a surge of lynching across the state. The convention foreshadowed future trends when it sought to create a more permanent organization. Delegates decided on the title "Anti-Class Legislation Organization of Texas"—after deciding against "Colored Men's Union"—in order to emphasize the goal of equality for all citizens.[27]

An analysis of the African American conventions in Texas leads to several conclusions. The delegates considered a great range of concerns in most meetings. While the emphasis shifted to some extent, several themes reoccurred in most conventions. Education in public schools and colleges received discussion in eight of the ten meetings. Race relations, including problems of violence, legal status, and segregation and political participation, attracted the attention of leaders in a majority of the conventions. Delegates in most of the meetings also expressed hopes and considered problems related to the availability of land. Texas leaders did not reflect uniform views on many of the questions before them throughout the period. Instead, they conducted lively debates about solutions to problems. In some instances their ideas varied from the dominant patterns in national conventions. For example, Texas conventions in 1879 and 1880 endorsed the possibility of migration, while encouraging settlements in West Texas.

These all-male conventions did on some occasions address issues related to women and gender roles. In the 1879 meeting, delegates criticized the Texas law against intermarriage because it did not speak to situations in which white men seduced black women but could not be required to marry and support them. Leaders in the 1884 and 1891 conventions expressed concern about divorces and urged women to be responsible mothers and wives, especially in raising children. These expressions of concern appeared in paternalistic terms. The 1895 convention showed more awareness of the expanding activities by women, however, when it allowed Mrs. M. R. Rogers Webb to speak to the delegates about "the national equal rights council," a forerunner of permanent civil rights organizations. The meeting also recognized several women visitors, some related to delegates and others, like Kizzie Miller and Marie Sharkie of Antioch Baptist Church in Houston, who led women's missionary societies that sought solutions for social problems. By visiting convention sessions the women showed their interest in public issues.[28]

Analysis of delegates to black conventions has received limited attention and has resulted in broad generalizations. August Meier suggests that political leaders dominated Reconstruction meetings in the early 1870s. In the Texas conventions, 572 delegates can be identified from incomplete lists, with most of them attending only one meeting—a strongly democratic pattern. Only twelve leaders attended three or more conventions. Jeremiah Hamilton, a member of the State Central Committee in 1866, served as a delegate in five meetings, the most of any Texas leader. Of the twelve, seven held political office at some point, but they formed a very small group. Merline Pitre, in her study of black political leaders in late nineteenth-century Texas, identifies fifty-two members of the state legislature or Republican Party conventions. Of those fifty-two leaders, only nineteen served as delegates at African American conventions in the state. In the 1873 meeting, seventeen men formed the largest group with political or government experience in a Texas meeting. Yet even then political figures did not dominate the black conventions.[29]

The convention delegates barely included any members of a black elite and clearly did not represent such a class, perhaps because Texas with its small, prewar, free African American population had too short a time period for the development of an elite. Historian Willard Gatewood in his volume *Aristocrats of Color* mentions only Norris Wright Cuney from Texas. Loren Schweninger in a study of *Black Property Owners in the South* counts thirteen Texans with $20,000 or more in property between the Civil War and World War I. Of those, only Cuney and Walter Burton appeared as convention delegates.[30]

Delegates in the early conventions from 1866 into the 1880s included significant numbers of farmers, craftsmen, ministers, and teachers. The growing number of businessmen in the later conventions, especially in the 1890s, represented the most important change in membership at the meetings. A more complex view emerges as the community roles of these leaders are considered. Jeremiah Hamilton, a carpenter by trade, served in the legislature and later edited a newspaper. Norris Wright Cuney, one of the few members of the black elite among the delegates, and a grand master of the state Masonic order, also helped organize dock workers in Galveston so they could get a fair share of the labor. Isaiah Scott, a minister, edited a Methodist newspaper and later served as president of Wiley College. Lee Campbell, who became president of the General Baptist State Convention, also organized St. John's Orphanage in Austin. Simon Turner, a San Antonio grocery and ice cream store owner, served as a captain of a black company in the state militia. Most delegates ranked as good examples of the growing black middle class in the state. Furthermore, many had established themselves as community leaders engaged in the variety of activities that sustained African Texans in towns and counties across the state. Those efforts in turn led to their selection as the best men to remind white Texans about African American progress as well as hopes of overcoming segregation and discrimination to achieve equal opportunity.[31]

White reactions to the conventions varied over time and depended on topics under discussion. Newspapers owned and edited by white Texans reported on the conventions from the 1870s to the 1890s. White reporters in the 1870s showed an inclination to stereotype African American leaders. A reporter discussing lively debate and efforts to pass motions in 1873 proclaimed, "Such a scene of confusion, imitating our views of Pandemonium, we never saw equaled." George Ruby, one of the two black state senators, responded later, "The confusion today was still not so great as the Democratic Convention of Corsicana and the closing scenes of the Thirteenth Legislature." The reporter also contrasted N. W. Cuney as a dignified presiding officer with Matt Gaines, a state senator, whom the reporter described as "little better than a corn-field hand at his best and owes his success in the party to his religious exhortations and pleadings." That concept seemed to ignore the revival style of some white ministers and politicians.[32]

The comments of Governor Ireland to the 1883 convention, suggesting the delegates focus less on civil rights and political issues, seemed to reflect the views of most white Texans. He also claimed that black workers did not need to migrate out of the state, which probably indicated labor concerns of white landowners. Yet Ireland found some common ground with the delegates in his endorsement of state support for education.[33]

By the 1891 convention, delegates expressed their appreciation to the *Houston Daily Post* and the *Galveston News* for being "courteous in reporting the proceedings of this convention" and for assigning as reporters "two of the brightest of our young men," Emmett J. Scott and D. Webster Wilson.[34]

White Texans did not respond favorably to black appeals for equal treatment as citizens. Instead, segregation and discrimination increased during the late nineteenth century. Yet descriptions of those problems by convention delegates may have slowed passage of state legislation, which included a separate railroad-coach law in 1891. Violence against people of color escalated as well, and Texas ranked third in the nation for the number of persons lynched in the late nineteenth century. Nevertheless, the state legislature dominated by Democrats supported successful legislation in 1897 to outlaw such mob violence. That reflected an awareness of black concerns, although the law received sporadic enforcement at best. As part of intense political campaigns in the 1890s, white men's associations supported by Democrats used violence and intimidation to reduce African American voting in some counties, which would evolve into the use of a white primary in the early twentieth century. Democrats also revived discussion of a poll tax requirement for voting that would win approval after the turn of the century.[35]

African American education, a major issue regularly discussed at conventions, received more positive treatment by white Texans, within a segregated system of public elementary and secondary schools. White funding support for black public education appeared stronger in Texas than in some southern states. The state government under Democratic leadership also created Prairie View College, an African American land-grant institution that focused on teacher and vocational training. Black advocates of a state liberal arts college for African Americans met disappointment, however, as promises for such an institution would not be fulfilled until the mid-twentieth century.

Despite these limits on the influence of African American conventions, they provided an important voice for the black community in Texas, the South, and the nation. The delegates represented the emerging middle class that included farmers, ministers, educators, and a growing number of businessmen, but hardly any members of the small black elite. A significant number of skilled craftsmen among the delegates ensured they would also address working class issues related to economic opportunity. Despite the all-male composition of the meetings, they addressed some women's issues, albeit in a paternalistic manner in the early years, and later began to recognize the expanding roles of women. The most significant role for the delegates became the preservation of hope by providing black Texans with examples of success—despite discrimination. These leaders then added firm and repeated reminders to their fellow citizens of Texas that African Americans would not accept a permanently subordinate status.

Finally, the conventions often reflected concern about greater organization. The first one in 1866 endorsed the Freedmen's Bureau that continued until 1870. Most conventions, from 1873, met in response to calls from a recognized leader or group of leaders from earlier meetings. At least three conventions sent delegates to national conventions in the 1870s and 1880s. The 1880 convention sought to create a Texas Farmers Association that would acquire land. Conventions in the 1890s foreshadowed the more permanent organizations developing in that period by forming an executive committee to function between the larger meetings. In 1891 and 1895, conventions included men who went on to become leaders in the more continuously active black organizational efforts of the twentieth century. Isaiah Scott, president of Wiley College, who presided at the 1891 and 1895 conventions, became a vice president by 1903 of the Afro-American Council, a civil rights group that foreshadowed the NAACP. Robert L. Smith, a legislator who created the Farmers' Home Improvement Society in the 1890s and was an organizer of the 1895 convention, served on the Afro-American Council executive committee, and in 1907 became the first president of the Texas branch of the National Negro Business League, established by Booker T. Washington. Emmett J. Scott, editor of the *Houston Texas Freeman* newspaper in the 1890s and an organizer of the 1895 convention, soon thereafter became the personal secretary to Booker T. Washington and secretary of the National Negro Business League.[36]

The African American conventions of late nineteenth-century Texas kept alive the goals of political and civil rights, as well as equal opportunities for education and economic advancement during an era of transition. The delegates recognized the value of organization through conventions, and by the 1895 meeting they began to seek more permanent forms of association to pursue their goals. Those efforts proved so effective that the organizations in which some became involved, such as the Afro-American Council and the National Negro Business League, replaced the convention movement. The new organizations provided leadership opportunities for members of the black community during the early twentieth century and became the means by which middle-class African Americans sustained their voice as they struggled to recover their rights as citizens.

NOTES

1. Howard H. Bell, *A Survey of the Negro Convention Movement, 1830–1861* (New York: Arno, 1969).

2. August Meier, *Negro Thought in America, 1880–1915* (Ann Arbor: University of Michigan Press, 1963), 4–10, 44, 69–71.

3. Randolph B. Campbell, *An Empire for Slavery: The Peculiar Institution in Texas, 1821–1865* (Baton Rouge: Louisiana State University Press, 1989): 54–58, 110–14.

4. Darlene Clark Hine, William C. Hine, and Stanley Harrold, *The African-American Odyssey,* 2nd ed. (Upper Saddle River, N.J.: Prentice Hall, 2003), 148–49; Leon F. Litwack, *Been in the Storm So Long: The Aftermath of Slavery* (New York: Random House, 1980), 502–14.

5. *New York Tribune,* April 9, 1866. A correspondent of the newspaper was at Austin, Texas, in the spring of 1866 to cover the state constitutional convention.

6. Ibid.

7. Ibid. Wilson Gregg, *Alexander Gregg: First Bishop of Texas,* ed. Arthur Howard Noll (Sewanee, Tenn.: University of the South Press, 1912), 91–98. In this book Gregg's son presents the bishop's view of these events, which reflects paternalism and white southern racial attitudes and assumptions of the period.

8. *Texas Almanac 1966–1967* (Dallas: A. H. Belo, 1965), 134.

9. U.S. Ninth Census, 1870, manuscript returns Travis County, Texas, Schedule 1, Inhabitants (microfilm, Southwest Collection, Texas Tech University); Census, Austin, Texas, 1875 (manuscript, Austin-Travis County Collection, Austin Public Library), 86, 91; *Gray and Moore's Mercantile and General City Directory of Austin, Texas, 1872–73* (Austin: S. A. Gray, 1872): 55, 73, 113; Jacob Fontaine III and Gene Burd, *Jacob Fontaine: From Slavery to the Greatness of the Pulpit, Press, Public Service* (Austin: Eakin, 1983).

10. Alton Hornsby, "The Freedmen's Bureau Schools in Texas, 1865–1870," *Southwestern Historical Quarterly* 76 (April 1973): 400.

11. Alwyn Barr, *Black Texans: A History of African Americans in Texas, 1528–1995,* 2nd ed. (Norman: University of Oklahoma Press, 1996), 43–49; Merline Pitre, *Through Many Dangers, Toils and Snares: Black Leadership in Texas, 1868–1900* (Austin: Eakin, 1985), 85; Alwyn Barr, "Black Legislators of Reconstruction Texas," *Civil War History* 32 (1986): 340–52; Ernest William Winkler, ed., *Platforms of Political Parties in Texas* (Austin: Bulletin of the University of Texas no. 53, 1916), 143.

12. Philip S. Foner and George E. Walker, eds., *Proceedings of the Black National and State Conventions, 1865–1900* (Philadelphia: Temple University Press, 1986), 349–50, 390–91; Pitre, *Through Many Dangers, Toils and Snares,* 166–73; *Washington New Era,*

January 13, 1870: U. S. Ninth Census, 1870, manuscript returns of Robertson County, Texas, 482 (microfilm, Southwest Collection, Texas Tech University). See also Carl H. Moneyhon, "George T. Ruby and the Politics of Expediency in Texas," in *Southern Black Leaders in the Reconstruction Era,* ed. Howard N. Rabinowitz (Urbana: University of Illinois Press, 1982), 363–92; James M. Smallwood, "G. T. Ruby: Galveston's Black Carpetbagger in Reconstruction Texas," *Houston Review* 5 (Winter 1983): 24–33; Randall B. Woods, "George T. Ruby: A Black Militant in the White Business Community," *Red River Valley Historical Review* 1 (1974): 269–80.

13. *Galveston News,* June 12, 26, 1873; Pitre, *Through Many Dangers, Toils and Snares.*

14. *Austin Daily State Journal,* July 5, 1873. Analysis of the delegates is based on several sources: the U.S manuscript censuses for Texas in 1870 and 1880; city directories for Austin, Galveston, and Houston; Pitre, *Through Many Dangers, Toils and Snares;* Ron Tyler et al., eds., *The New Handbook of Texas* (6 vols.; Austin: Texas State Historical Association, 1996); Clyde McQueen, *Black Churches in Texas: A Guide to Historic Congregations* (College Station: Texas A&M University Press, 2000); and David A. Williams, ed., *Bricks Without Straw: A Comprehensive History of African Americans in Texas* (Austin: Eakin, 1997).

15. Winkler, *Platforms of Political Parties in Texas,* 148–51.

16. Nell Irvin Painter, *Exodusters: Black Migration to Kansas after Reconstruction* (New York: Knopf, 1976): 221–24; Lawrence Rice, *The Negro in Texas, 1874–1900* (Baton Rouge: Louisiana State University Press, 1970), 199–201.

17. *Galveston News,* July 4, 5, 1879.

18. *Galveston News,* July 5, 1879. Analysis of the delegates is based on several sources: the U.S. manuscript censuses for Texas, 1870 and 1880; city directories for Austin, Galveston, and Houston; Tyler, *New Handbook of Texas;* Pitre, *Through Many Dangers, Toils and Snares;* McQueen, *Black Churches in Texas;* Fountain and Burd, *Jacob Fontaine;* and Bill Moore, *Bastrop County, 1691–1900* (Wichita Falls, Tex.: Nortex, 1977); Patricia Smith Prather and Jane Clements Monday, *From Slave to Statesman: The Legacy of Joshua Houston, Servant to Sam Houston* (Denton: University of North Texas Press, 1993).

19. *Galveston Daily News,* February 17, 1880. Analysis of delegates is based on several sources: the U.S. manuscript census for Texas, 1880; city directories for Dallas; Tyler, *New Handbook of Texas;* and McQueen, *Black Churches in Texas.*

20. *Galveston Daily News,* February 18, 22, 1880.

21. Painter, *Exodusters,* 221–24; Rice, *Negro in Texas 1874–1900,* 198–204. Painter, *Exodusters,* 184, 256, estimated 15,000 to 20,000 migrants, while Rice thought up to 60,000 had migrated with 12,000 from Texas. Robert A. Athearn, *In Search of Canaan,* 261–62, estimated 20,000 to 25,000 migrants. Painter and Athearn mention higher estimates in 1879–1880 of 40,000 to 50,000 migrants that they believe were exaggerated.

22. *Galveston Daily News,* July 10–13, 1883; *Austin Statesman,* July 11–12, 1883. The "Report of the Committee on Grievances at the State Convention of Colored Men of Texas, 1883" is reprinted in *Afro-American History: Primary Sources,* 2nd ed., ed. Thomas R. Frazier (Chicago: Dorsey, 1988), 165–70.

23. *Galveston Daily News,* August 6–8, 1884; Alwyn Barr, "The Texas 'Black Uprising' Scare of 1883," *Phylon* 41 (1980): 179–86.

24. *Brenham Daily Banner,* September 8, 10, 1886.

25. *Galveston Daily News,* August 21, 23, 1889.

26. Analysis of the delegates to the conventions in 1883, 1884, 1886, and 1889 is based on several sources: the U.S. manuscript census for Texas, 1880; city directories for Austin, Dallas, Galveston, Houston, and San Antonio; Tyler, *New Handbook of Texas;* Rice, *Negro in Texas, 1874–1900;* McQueen, *Black Churches in Texas;* Prather and Monday, *From Slave to Statesman; The Red Book of Houston: A compendium of Social, Professional, Religious, Educational and Industrial Interests of Houston's Colored Population* (Houston, 1915).

27. *Houston Post,* September 1–3, 1891; *Galveston Daily News,* May 24, 1895; Theda Skocpol, Ariane Liazos, and Marshall Ganz, *What a Mighty Power We Can Be: African American Fraternal Groups and the Struggle for Racial Equality* (Princeton, N.J.: Princeton University Press, 2006). Analysis of the delegates at the 1891 and 1895 conventions is based on several sources: city directories for Austin, Dallas, Galveston, Houston, and San Antonio; Tyler, *New Handbook of Texas;* Winkler, *Platforms of Political Parties in Texas;* McQueen, *Black Churches in Texas;* Williams, *Bricks Without Straw;* Pitre, *Through Many Dangers, Toils and Snares; Indianapolis Freeman;* Prather and Monday, *From Slave to Statesman;* Kenneth Mason, *African Americans and Race Relations in San Antonio, 1867–1937* (New York: Garland, 1998); A. W. Jackson, *A Sure Foundation and Sketch of Negro Life in Texas* (Houston: A. W. Jackson, 1936).

28. *Galveston Daily News,* May 24, 1895; Ruthe Winegarten, *Black Texas Women: 150 Years of Trial and Triumph* (Austin: University of Texas Press, 1995), 62. The group discussed by Mrs. Webb probably was the American Citizens' Equal Rights Association, which formed in 1890. Meier, *Negro Thought in America,* 70–71.

29. Meier, *Negro Thought in America,* 9–10; Pitre, *Through Many Dangers, Toils and Snares.*

30. Willard Gatewood, *Aristocrats of Color: The Black Elite, 1880–1920* (Bloomington: Indiana University Press, 1990): 19, 176, 267; Loren Schweninger, *Black Property Owners in the South, 1790–1915* (Urbana: University of Illinois Press, 1990), 295–300.

31. Tyler, *New Handbook of Texas,* III, 429, and V, 936–37; Douglas Hales, *A Southern Family in White and Black: The Cuneys of Texas* (College Station: Texas A&M University Press, 2003); San Antonio city directory for 1891; Mason, *African Americans and Race Relations in San Antonio,* 167.

32. *Galveston Daily News,* July 5, 1873.

33. *Austin Statesman,* July 12, 1883.

34. *Houston Post,* September 3, 1891.

35. Barr, *Black Texans,* 79–80, 84–85.

36. "The Afro-American Council," *Colored American Magazine* VI (March 1903): 335, 337; Tyler, *New Handbook of Texas,* V, 935, 936–37, 1108–9.

CHAPTER TWO

Crucial Decade for Texas Labor

RAILWAY UNION STRUGGLES, 1886–96

George N. Green

During one crucial decade for the workers of Texas, the Knights of Labor reached its peak, was defeated in a dramatic railroad strike in 1886, and was transformed into an agrarian and mechanics' organization, cooperating with the Farmers' Alliance. Out of the turmoil of the era, a general farm-labor movement eventually led by the Populists—stronger in turbulent Texas than in most states—challenged the existing political order, went down to electoral defeat in 1896, and took the Knights of Labor with them. Farm-labor movements revived after the demise of Populism, but within the Democratic Party structure.

Craft unionism, including the railroad brotherhoods, came of age that same decade and took on a more narrow focus than the Knights. The more job-oriented railway brotherhoods and other crafts in Texas joined the farm organizations and the transformed Knights in some political battles, but they were more involved in confronting corporations over wages, hours, and working conditions. They resisted corporate hegemony through some strikes, often in the news, through lobbying efforts before the legislature, negotiations with employers, seldom in the news, and through law suits, especially hundreds of personal injury court cases, almost never newsworthy. It was the railway brotherhoods that launched the first legislative lobbying efforts on the part of unions in Texas, achieving some results. Injuries and deaths were part of a daily toll on railroad employees, and while the incidents that made it to court were only a fraction of the total number, here too laborers made some progress in protecting their rights.

Most workers in the United States believed in the short-run goals of the right to living wages, decent working conditions, workdays shorter than from daylight to dark, and unemployment relief. Regarding conditions, railroad workers included increased crew sizes as trains became heavier and longer,

Fig. 2.1. Texas South-Eastern train loaded with logs ready to be shipped. Photograph in East Texas, date unknown. Temple Industries (Diboll, Texas). Credit: UTSA's Institute of Texan Cultures, No. 068-2853, Courtesy of Temple Industries, Diboll, Texas.

and they asserted the right to demand the firing of abusive supervisors. Workers held a strong belief that the human factor in industrial relations was being ignored. Corporations believed that laborers should accept their fate, submitting to whatever conditions prevailed in industry, and they proved willing to suppress union activities through federal and state legislation and utilization of the courts, as well as the deployment of strikebreakers and public and private armed forces. State courts, and later the federal courts, obligingly twisted the due process clause of the Fourteenth Amendment—designed to protect the legal rights of former slaves—into a doctrine that protected private business from public regulation. (American Federation of Labor president Sam Gompers considered this approach a "judicial reenactment of slavery.") Judge Thomas Cooley and Christopher Tiedeman were foremost among the legal commentators who devised general prohibitions against everything that conservative interests regarded as unreasonable, all of which was labeled class legislation. Laissez-faire became a pervading doctrine by 1886, and Tiedeman openly admitted that his mission was to "awaken the public mind" about the "constitutional limitations . . . against the radical experimentations of social reformers."[1]

Meanwhile, factionalism and racism (in a Texas incident) deterred one nationwide brotherhood attempt at unity. Another such endeavor was launched by the American Railway Union (ARU), which attempted to supplant the brotherhoods, but it was crushed by the federal government and the railroad corporations. Railway labor relations was the most disturbed sector of the Texas labor movement in the late nineteenth century, but unlike the Knights and the ARU, the brotherhoods by the 1880s were not perceived by the corporations or the state and federal governments as communist revolutionaries. The brotherhoods' existence was never on the line in any given strike or political campaign. Governments and corporations could not suppress all voluntary organizations or strikes or win all court cases in the face of local juries, so the railway brotherhoods remained standing in 1896 (along with other craft unions, some of which belonged to the American Federation of Labor), outlasting the more aggressive and idealistic Knights, ARU, and Populists. The very pace of the change hindered the growth of class consciousness in the United States, especially since the courts responded quickly to the labor-management violence of the era as well as the astounding number of industrial injuries. (When industrial unionism revived later, it was in a less ambitious form than the Knights of Labor, which attempted to organize virtually everyone, or the ARU, which attempted to organize a multitude of crafts and unskilled trades in one union). Texas was a hotbed of railway labor activity and the decade of tumult, 1886–96, helped shape labor in Texas for decades thereafter.[2]

The wretched wages, hours, and conditions reached their nadir during the depression of the 1870s. After the collapse of the violent national railway strikes in 1877, the Knights of Labor attempted to peacefully organize all hands and craftsmen who worked for the railroads. The Knights' apparently successful sympathy strikes on two Texas railroads in 1885, as well as their bold move in taking charge of a walkout on the Gould lines fending off wage cuts, appeared to give some hope of a new age.[3]

As a result of the 1885 strike, the Missouri Pacific pioneered guaranteed pay for what it perceived to be its most crucial employees, the engineers. They were usually limited to twelve hours per day and earned about $1,000 per year, which would support a middle-class lifestyle in an era when about $500 to $600 per year would suffice to allow a family of four the very minimal health and decency budget. But on all the Texas roads, a third or more of the hands were trackmen and laborers, nearly all of whom earned $1.15 per day, or about $30 a month or $360 a year. Just paying board to the railroad section house would take $15 a month. These starvation-level wages were the underlying cause of another fateful strike.

Wall Street tycoon Jay Gould controlled the Missouri Pacific, Texas and Pacific, International and Great Northern, and the Missouri-Kansas-Texas

(Katy) railroads. The Great Southwest Strike was brought on by unrest over wages, mismanagement, corporate contract violations, the use of convict labor, and by the triggering incident—the firing of Knights of Labor leader C. A. Hall in the Texas and Pacific shop in Marshall. Mobs of men, many of whom were strike sympathizers rather than strikers, prevented most freight trains from moving. The railroads had recruited some strikebreakers but deliberately waited three weeks until towns felt the economic pinch before asking the state for help in dispersing the crowds. There was no hurry, since Gould had already looted three of his southwestern lines and driven them into bankruptcy, yet he retained control even during the government's receivership. More than one newspaper observed that the strikers did not understand that Gould "does not care whether his roads are operating or not." While many members of the railroad brotherhoods were sympathetic, their unions refused to endorse the strike and thereby helped break it—they moved the trains once the crowds were kept at bay by militia, Texas Rangers, and U.S. marshals. Many Knights blamed their defeat on circuit judges, especially U.S. District Judge Pardee's ruling that the employees of railroads in receivership were officials of the court and that all ten thousand would be in contempt if they merely walked off their jobs peacefully. He dispatched marshals as though they were the cavalry. Independent editor Charles DeMorse mused, "If the position of Judge Pardee is correct, the citizens of Texas will have to take to the woods, or avoid railroad employees as they would vipers, or run a continual risk of imprisonment for contempt." It was the Knights' first serious defeat and seemed to unleash a chain of losses that brought about the virtual demise of the order nationwide within five years.[4]

Texas membership, however, seemed to decline more slowly from its peak of about twenty thousand in the spring of 1886. The Noble Order in Texas included scores of farmers' and small town mechanics' groups and was consequently less dependent on sizeable industrial assemblies. In fact, some 202 assemblies were begun in 1886 and 1887. Of the twenty-one known railway-dominated assemblies, most of which were undoubtedly composed of shop craftsmen and yardmen and other laborers, fourteen survived the carnage of 1886. But the Texas Knights faced more than just defeat in one strike. The Knights in Chicago had been infiltrated by anarchists and communists, allowing corporate interests and such newspapers as the new *Dallas Morning News* to tar Texas Knights with the same brush. The *Houston Post,* though more accepting of local labor, believed that the alleged Haymarket Square bombers in Chicago were legitimate targets for execution. Indeed, the Haymarket Riot triggered the first nationwide red scare.[5] (The deployment of this smokescreen weapon by antilabor corporations, the press, and their political friends became habit-forming through the decades).

The national leadership of the Knights did not approve of strikes and did not attempt to organize assemblies along craft or occupational lines, though some were so constituted. Though favoring the eight-hour day, national leaders like Grand Master Terence Powderly were far less interested in collective bargaining for workers than in vast, future economic and political reform. Since this largely visionary approach did not appear to be succeeding by 1886, in the wake of the Great Southwest Strike, the four big operating brotherhoods, the first four organized, were supplanting the Knights on the railroads. The brotherhoods were dedicated to challenging employers regarding daily problems like wages, hours, and conditions. These craft unions did not attempt to organize shopmen and laborers who were not operating the trains. They were the Brotherhood of Locomotive Engineers, founded in 1863, the Order of Railway Conductors, 1868, the Brotherhood of Locomotive Firemen and Enginemen, 1873, and the Brotherhood of Railroad Trainmen (including brakemen and sometimes switchmen and others), 1883. Unlike the brotherhoods, the Knights exercised no real control over its regional offices or district assemblies. The failure of the great strike, the negative publicity in the aftermath of the Haymarket Riot, and the organizational successes of the brotherhoods eventually undermined the Knights' influence on Texas railroads and elsewhere. Also, Powderly turned even more against strikes and labor assemblies in general after the events of 1886 and moved the organization to the countryside and small towns. Rank and file union members in the Knights became disgusted with the national leadership. After 1890 in Texas only four of the Knights' known railroad assemblies survived.[6]

At the time of the nationwide railroad turmoil of 1877, which spread into Texas, some of the brotherhoods had agreements with a few Texas lines, but many Texas roads had not yet been built. It was in the 1880s and 1890s that the state's railroad employment grew prodigiously. Over 25,000 Texans worked for railroads in 1888.[7] The brotherhoods moved cautiously in the face of railroad power. The Brotherhood of Locomotive Firemen (BLF) on the Santa Fe Railroad organized Lodge 147 in Temple in 1883. With walkouts occurring on various roads in 1884, the lodge first voted to approve strikes, but only "in cases of absolute necessity." Upon receiving a proposed contract and resolutions from Galveston BLF Lodge 115, the Temple assembly approved them unanimously but warned their brothers not to present a copy to Santa Fe's General Manager. The Temple lodge reminded the Galveston local that the shop employees in Galveston had recently laid their grievances before the general manager and that every member of the shop committee had been fired. The Temple firemen were waiting on the Engineers so that they could inaugurate a joint discussion of grievances. As the Great Southwest Strike swept through Texas in the spring, 1886, the Temple firemen made no mention of it in their minutes.[8]

But if opportunities arose, some brotherhoods would act. Houston brakemen organized in 1885 with about fifty members on their division of the Southern Pacific System. Taking advantage of a seemingly successful brakemen's strike on the Louisiana and Morgan divisions of the Southern Pacific, February 15, 1886, Houston brakemen walked out two days later with the same demand—a pay raise from $50 to $65 per month. Southern Pacific business in the area suffered considerably, and by February 22, when Houston's striking brakemen now numbered 250, the company yielded.[9]

Four divisions of the Brotherhood of Locomotive Engineers, by far the strongest of the brotherhoods, launched a General Grievance Committee on the Texas and Pacific Railway in 1886, but the delegates expressed concern in their first meeting that they might be discriminated against. They saw the benefits of a semblance of unity, working out a joint contract with the firemen in 1890, which the Texas and Pacific signed and then renewed in 1891. They worked out an arrangement with the BLF that engineers (and presumably firemen) who were too "old or disabled for running a road engine should have the privilege of running switch engines."[10]

The Brotherhood of Locomotive Engineers, meanwhile, began trying to influence the legislature, just as the railroads had been doing for years. The BLE evidently had lobbyists on hand for the 1887 session of the legislature and formally organized their State Legislative Board in Austin on February 5, 1889. The BLE claimed credit for lobbying successfully for the 1887 measure that required railroads to provide thirty days' notice for wage reductions with full pay for the thirty days and to pay a worker back wages within fifteen days of his leaving employment on the line. These actions were sufficient to make railroad workers the state's most favored body of wage hands, though it was merely in relation to other downtrodden wage earners. In 1889, another law strengthened mechanics' liens, i.e., workers' efforts to gain their wages from defaulting employers. By 1895, the conductors, firemen, and brakemen's unions began to coalesce in a joint lobbying effort.[11]

The railroads, meanwhile, had earned the ire of the public. James S. Hogg took office as attorney general in 1887 and, with the help of irate farmers, the Knights, and undoubtedly the railroad brotherhoods, pushed through a state antitrust law aimed at the railroads' monopolistic practices. The railroads' pooling agreement was busted. In 1890, Hogg was the first Texas gubernatorial candidate to face vilification as an alleged communist because of his farm-labor support. And, as he anticipated, railroad construction was slowed in an effort to blame him for it. The Missouri-Kansas-Texas laid off engineers in North Texas while the *Dallas News* and *Galveston News,* owned by the same company, smeared Hogg's followers as "Union Laborites, Anarchists and Communists." Hogg was elected anyway and soon established the state railroad commission with the power to regulate freight rates and fares. The

Dallas News and *Galveston News* believed the commission marked the state government as "an engine of communism."[12]

The battles for working people's rights were also fought in the courts, supposedly in quiet neutrality. The 1880s was the decade that the U.S. judiciary—terrified of the class struggle as well as lawsuits that might hold corporations liable for widespread damages they inflicted on society—invented devices to limit damages suits and curb workers' rights. To cope with the astounding number of injuries generated by the industrial revolution, the courts concocted the doctrines of contributory negligence, the fellow-servant rule, and assumption of risk. If the plaintiff was negligent, even slightly, he could not recover from the defendant. This harsh doctrine was the favored method by which judges kept tort claims from the deliberations of juries, which tended to sympathize with crippled men suing giant corporations. A plaintiff, whether a railroad employee or the survivor of one of the innumerable railroad crossing accidents, not only had to prove that the railroad was negligent, but also that he was faultless himself. Assumption of risk meant that a worker could not recover if he had put himself willingly in a position of danger, which seems just until one considers that railroad men, miners, and factory hands put themselves in grave danger merely by accepting their jobs. Under the fellow-servant rule an employee (the servant) could not sue his employer (the master) for injuries caused by the negligence of another employee (and, usually, even if the employer was also negligent). Since most accidents came about in this manner, an injured workman frequently could only sue another equally impoverished fellow worker, a meaningless recourse to law. So the cost of industrial accidents had to be borne by the workers themselves and their destitute families rather than by the most productive sector of the economy. Not all states or different courts within a state carried these techniques to the extreme and, of course, laws changed along with court interpretations as the years passed. The common-law doctrines of Texas operated to the prejudice of some 80 percent of all employees injured on the job.[13]

In Texas, the doctrines of fellow servant, assumed risk, and contributory negligence began to be put into place under the common law in the 1870s, then into written law in the 1890s and later. But the power of the railroads in Texas was slowly eclipsed after 1886 and under continuous challenge for the next decade (and after), and many Texas juries and judges riddled the state's tort policies and laws. The "Master and Servant" section of the *Texas Digest,* the index for the Texas judiciary, contains scores of pre-1900 cases, the great majority of railroad cases, wherein injured workers often collected accident compensation from their employers in spite of policies and laws that were designed to prevent them.[14]

The Texas and Pacific Railway established the fellow-servant doctrine in Texas through the U.S. Circuit Court and U.S. Supreme Court in 1876. Cases followed in which trackmen were considered fellow servants of the craftsmen operating the trains. But there were also cases in which brakemen injured by the negligence of conductors, car inspectors, telegraph operators, road masters, and section hands were judged not to be fellow servants, so the railroads were often liable to the brakemen. Company officials with control and supervisory power could be fellow servants of wage hands. Texas demanded, unlike many jurisdictions, that only those corporate representatives with hiring and firing power were not fellow servants with workers. On the foggy morning of November 30, 1886, in Colorado County, a section hand, Michael Smith, was riding in the caboose of a train controlled by a roadmaster. Their jobs, of course, had nothing in common. A special freight train smashed into the caboose, injuring Smith. The local district court upheld Smith's claim for compensation, but four years later the Texas Supreme Court ruled that the negligent roadmaster was Smith's fellow servant and overthrew the claim.[15]

The first Texas fellow-servant law was passed in March 1891, providing broadly that those railroad employees with authority (hiring and firing authority as interpreted by the courts at that time) were vice principals and that all others were fellow servants, who assumed the risks of each other's negligence. But definitions were narrowed in 1893, specifying that fellow servants worked in the same grade of employment, the same time and place, and in the common service for a common purpose.[16] Texas courts, juries, labor attorneys, and the legislature shredded the fellow servant doctrine in the 1880s and 1890s.

The common law doctrine of assumed risk, developed in the 1880s in Texas, had a checkered history also. Common law supposedly held employers responsible for providing safe equipment, but the Texas and Pacific recognized no such obligation. Section foreman I. C. Bradford, upon receiving stern orders from the roadmaster to straighten a badly bent rail immediately, faced an impossible dilemma. The rail needed to go to the shops, or if repaired on site it could be heated or straightened with a curving hook. Even the roadmaster admitted that Bradford had no proper tools and no time. Bradford improvised and was injured in the process. The Red River County jury decided he could collect compensation, but the Texas Supreme Court ruled that it was Bradford's fault for using tools that he knew to be inadequate. However, railroads failed to spread a worker's risk to machinery beyond which his particular line of duty would require him to inspect or deal with. And even though charged with using and inspecting machinery, workers could not be held responsible for searching for latent defects. The Houston and Texas Central and the Santa Fe vainly attempted to require brakemen to assume the risk of inspecting tracks and cross ties on the road beds.[17]

Contributory negligence, like assumed risk, was devised in the 1880s and was more reliable for the railroads than the fellow-servant doctrine. In an 1891 case before the Texas Supreme Court, for instance, the International and Great Northern was not liable for an accident even though an employee had notified the company of a defective machine. The worker was guilty of contributory negligence because he used the machine. Yet this doctrine also met spirited resistance from the beginning. In 1893, the U.S. Court of Civil Appeals ruled that the Southern Pacific's promise to remedy a defect complained of by a worker relieved the servant of the charge of contributory negligence. On several occasions, servants' violations of rules were not negligence per se. In one case in 1895, for instance, the Texas and Pacific had made no effort to enforce an openly disregarded rule and, after an injury, could not pin contributory negligence on any employee.[18]

In other labor cases, some judges seemed anxious to smash the working class. In a Missouri Pacific case involving a veteran conductor in 1889, the Texas Supreme Court tossed out a McLennan County jury's decision and sanctioned the notorious blacklist. And when a construction worker sued the San Antonio and Aransas Pass for back wages, the DeWitt County court ruled in his favor, citing the 1887 law. Judge J. Simkins struck down the law, observing that, "Unquestionably so long as men must earn a living for their families and themselves by labor, there must be, as there always has been, oppression of the working classes."[19]

The Texas courts handled hundreds, if not thousands, of complicated railway injury cases in the late nineteenth century. The brotherhoods, specifically oriented toward railway workers and their problems, were undoubtedly better able to serve these men than an all-purpose organization like the Knights of Labor. It was a duty for the brotherhoods, of course, to retain lawyers for their injured or fired members, or at least direct them to appropriate attorneys. The Firemen's Lodge No. 147 in Temple allowed Engineers' Division No. 206 to handle some of its affairs, notifying the BLE on one occasion that it would pay "all expenses" for an unjustly discharged fireman.[20]

Racism affected strikers during the upheaval of 1886 and thereafter because a number of African Americans worked as firemen, brakemen, switchmen, and shopmen. The question of how to treat black railroad employees bedeviled the brotherhoods more than the Knights because the brotherhoods favored the impossible task of expelling blacks from the industry. Railway unions from the Mississippi Valley and westward were much more strike-prone after 1877 than in the Northeast or in the South, but Texas—uniquely—was southern as well as western. It was certainly appropriate, then, that a strike action characteristic of the West that foundered on the race issue, propelled mostly by southern members, would occur in Texas. Moreover, it occurred in this crucial era when many workers in the industry were searching for unity. The racist incident contributed to the demise of that potential national unity.

The Brotherhood of Railroad Trainmen, which would not admit black brakemen or switchmen, and the equally white Switchmen's Union, called a strike against the Houston and Texas Central Railroad in September 1890 demanding that black switchmen be fired and decrying the situation wherein white workers had to associate with blacks "to an unbearable extent." The presidents of the two brotherhoods journeyed to Houston to show their support, and the other brotherhoods endorsed the walkout. The railroad responded by giving white employees jobs where they would have no contact with blacks.

The issue was brought before a special session in Houston of the new Supreme Council of the United Orders of Railway Employees under the chairmanship of the Firemen's Treasurer, Eugene Debs, in October 1890. The two international presidents demanded the blacks be removed on the same principle as it "would ask for the removal of an obnoxious yardmaster or a 'scab.'" Debs noted that the brotherhoods ultimately faced a choice between calling a general strike or accepting black membership. In Debs's absence, the Council voted to ask the Houston and Texas Central to fire the blacks, but the railroad again refused. Debs lamented that the southern branches of the brotherhoods, where racism was most deeply entrenched, were weakening themselves and the international union with the exclusionary policies. He was so discouraged by the racism, as well as by bitter jurisdictional disputes that also plagued the Council, that at the annual session in Chicago during June 1892, Debs took the lead in dissolving the organization.[21]

Skilled railroad workers in Texas appear to have been reasonably well paid by the 1880s and thereafter. From June 30, 1890, to June 30, 1891, the Texas and Pacific's ninety-two conductors earned an average $3.89 per day, some $1,218 per year. They had surpassed the pay of the 174 engineers, who earned $3.69 and $1,155. The 208 trainmen made $2.39 and $748, and the 175 firemen $2.11 and $660. The 141 machinists earned $3 and $939, and the 133 other shopmen $3.21 and $1,005. Western railroads paid the operating crafts better than those east of the Mississippi, and these levels were far above the national average. The one hundred switchmen, flagmen, and watchmen earned a bit more than the machinists. The 294 carpenters, 149 section foremen, and the 207 station men other than station agents made about what firemen did. The 1,186 other hands—the 38 percent of the workforce who were trackmen and laborers—earned $366 and $438 respectively, well below a living wage for a family. Moreover, a single injury or death could plunge any family into poverty. In one fiscal year on the Texas and Pacific (1890–91), fifteen railroad employees were killed and 192 injured, while twenty-one passengers, trespassers, and bystanders were killed and forty-five injured. In the year ending

Fig. 2.2. Group of Italian railroad workers who worked on the New York, Texas, and Mexican Railroad, 1880–90. L-R: Ignarzo Toss; Giacomo Zandonatti; Giacomo Zambelli; Antonio Bartoni; Massimo Tasin; and Eugenio Depine. Bartoni and Tasin were stone cutters. Credit: UTSA's Institute of Texan Cultures, No. 073-0271, courtesy of Mr. & Mrs. Charles Innocenti.

September 30, 1888, 163 people were killed by Texas railroads and 814 injured. Judging by national statistics of that year, railway men were the victims of one-third of the fatalities and three-fourths of the injuries.[22]

After the nation sank into depression in 1893, the railroads and their unions were drawn into one of the most tumultuous events in U.S. history. Eugene Debs had resigned his treasurer's position with the Firemen and organized another attempt at unity, the American Railway Union. It was an effort to bring all railroad hands, operating crafts, machinists, and unskilled alike into one big railway union whose members would not crash each others picket lines and boycotts as the brotherhoods did. To Debs's bitter dismay, the delegates (including those from the Southwest) at the founding convention, June 1893, narrowly voted to exclude blacks from membership, though they encouraging them to organize a separate union.[23]

American Railway Union (ARU) growth came partially at the expense of the older railway unions. In January 1894, a Firemen's official bemoaned that Texas lodges were restless and very receptive to the new union. Many members of the International Association of Machinists in the railway shops joined the new industrial organization. Knights' membership in Texas was estimated at 19,000 in January 1893, but it was more likely half that or less, a decline hastened in all probability by growth of the ARU. Even so, it was likely that the Knights of Labor was larger than the ARU or the combined membership of the brotherhoods in Texas in 1893–94.[24]

During the famous ARU strike against the Pullman Palace Car Company (June and July 1894), virtually all trains in the West, except for mail trains, stopped running for a time. The railroads refused to run the trains without Pullman sleeping car coaches, and the hands refused to run trains with them. The brotherhoods did not accept the strike or even the existence of the ARU. Texas had some 2,500 to 3,000 members in twenty-two ARU locals, out of 453 nationwide, more than any state west of the Mississippi save Minnesota. Many members were also enrolled in the brotherhoods or the Knights of Labor, and in Texas they were best organized on the Santa Fe, with over 1,600 members. They had no contracts. While the Knights had no objection to the ARU, the brotherhoods threatened dual members with expulsion if they observed the boycott against Pullman coaches. Most brotherhood members believed they could not participate, or could not do so very long. Probably between 10 and 20 percent of all Texas railroad employees were ARU members, and they were mostly the unskilled who could be replaced even more easily in the hard times than was usually the case. Also, the Grover Cleveland administration was determined to smash the union.[25]

The boycott of coaches began on June 27 and spread across the West, Midwest, and Southwest. Freight traffic across Texas slowed considerably, especially after the Galveston, Temple, Dallas, Cleburne, and Gainesville locals of the ARU were called out effective July 9 on the Santa Fe line. They constituted coach cleaners, car repairmen, section hands, boilermakers, helpers, switchmen, painters, and some members of the Machinists union. Probably they were not sufficiently numerous or so crucial to daily operations that their walkout alone would have made much of an impact, but they were joined by a number of firemen and several engineers who would not run with a nonunion fireman or who would impose very high standards in testing presumably incompetent firemen. In Dallas on July 12, the Santa Fe offered $500 and a lifetime job to anyone who would fire up Number 74, but there were no takers. During the first days of the Texas strike, in Galveston, Temple, and Dallas, large crowds of workers, sympathizers, and onlookers gathered at the Santa Fe depots, but they were soon stymied by police and militia. Most of the brotherhood members and machinists who worked for the railroads would not join the strike, and by July 15 most Santa Fe trains were moving. Many strikers were replaced and those reemployed had to pledge that they would never join the ARU again. The *Dallas News* compared Debs to Attila the Hun.[26]

During the Pullman strike, Governor Hogg denounced the dispatch of federal troops to Illinois over the protest of that state's governor, denied the legality of the sweeping court injunction against Debs and the ARU, and called attention to the jailing of men without jury trial. While the strike was broken in 1894 by federal military and legal action in Chicago, the Texas Democratic Party adopted a plank in 1894 recognizing the right of labor to organize. Hogg, who noted that capitalists, railroads, and farmers already enjoyed that right, believed the plank authorized the legislature to create a board of arbitration to settle labor-management differences on the railroads.[27]

Also by the 1890s, the operating brotherhoods succeeded in more or less stabilizing their wages throughout the territory of each carrier or system in the nation. Brotherhood grievance and adjustment committees were functioning on Texas lines during the 1890s. Firemen, hostlers, and switch engineers on the Texas and Pacific, in 1893, for instance, were able to negotiate an appeals process. They received six hours' rest after eighteen hours of continuous service, if they desired it and if there was no emergency. They got seniority, guarantees of no fines for lost or damaged company property, and a call to service at least an hour before departure, among other provisos.[28]

Meanwhile, the Populist Party had been founded in 1891 because of widespread belief among southern and western farmers and wage hands that the two existing political parties were not meeting their demands. Jim Hogg announced his retirement in 1894, and in the governor's race that year Democratic attorney general Charles Culberson defeated Populist judge Tom Nugent, 216,000 to 160,000. Populists always did best in the countryside, but organized labor allowed Nugent to increase his urban vote from 10 percent in 1892 (against Hogg) to 25 percent in 1894. In Tarrant County, home of Ft. Worth, the farm-labor alliance (supposedly representing some 1,800 to 2,000 out of 5,215 registered) allowed different unions to select candidates for public office. The railroad brotherhoods selected a district clerk candidate, the building trades a legislative candidate, the ARU a justice of the peace, and the machinists a constable—apparently all were Populists. But the city's building trades locals were angered that the Populists challenged preferred, pro-labor Democrats for three other county offices. Nugent apparently carried Ft. Worth's working class third ward, but only with a plurality. Nugent came closest to carrying Austin and Houston in the working-class precincts, losing Houston's first ward by only ten votes and running well in the forth ward north. Texas labor supported the Populists better than previously, in part because Culberson did not agree with Hogg's sympathetic stand on behalf of railroad workers in the Pullman Strike that year and because of a new state Democratic plank, a backlash against the ARU strike, that promised penal sanctions against even peaceful persuasion aimed at preventing strikebreakers from taking workers' jobs. But late in the campaign Culberson deftly stemmed labor's desertion of the Democrats by pledging not to sign any bill that abridged labor's right to peacefully ask men not to take strikers' jobs. Democrats generally swept Texas in 1894, but there is evidence in some states, including Georgia and Texas, that Populist candidates won their elections, yet were counted out by the Democrats who controlled the election machinery. Some Populists were also murdered.[29]

In 1896, the Democrats nominated former Nebraska congressman William Jennings Bryan for the presidency and most western Populists were attracted to him. His potential nomination by the Populists represented a highly controversial fusion of parties at the national level that dismayed Texas Populist delegates who searched frantically for another candidate, Eugene Debs among them. The barrier that separated the two parties in Texas was said to be a line of bloody graves, but Bryan received the Populist nomination regardless. Bryan talked mostly about his free-silver plank, a gimmick to inflate the nation's currency and thereby assist debtors and others suffering from the hard times. The Populists dared to court black voters and also brought Debs, recently released from jail, into Texas to speak to workingmen in Dallas and Galveston. The Texas farm-labor political alliance reached its peak in the fall of 1896 behind the gubernatorial candidacy of Dallas attorney Jerome Kearby.[30]

But free silver (as well as Debs's presence in the campaign, perhaps) was possibly too extreme for the brotherhoods to embrace. In August, the Sound Money Clubs made up of railroad workers in Dallas, Houston, Fort Worth, and El Paso denounced the prospect of free silver as undermining the wage scale. Sound Money Club pledge cards had been distributed by the railroad corporations in an effort to control their employees, but the brotherhood members, not necessarily intimidated, may have simply become accustomed to their stabilized wages. Many other craft unions did not bolt to the Populists, no doubt in part because the Democratic legislature and governor in 1895 had reconciled their contradictory labor planks by establishing a voluntary arbitration board and promising to exempt unions from the anti-trust laws.[31]

Bryan easily carried Texas as a Democrat, though Republican William McKinley won the presidency. Kearby took 44 percent of the gubernatorial vote in a huge turnout in which the rest of the labor movement helped him carry Austin and Dallas. He carried the working-class fourth ward in Houston (947 to 770) and narrowly lost the first and second wards; he captured the mining towns of Strawn, Mingus, and Gordon. Yet it was the last gasp for the Texas Populist Party, which had alienated many of its own supporters through fusion and appeals to blacks. It was the end of the trail for the Knights of Labor as well. Both the sizeable assemblies of mixed trades railroad shopmen in Dallas and Houston—the only known railway locals remaining to the Knights in the state—either closed their doors in 1896 along with a dozen other assemblies or at least ceased their national affiliations as they faded away.[32]

Over the long haul, the Knights of Labor were killed off in part by inept and unintelligent national leadership and internal divisions, especially after 1886. Internal divisions crippled the Supreme Council of Railway Employees between 1890 and 1892 as well as farmers' efforts to unify in the 1890s. Lack of organizational unity and uninspired leadership doomed the laborers' challenges to business exploitation. Even if the brotherhoods and unions had come closer to achieving stated goals, they would likely have been crushed by force just as the southwestern and midwestern Knights had been in 1886, the American Railway Union in 1894, and the Populists in 1894 and 1896. The corporations, the two old political parties, the federal and state governments, and the courts were not going to tolerate parties or unions if they organized across classes or industries, if they accepted blacks into membership, or if they appeared on the verge of success. During the late nineteenth century, constitutional provisos for individual liberties, freedom of assembly, and the right of peaceful petition yielded to raw power. The railway brotherhoods were well aware of their vital services in the emerging industrial order and cautious of engendering a backlash in public opinion. They were agreeable to wage and work-rule revisions during the depression.[33] They survived the political and economic purges of the mid-1890s, including a plethora of court cases. So did the AFL craft unions, especially in the construction and printing trades, which won shorter work days—around nine hours—in a number of Texas cities by 1896. The brotherhoods and the AFL unions had survived and were better grounded (which included being more amenable to the prevailing racism of the era) than the more visionary and idealistic Knights. The brotherhoods looked particularly strong, since the railroads—after their ARU experience—were almost grateful for the presence of the brotherhoods and more contracts were signed. The AFL crafts and the railway brotherhoods were better adapted to endure in America's acquisitive capitalist system of that era and set most of the patterns for unionism until the Great Depression of the 1930s.[34]

NOTES

1. Melvyn Dubofsky and Foster Rhea Dulles, *Labor in America,* 7th ed. (Wheeling, Ill.: Harlan Davidson, 2004), 105, 127, 111, 133; Clyde Jacobs, *Law Writers and the Courts: the Influence of Tomas M. Cooley, Christopher G. Tiedeman and John F. Dillon Upon American Constitutional Law* (Berkeley: University of California Press, 1954), 20–27, 31–32, 58–64, 96–97 (Tiedeman quote on p. 60); William Forbath, *Law and the Shaping of the American Labor Movement* (Cambridge, Mass.: Harvard University Press, 1991), 76, 136 (Gompers quote); Samuel Hays, *The Response to Industrialism, 1885–1914* (Chicago: University of Chicago Press, 1995), 86–87, 159.

2. For national background on this era, see Hays, *Response to Industrialism, 1885–1914,* and Lawrence Friedman, *A History of American Law* (New York: Simon & Schuster, 1985), especially 467–87.

3. Robert Zeigler, "The Workingmen in Houston, Texas, 1865–1914" (PhD diss., Texas Tech University, 1972), 129–31. See Robert Bruce, *1877: Year of Violence* (Indianapolis: Bobbs-Merrill, 1959), 44–47, and Walter Licht, *Working for the Railroad* (Princeton, N.J.: Princeton University Press, 1983), 64, 90–91, 181–97, for wages, hours and conditions, including brakemen hurled off cars due to faulty handhold brackets, firemen coping with furnaces hot enough to melt glass, and engineers on alert through fog and night, hour after hour without rest.

4. Reed Richardson, *The Locomotive Engineer, 1863–1963* (Ann Arbor: University of Michigan Bureau of Industrial Relations, 1963), 223–25; *Waco Daily Examiner,* March 11, 1886; *Temple Times,* April 17 and 25, 1886; *San Antonio Light,* March 5, 6, 11, 1886; F. W. Taussig, "The South-Western Strike," *Quarterly Journal of Economics* 1 (January 1887): 199, 204–205; Julius Grodinsky, *Jay Gould, His Business Career, 1867–1892* (Philadelphia: University of Pennsylvania Press, 1957), 351, 354, 399–407; *Clarksville Standard,* April 16, 1886 (quote from the *Western Rural*), April 30, 1886 (second quote); Forbath, *Law and the Shaping of the American Labor Movement,* 95; Dubofsky and Dulles, *Labor in America,* 133–36. See also Theresa Ann Case, "Free Labor on the Southwestern Railroads: The 1885–1886 Gould System Strikes" (PhD diss., University of Texas at Austin, 2002), and Ruth Allen, *The Great Southwest Strike* (Austin: University of Texas Bureau of Research in the Social Sciences, 1942). When the president of one Texas road wanted new equipment, since the cars leaked, Gould suggested that the passengers provide themselves with umbrellas—Grodinsky, *Jay Gould,* 407.

5. *Fort Worth Gazette,* March 25, 1886, estimated Texas Knights at 25,000; Texas KOL leader Pat Golden in 1893 estimated that in 1886 there had been 30,000 Knights in Texas—see *Dallas Morning News,* January 2, 1893; Ray Marshall, *Labor in the South* (Cambridge, Mass.: Harvard University Press, 1967), 22–24; Shelton Stromquist, *A Generation of Boomers* (Chicago: University of Chicago Press, 1987), 64–65; Robert C. Cotner, *James Stephen Hogg: A Biography* (Austin: University of Texas Press, 1959), 172; Jonathan Garlock, *Guide to the Local Assemblies of the Knights of Labor* (Westport,

Conn.: Greenwood Press, 1982), 491–513; Zeigler, "Workingmen in Houston," 4–5, 87, 134–39 on *Houston Post;* Melvyn Dubofsky, *Industrialism and the American Worker, 1865–1920* (Arlington Heights, Ill.: Harlan Davidson, 1985), 48.

6. Nathan Fine, *Labor and Farmer Parties in the United States, 1828–1928* (New York: Rand School of Social Science, 1928), 148; Garlock, *Guide to the Local Assemblies of the Knights of Labor,* 491–513; Philip Foner, *History of the Labor Movement in the United States: From the Founding of the A.F. of L. to the Emergence of American Imperialism* (New York: International Publishers, 1975), 158–67; Norman Ware, *The Labor Movement in the United States, 1860–1895* (New York: Vintage, 1929), 149, 365–70; Gerald Grob, *Workers and Utopia* (Chicago: Quadrangle Books, 1961), 37–38.

7. Zeigler, "Workingmen in Houston," 4–5, 87, 134–39. Railroads were male bastions, of course. Belle Archer, hired by the Texas and Pacific as a stenographer in 1889, was the first woman hired by a railroad in Dallas—*Dallas Morning News,* March 20, 1889.

8. Brotherhood of Locomotive Firemen Lodge 147 Minutes, Temple, Texas, August 30, 1884, May 10, 1885, and March and April 1886, Texas Labor Archives, AR 50, Special Collections, University of Texas at Arlington Library.

9. Zeigler, "Workingmen in Houston," 133.

10. Brotherhood of Locomotive Engineers General Grievance Committee Minutes. January 2, 1886, January 26, and February 3, 1891, and November 8, 1892 (the quote), Texas Labor Archives, AR 72, UTA Library.

11. *Texas Railway Journal,* January 1907, contains a brief history of the legislative board; See also Irwin Yellowitz, *The Position of the Worker in American Society, 1865–1896* (Englewood Cliffs, N. J.: Prentice-Hall, 1969), 49–50. Yellowitz notes that legislation at the state level rather than national reduced the scope of the legislation that passed and created new groups of favored workers, but that most labor leaders were wary of political efforts since they mostly failed.

12. Cotner, *Hogg: A Biography,* 163, 166–67, 170–74, 201–206 (quotes); *Texas Railway Journal,* January 1907.

13. Friedman, *History of American Law,* 467–87; John Peace, *Selected Cases and Materials on Texas Workmen's Compensations Law* (San Antonio: St. Mary's University Book Store, 1950), 11–12, on the 80 percent figure.

14. See *Texas Digest, Master and Servant* (St. Paul, Minn.: West, 1969), Vol. 27, 130–645 and Vol. 27A, 31–344.

15. Ibid., Vol. 27, 281, 284, 300–301, 324–25. Even if there was any employer negligence in a particular accident, which there very frequently was, the only way to be certain of accident compensation was to die—see *Gulf, Harrisburg and San Antonio Railway v. Smith,* 76 Tex 611, 13 S.W. 562 (1890), and Peace, *Selected Cases,* 11–12.

16. *Texas Digest, Master and Servant,* Vol. 27, 279, 282, 289–91, 325. Even workers' known abilities became part of the definition. In 1896, the Texas and Pacific attempted to blame an accident on various fellow servants only to be held liable itself for maintaining a negligent worker who was known to be incompetent.

17. Ibid., Vol. 27, 359–60, 374–77; *Texas and Pacific Railway v. I. C. Bradford,* 66 Tex 732, 2 S.W. 595 (1886). In one case, strapping young brakeman John McNamara was smashed up and rendered permanently feeble by the Houston and Texas Central's

shoddy equipment, and the company tried to hold him responsible for the defective, rotten railroad ties and the resulting derailment—see 59 Tex 255 (1883).

18. *Texas Digest, Master and Servant,* Vol. 27, 441, 458, 464, 466.

19. *Missouri Pacific Railway v. Richmond,* 11 S. W. 555–558 (1889); *San Antonio and Aransas Pass Railroad v. Wilson,* 19 S.W. 910–914 (1892), quote on 912. This Texas Court of Appeals decision in the Wilson case was the first in the nation to strike down a required payment law, which Judge Simkins labeled as class legislation—see Jacobs, *Law Writers and the Courts,* 185, and Forbath, *Law and the Shaping of the American Labor Movement,* 178–79.

20. Brotherhood of Locomotive Firemen No. 147 Minutes, February 13, 1888, AR 50, Texas Labor Archives, UTA Library. Judging by the general legal guidelines of the era, passengers were held to the contributory negligence doctrine, but they assumed no risks for injuries traceable to railroad negligence. Livestock also fared better than employees. As of 1884, carriers were "liable absolutely for the loss of, or injury to, stock entrusted to them for transportation," though the railroads were not held responsible for acts of God or outlaws or unruly actions by the animals. See *Texas Digest, Carriers,* Vol. 7, 280, 669–70.

21. Charles Gibson, "Organized Labor in Texas From 1890 to 1900" (master's thesis, Texas Tech University, 1973), 188–91; Foner, *From the Founding of the A.F .of L.,* 252–53 (the quotes); *The Nation* 51, October 30, 1890, 334; Stromquist, *A Generation of Boomers,* 81; Marshall, *Labor in the South,* 58; George N. Green, "Militant Railroad Workers and the Closing of the Frontier, 1870s-1920s," *Red River Valley Historical Journal* 2 (Fall 2001): 14–36.

22. *Annual Report of the Texas and Pacific Railway Company to the Railroad Commission of the State of Texas for the Year Ending June 30, 1891,* 59, 73, Box 455–597, Texas State Archives, Austin; L. L. Foster, *Forgotten Texas Census* (Austin: Texas State Historical Association, 2001), 318; Licht, *Working for the Railroad,* 190. Some twenty-five to thirty Texas and Pacific "extra men" among operating brotherhood members living in Longview were described as "all, or nearly all, settled men and householders" by the *Dallas Morning News,* June 14, 1887.

23. Nick Salvatore, *Eugene V. Debs* (Chicago: University of Illinois Press, 1982), 115–16, 227; Foner, *From the Founding of the A.F. of L.,* 255; Richard Boyer and Herbert Morais, *Labor's Untold Story* (New York: Cameron Associates, 1955), 122; Stromquist, *Generation of Boomers,* 81.

24. Salvatore, *Debs,* 117; John Laslett, *Labor and the Left* (New York: Basic Books, 1970), 150; *Dallas Morning News,* January 2, 1893.

25. See Ray Ginger, *The Bending Cross* (New Brunswick, N.J.: Rutgers University Press, 1949), 108–51; Stromquist, *A Generation of Boomers,* 84–85; Gibson, "Organized Labor in Texas," 147–57; membership estimates from *Dallas Morning News,* July 7, 9, 10, 1894, and *Temple Times,* July 10, 1894.

26. Gibson, "Organized Labor in Texas," 209, 217–18; *Dallas Morning News,* July 7, 11–14, 16, 1894; *Fort Worth Gazette,* July 13, 14, 1894; *Marshall Evening Messenger,* July 12–13, 1894; Ginger, *The Bending Cross,* 180.

27. Cotner, *Hogg: A Biography,* 388–90, 433; *Dallas Morning News,* August 24, 28, September 25, 1894.

28. Marshall, *Labor in the South,* 50–51; Philip Taft, *Organized Labor in American History* (New York: Harper and Row, 1964), 264; "The Texas and Pacific Railway Co. Schedule of Pay and Rules and Regulations Governing Firemen, Hostlers and Switch Engineers," Dallas, May 24, 1893, G O 3/3, Texas Labor Archives, Special Collections, UTA Library.

29. Martin, *People's Party,* 137–39, 184–85; Barr, *Reconstruction to Reform,* 150–51,157–58; Zeigler, "Workingmen in Houston," 180; Gibson, "Organized Labor in Texas," 147–57; *Fort Worth Gazette,* October 2 and November 6, 1894; *Dallas Morning News,* August 24, 28, and September 25, 1894; Lawrence Goodwyn, *Democratic Promise: The Populist Moment in America* (New York: Oxford University Press, 1976), 332–33. In Fort Worth's third ward, Culberson received 214 votes, Nugent 2_5 and other candidates 108. There is a 90 percent chance that the missing integer in Nugent's total is higher than zero, meaning that he probably carried the ward, but only with a plurality. See the *Fort Worth Gazette,* November 9, 1894. Of the nine relatively modest Texas labor demands put forward in 1894, three directly concerned railroad workers—the passage of an anti-blacklist law, a better fellow servant statute, and the abolition of child labor among railroad telegraphers. See *Dallas Morning News,* September 21, 1894.

30. Barr, *Reconstruction to Reform,* 165–67, 170; Gibson, "Organized Labor in Texas," 163–70; Ginger, *The Bending Cross,* 189; Goodwyn, *Democratic Promise,* 490–92. Just after the Populist convention nominated Bryan, the Texas delegates refused to join in the demonstration and "repulsed with drawn pistols an effort to carry their banner into the procession"—see Barr, *Reconstruction to Reform,* 167.

31. Fine, *Labor and Farmer Parties,* 85; Milton Garner, "The Application of the Anti-Trust Laws of Texas to Labor Unions," *Southwestern Law Journal* 2 (Spring 1948): 112; Gibson, "Organized Labor in Texas," 157–58, 169–70.

32. Barr, *Reconstruction to Reform,* 171; Zeigler, "Workingmen in Houston," 180–81; Garlock, *Guide to the Local Assemblies of the Knights of Labor,* 491–513; *Stephenville Empire,* November 13, 1896, for mining-town votes. The Populists may have done better than the figures suggest, of course, since they continued to be routinely defrauded by Democrats, who arranged votes for dead people, droves of mules and Jefferson Davis, among others—see Martin, *The People's Party,* 184–85.

33. Taft, *Organized Labor,* 59; Stromquist, *A Generation of Boomers,* 263.

34. Stromquist, *A Generation of Boomers,* 264–65; Dubofsky, *Industrialism and the American Worker,* 67–68, notes the weakness of the AFL in 1897.

CHAPTER THREE

Racism and Sexism in Rural Texas

THE CONTESTED NATURE OF PROGRESSIVE RURAL REFORM, 1870s–1910s

Debra A. Reid

Robert Lloyd Smith, educator and founder of the all-black Farmers Improvement Society of Texas (FIS), and Seaman Knapp, educator and designer of the U.S. Department of Agriculture's cooperative demonstration work, shared progressive ideals. Both believed that much could be accomplished with education and government influence. Smith told FIS members in 1902 that nothing was impossible to attain "under the protection that is vouchsafed unto us by a humane state and national government." Knapp believed that "the people on the farms in our country shall have an equipment [provided by land-grant colleges] so broad and thorough that they are qualified for the highest requirements of our citizenship." Both shared traditional male views regarding men's and women's roles in rural reform, believing that men of character held responsibility for economic, social, and political issues, and that women needed to focus on the domestic economy. Smith believed that the African American family was "the unit of civilization" most assailed by slavery and most needed by black Texans: "No influence this side of heaven can begin to compare with that of a well ordered domestic fireside." Knapp went so far as to claim that "the home itself upon the farm, and the women and girls of the home, [constituted] one of the problems of rural uplift . . . [and] one simple and straightforward lesson to girls . . . will . . . open their eyes to the possibilities of adding to the family income."[1]

Needless to say, socialization affected rural women as well as men, and this caused many women to share gender biased views that relegated them to the home. Their duties to raise children, procure and process food, and contribute to the economic viability of the farm dictated their routines. Yet, many women refused to settle for public isolation, and they lobbied for rural economic development, education, and suffrage. In 1912, Mrs. O. L. Helm told Texas State Farmers' Institute attendees that beautifying the home should

Fig. 3.1. Mrs. McGee's Home Demonstration Club, McKinney, Texas, preparing carrots, corn, apples, and tomatoes for canning in glass jars. The club lived in a truck-farming area, and canning supplemented farm-family income. A USDA photographer documented the activity in 1917. Credit: North Texas History Center, McKinney.

involve both sexes: "if the girls and boys feel that they are home-makers, . . . they will be home-makers." Mrs. Albert W. Brown described the work of girls on the farm, but she expanded considerably beyond one simple lesson, as Knapp had suggested. Instead, she urged girls and women to can vegetables and fruits and sell them. She reported on raising cattle, making butter, and fattening calves and hogs on residual skim milk. African American women went a step further to try to educate rural youth in the source of justice and to encourage citizens to take their grievances to court. Smith's wife held administrative responsibility for the FIS Juvenile Division, and she wrote a play that complied with the gender bias that Smith had expressed, but it also indicated additional roles that women could take to change rural life. *Trial of Old King Credit* included only one woman character, Mrs. Good Family, and she appeared as a victim of her husband's manipulation by King Credit, but the play featured a courtroom and jurors such as Negro Manhood, Self Respect, and Justice. They found "King Credit" guilty of destroying the race. The FIS published the play so that communities could perform it "to help inspire the people to be more progressive."[2]

Rural Texans shared much, but not all, in their quest to improve their standards of living and realize full citizenship. Reformers, black and white alike, male and female alike, believed that education and economic stability could help farm families secure personal liberty and contribute to the public good. Once trained in scientific agriculture and home management, they wanted outlets to share the information and influence economic, political, and social decisions. All used grassroots activism, direct appeals to elected and appointed officials, and moral suasion to leverage white male decision-makers. But they did not work together to realize such goals. Instead, racism and sexism divided them. Collaboration not cooperation resulted, and without a united effort, women could not overcome gender bias, and blacks could not overcome race bias.[3]

Government legislation at the national and state levels codified race- and gender-biased reform, and Texans facilitated its development. Kathleen Hilton considers the U.S. Department of Agriculture (USDA) the main culprit: "The Office of Extension Work South deliberately chose a gender-segregated pattern for the work . . . [and] reflected the USDA's determination to revolutionize agriculture but maintain male control of gender relations within rural society." African American historians have likewise charged the USDA with racist tendencies, but individual southerners and state land-grant college administrators called for and then implemented segregated rural reform. White males in Texas led the assault, and they defied Fourteenth Amendment guarantees and perpetuated inequality in their quest to retain their control of rural Texas.[4]

More than 90 percent of all Texans lived in rural areas during the late nineteenth century, and rural concerns galvanized them, particularly the goals of retaining inexpensive black labor and creating markets. Between the mid-1870s until 1905, the strongest southern branch of the National Grange of the Orders of Patrons of Husbandry, a nonpartisan organization devoted to farm family interests, operated in Texas. Members adopted an antiblack and pro-capitalist stance that rural whites believed could help them retain their hegemony. Archibald J. Rose, a Confederate veteran, leading educational reformer, and Grange organizer served such conservative rural Texans well. He supported congressional aid for the Texas & Pacific Railroad, because the railroad gave them critical market access, and thus afforded them an opportunity to "have . . . the rights and facilities to develop their material wealth and increase their production."[5]

While the railroad ensured market access, farmers also needed cheap labor, and this led them to essentially replicate pre–Civil War white-black economic relationships. The experiences of the Porter and McQuinney families indicate how the relationship evolved, and the roles that men and women of both races played in it. John Brooks Porter, a native of Kentucky, an ex-Confederate, and resident of Morringsport, Louisiana, took advantage of opportunities afforded by railroad expansion into Texas after the war. He and his extended Louisiana family relocated en masse, reputedly traveling on one of the first Texas & Pacific trains heading west. Porter purchased forty acres in Terrell around 1872, and after he permanently settled in the area, he established various businesses and accumulated farm land.[6]

Around 1878, Porter moved an African American tenant family, Ben and Agnes McQuinney and their children, from Morringsport, Louisiana, to Texas. Both Ben and Agnes had been born slaves, and according to Porter descendents, they came to Texas to "get a new start." The family lived on Porter land for most of their lives, and the Porters valued their service. The McQuinney family included eight surviving children, and they provided labor in exchange for lodging, foodstuffs, and shares of the crop on the Porter farm. The McQuinneys lived in close proximity to the Porters, and they farmed between seventy and one hundred acres adjacent to the Porter homestead. This gave the Porter family a steady view of McQuinney-family pursuits. Though the children played together, race and class divided the families. Black and white tenants performed the labor—the Porters owned the land.[7]

The heads of the McQuinney and Porter households were nearly the same age, they fathered many children at similar intervals, and they both pursued farming as their occupation. Sons in the families, Walter C. Porter and John McQuinney, were born within six months of each other in 1868, in Louisiana. They followed in their fathers' footsteps, with the younger Porter maintaining a large farming operation, and the younger McQuinney providing labor. They both married and started families during the 1890s. Walter C. Porter

Fig. 3.2. Unidentified African Americans on a wagon near Kaufman, Texas, standpipe. The original image was printed on postcard stock, c.1915. Credit: Kathey Kelley Hunt, The Kaufman County TXGenWebProject Site, http://www.txgenweb5.org/txkaufman/.

married Elizabeth Mary "Bessie" Crumbaugh in December 1891, and the family grew to nine children. John Quinny [McQuinney] married Sue Hodge in December 1895. The family grew to nine children, as well. The high survival rate implies that each family enjoyed generally good health, and indicates that both families apparently satisfied their basic food, clothing, and shelter needs. Aspects of inequality extended beyond economics. All of the Porter family members had the opportunity to receive an education. None of the McQuinney children attended school through Sue Hodge McQuinney, and the McQuinney children could read and write at the turn of the twentieth century.[8]

In fact, education motivated white as well as black reformers. White Texans had selected a site for the white land-grant college, Agricultural and Mechanical College of Texas (hereafter Texas A&M) by 1871. Black reformers lobbied for access, and only five years later, in 1876, the Texas legislature authorized the Alta Vista Agriculture & Mechanical College of Texas for Colored Youth (hereafter Prairie View A&M). Despite gains of black reformers, racism persisted but so did black rural activism.[9]

Robert Lloyd Smith came to Oakland, Texas, from South Carolina around 1878, about the same time that the McQuinney family had relocated. Yet, Smith and the McQuinney family had little in common. Smith, born free, did not have the patronage of a white family to limit his choices, though he faced other challenges. He settled in an all-black community, Freedmantown, at the edge of Oakland, Texas, and he immediately set about helping black sharecroppers and tenants gain a sense of economic independence. He modeled Republican aspirations, living a pious and morally upright life while committing himself to educational reform and mutual aid. He successfully blended his educational responsibilities with political aspirations during a turbulent era. The Colored Farmers National Alliance and Cooperative Union had originated in nearby Houston County, Texas, in 1886. It offered rural blacks a voice in local, state, and national politics. When Smith founded the Village Improvement Society three years later, it stood as a Republican alternative for rural black families not engaged with the alliance and populist challenge.[10]

Smith spent much of his first ten years in Oakland improving educational opportunities for children and adults. He reformed the public schools, became principal of the high school, and developed a normal school to train teachers. He helped the community build a new school and a new church and, in late 1889, he organized African Americans into the Village Improvement Society of Oakland to encourage the purchase and improvement of homes. Yet, educated Freedmantown residents had to answer to the landlords for whom they labored and then to the white owners of any property they sought to acquire, so they could do only so much to build their separate community.[11]

Smith promoted his Village Improvement Society as a means to circumvent exploitation by whites, "a class," according to Smith, "that calculated, almost to the pound, his productive capacity, and then gave him credit up to this estimate and occasionally beyond it." Women played a key role in this effort, particularly after Smith married Francis Isabella Isaacs in 1890. Mrs. Smith administered the Women's Barnyard Auxiliary, which implied the subordinate status of women in the organization but also reflected the real contribution rural black women made to their farms. Mrs. Smith and her cohort raised food and tended stock that helped families realize two goals—avoidance of crop liens and improved standard of living that visibly indicated economic independence. The women allied with the men to engage in economic warfare, encouraging black farm families to practice improved methods of farming, invest their egg, poultry, and butter income in their own homes and land, and thus distance themselves from white control. Farmers could improve their status from sharecropper to tenant to farm owner, and gain personal security as a result. Landowning families influenced local decision-making; they could hire educators, ministers, tradesmen, doctors, and even lawyers to work in their interest. Property ownership, particularly land ownership, assured them some influence, even during an era of increased disfranchisement and de facto discrimination. At the same time, though, landowners paid more taxes, including poll taxes, and they committed limited resources toward education. Reformers allied with landowners to improve conditions in Texas, bringing to rural blacks the gleanings from their own education. Thus, land became a tool that black men and women used to secure personal liberty. White Texans could support such conservative goals as private property ownership and self-improvement because they believed in the free market capitalism, but black reformers such Robert and Belle Smith carefully shielded the ways that such economic independence could further local autonomy, a right that white Texans did not want to extend to black Texans.[12]

The Smiths' reform agenda resonated with black women who, despite their impoverished circumstances, could more easily secure an advanced degree from a public institution than could white women. Ironically, black women could attend Texas' black land-grant college, Prairie View A&M, and take classes in cooking, sewing, and other domestic science topics beginning during the 1880s. White women faced more resistance as they lobbied for equal access to education. They could not attend the state land-grant university, and a separate college did not exist for them until 1901 when legislators finally authorized the Girls' Industrial College.[13]

The Smiths challenged FIS members, men, women, and children alike, to do more with less, and they believed that public research institutions could help them rise above. In 1900, Mr. Smith chided black farmers: "Well, really, to sum up, if there's anything like scientific methods among the vast majority of our people I don't know it." Then he urged them to turn to "the agricultural department [that] has established and maintains at great cost experimental stations, for the purpose of disseminating useful knowledge among the common people. Literature is distributed free of costs. I venture to say that not one negro farmer in a hundred ever saw the back of one of these bulletins, much less the inside." Smith obviously read the literature because he summarized the integrated pest management approach that the USDA recommended to eradicate the boll weevil in 1902, but his sustained discussion of the value of government publications implied that black farm families did not heed his advice.[14]

Smith praised private as well as public educational opportunities. In 1902, he informed FIS members that *Texas Farm and Ranch* had begun offering farmers' institutes, "footing the bill out of its own pocket." Actually, Franklin Pierce Holland, the agricultural journal's publisher, sponsored institutes in Louisiana and Oklahoma, as well as Texas, and helped organize special interest groups such as the Texas Swine Growers Association. Smith believed that black farmers had to take advantage of every opportunity available because they had to "hold [their] own by DOING better." Unless black farmers improved their methods, "Yes, sir, . . . we shall lose our place in the industrial world. Already we are being elbowed out by German, Bohemian, Swede and Mexican renters."[15]

Smith constantly urged FIS members to focus on independence realized through hard work, education, and economic management. By 1909, he believed that the FIS "army . . . of men and women . . . who want more stock and better stock" would prosper if they worked hard and gained "practical training in the noble occupation of agriculture." Yet, the crop lien system continued to conspire against them. This caused Smith to encourage members to participate in FIS's cooperative purchasing program, which he described as "the central arch in our bridge from Slavery to Freedom. By this we expect to lead the people out from the land of Bondage into the land of Independence." A combination of government support, education, and personal acquisitiveness would ensure their success.[16]

Black rural reformers such as the Smiths, working through private organizations, encouraged farmers to seek information on scientific agriculture. At the same time, white Texans strengthened their authority over publicly funded scientific agriculture, even as they disfranchised poor rural and black citizens by instituting poll taxes and white primaries. Edward Reeves Kone, a leading Democrat from San Marcos and one of many committed white supremacists who supported such legislation, helped codify agricultural reform as well. He became the first elected commissioner for the Texas Department of Agriculture (TDA) in 1908, and held the position to 1915. Democrats such as Kone left little doubt about which race should control Texas.[17]

The national government likewise became involved in rural reform as agents began working directly with Texas farmers and reformers by 1903 when Seaman Knapp undertook an experiment in crop cultivation near Terrell, in Kaufman County. This helped launch Farmers' Cooperative Demonstration Work (FCDW), which, by 1914, evolved into the Cooperative Extension Service, a state-based service authorized by the Smith-Lever Act and run out of land-grant universities across the nation. Significantly, the origins of the service involved black Texans, an oft forgotten contribution to rural reform. John "Jack" McQuinney, African American tenant farmer to the Porter family, actually implemented FCDW guidelines that resulted in yields that reporters claimed "far exceeded expectations."[18]

The McQuinney family had farmed the field designated for the experiments since they had come to Texas, and reporters indicated that the acres had "been planted in cotton or corn every season for twenty-eight years without any fertilizer or any renovating crops." Knapp planned to "investigate the effect of fertilizers, methods of cultivation and planting without any special attempt to produce large crops," but nearly one-half of the acreage was planted in the state's major cash crop, cotton, and most of the remainder in the major feed crop, corn. Porter, the landowner, garnered high praise from local reporters who described him as "one of the best" and "one of the most thorough and reliable farmers" in the area. Local media and posturing government agents and private interests ignored the black tenant as they privileged the white owner. This obliterated McQuinney from the project, preventing him from claiming any legitimate role in the endeavor.[19]

The first five USDA agents received their appointments to conduct demonstration work in late January and February 1904, and they spent about one-quarter of their time serving black farmers. African Americans accounted for approximately 20 percent of all Texas farmers in 1905, and most of them depended on cotton as their principle cash crop. Yet, they cultivated only about 14 percent of all land devoted to cotton in Texas. Given the degree to which black farmers depended on cotton, they warranted at least the attention they received, if not more. Despite the obvious responsibility that black farmers bore for the crop, and thus the livelihood of white Texans, racist attitudes affected Knapp's judgment. He believed that "the colored race . . . [must] start at the bottom. In attempting to raise the condition of the colored man we frequently start too high up, and in talking of the higher progress talk right over his head. When I talk to a negro citizen I never talk about the better civilization, but about a better chicken, a better pig, a white-washed house." Knapp did not want to hire black agents because he believed whites would serve both races while blacks would concentrate only on programs for members of their race. Racism as well as carefully constructed segregated rural relations confirmed Knapp's assumption that blacks would serve only their own race. Yet, some evidence of white and black Texans working together appears in the historic record. The county agent in Kaufman County, home of the first demonstration and the McQuinney family, worked with forty black tenant families by 1907.[20]

Successful reform depended on youth involvement, and black and white reformers, male and female alike, organized youth clubs. The Texas Farmers' Congress, a Texas A&M offering that began in 1898, supported the Farmer Boys' and Girls' League in 1903, and enrolled 1,200 white youth by 1904. Its funds were cut in 1905. Belle Smith organized the FIS's Juvenile Branch in 1907, which included boys and girls. USDA agents likewise believed that training youth could further the agricultural reform agenda efficiently, though men provided the instruction during the early years. J. L. Quicksall, state agent in Texas, recounted how Capt. F. S. White, the Horticultural Commissioner of the Rock Island and Frisco Railroad lines, visited Jacksboro, Texas, in 1907, and suggested the establishment of corn clubs. Tom Marks, the agent in Jack County in West Texas, enrolled 111 white boys by spring 1908. He involved the county superintendent, teachers, and parents in organizing viable corn contest clubs.[21]

White Texans celebrated the youth that participated in the clubs. Reformers impressed upon the boys and girls that "the time has come when the farm needs men and women well educated . . . to succeed and become great broadminded citizens, progressive and fully alive to the advantages offered on the farm." This coincided with a national effort to improve rural conditions to stem the out-migration, and improving the farm home and rural conveniences became central to women's work. Thus, boys and girls were reminded of the proper roles in rural reform. A photograph of a parade in Brenham, Texas, in 1910, included a float bedecked with corn, flags, and Boys' Corn Club members. The president was a boy being groomed to assume scientific farm management. The girl next to him was the club's princess.[22]

Other public displays had to maintain racial hierarchy, so even though white agents could work with African American boys, the boys could not compete against white boys at fairs. For example, in 1910, R. P. Elrod, the agent in Lee County in south central Texas, organized all-black corn clubs. Forty-two enrolled, and the agent reported that he had "equally good results shown with them as with the white boys." Nearly one-third of the Lee County population was black, so the ratio of black to white youth in the clubs reflected county demographics. Yet, black youth could not exhibit their "equally good results" unless separate competitions and separate premiums for "Negro" entrants were awarded at fairs or if separate "Negro fairs" occurred. The FIS facilitated Elrod's program by sponsoring corn and cotton exhibits at the Lee County fair and providing a platform for Elrod and the county superintendent of public instruction, C. M. Bishop, to speak.[23]

Fig. 3.3. L. A. Nieburh, agent for Farmers Cooperative Demonstration Work in Brenham, Texas, in 1910, worked with several boys enrolled in corn clubs. This photograph, included in *Farmers' Cooperation Demonstration Work for 1910,* 424, depicts "a float in parade at Brenham, Texas. Boy standing by girl who represents 'The Corn Queen' is the President of Corn Clubs in the County, May 26, 1910." Credit: Personal Papers of Wayne Rasmussen, USDA History Collection, Special Collections, National Agricultural Library, Beltsville, Maryland.

The FIS provided considerable structure for its youth members, but it apparently followed less strict gender divisions in its Juvenile Department. Mrs. Smith conceived the organization as one that would educate the black youth to face the demands "made upon . . . our race." The constitution described the protocol for meetings, thus providing members experience in organizational structure. Girls could assume officer positions in local branches, but some gender distinctions persisted. Only "a grown person or young lady of good moral character, a Christian if possible" could serve as preceptress of a branch. This person served as the moral barometer for the camp, a responsibility typically ascribed to and assumed by women. Mrs. Smith, as Grand Preceptress of the Juvenile Branch, left no question about the centrality of religion to the morality of the members, nor about the importance of agriculture. Members raised money by tending one to three acres of cotton and keeping chickens, thus earning funds adequate to pay for their college education. Both boys and girls bore responsibility for such chores.[24]

Despite the effort the Smiths put into FIS, they became frustrated as they preached self-determination. Concomitantly, the farmers lost faith with agents who implied that they, and not the economic system that entrapped them, were responsible for the South's social and economic shortcomings. Black farmers also understood that improvements could have repercussions. Better homes led to increased rents, thus allowing the white landlord to reap additional rewards from the tenants' labor. Class conflict within the black community also challenged agents. They appeared as representatives of the landlord class, the ones sapping the strength out of the poor rural blacks, and tenant farmers and sharecroppers resented their advice. Some tenants showed their lack of support for the program by choosing migration.[25]

White women engaged in the same struggle that African American men and women undertook to gain authority over rural reform, and gender discrimination compromised their quest as racism conspired against African Americans. White Texas women could secure a degree from the Girls Industrial College, which had a curriculum in household arts by 1903, or from the School of Domestic Economy at the University of Texas (hereafter UT). This provided credentials they needed to improve women's and families' lives, but not necessarily access to paying positions. Some found outlets through extension courses offered at UT, but officials with the Texas Extension Service still resisted hiring women full time to deliver rural reform. By 1911, girls obviously participated in clubs that local farmers' institutes sanctioned. John S. Kerr of Sherman, Texas, spoke on the history of institutes in 1911, and he indicated that adults taught boys and girls about scientific agriculture. He expressed traditional gender bias by identifying boys as future farmers and relegating girls to the role of farm wife. But he also indicated that girls participated in corn clubs, along with the boys: "When these boys and girls, to whom we are offering prizes to beat us raising corn—when these boys and girls come along to take our places in the government, they are going to see these things more intelligently, and there will be an uplift in Texas of everything pertaining to agriculture." Doubtless many women and girls intended for the uplift to extend beyond agriculture.[26]

In 1912, a few women became involved as temporary employees of the USDA's Cooperative Demonstration Work in Texas, and the programs they initiated offered some flexibility in traditional gender roles. The women worked two months during the summer to instruct girls in growing one-tenth acre of tomatoes and canning them. In 1912, girls' tomato clubs existed in eight counties. The president of Texas A&M, R. T. Milner, reported enthusiastically to Farmers' Congress attendees in July 1912 that 2,000 girls enrolled in club work and "they . . . helped to solve the problem of the high cost of living in their homes [and] earned a neat sum of money." Mrs. Edna W. Trigg, a rural high school principal from Milam County, accepted appointment as a girls' tomato club collaborator for seventy-five dollars for her two months of summer employment. The Cameron Chamber of Commerce matched that amount. She worked with the network of rural teachers that she knew as well as the Truck Growers Association in the county. These existing support systems, plus a predisposition for tomato truck farming among rural families, helped her realize initial success. She organized eleven clubs with around ten girls in each club. Successful exhibitions and local and regional fairs helped acquaint other farm families with the program. Trigg remembered that by 1913, the clubs expanded to "Canning and Poultry Clubs," and boys could join and thus learn new information about diversified agricultural production. Yet, adequate salaries for the collaborator proved difficult to secure. The Commissioners Court in the country refused to match the salary provided through the USDA, and the club work ceased after 1914. Thus, opportunities to challenge gender barriers existed, but individual and community support in the form of adequate funding proved lacking.[27]

Farm girls and women participated regularly in local farmers institutes—they did not depend on the temporary offerings provided under the auspices of the USDA. Activities indicated the vital role that farm women and rural reformers could play in the local economy, and the degree to which they engaged in local politics. Knapp's perception that rural women needed simple instructions proved unfounded. Mrs. Rebecca H. Hayes of Alvin, Texas, commented at the 1912 institute that women in Brazoria County received permission to use their local dues to pursue their own interests. They invited speakers to meetings but also organized an information meeting in partnership with the Truck Growers' Association that helped keep the fig preserving factory from closing. This allowed them to retain an important element of their rural economy. Yet, the TDA steered clear of controversial topics. Mrs. Hayes broached the topic of woman suffrage as a "simple" request for "right and justice toward women" at the 1913 institute, and her request was ruled out of order even though several male delegates seconded her motion to discuss the topic.[28]

Lest other organizations come to dominate rural reform, the USDA and Texas A&M signed a Memorandum of Understanding on October 1, 1912, thus consolidating responsibility for agricultural reform at Texas A&M. The memorandum gave Texas A&M authority over farm demonstration and boys' and girls' club work in the state, conducted via the auspices of Texas Agricultural Extension Service (hereafter TAEX). This effectively eliminated UT from involvement in rural reform and undermined Texas Farmers Institute offerings. By 1915, the TAEX emerged as the dominant force in Texas rural reform.[29]

White women did not celebrate this agreement because Texas A&M prohibited women from enrolling in the university. Many saw little potential

Fig. 3.4. Women hired in 1912 through the USDA's Farmers Cooperative Demonstration Program to work with Girls' Canning & Poultry Clubs in eight Texas counties included: L-R, row 1: Miss Bernice Carter, Denton County, Miss Lizzie Thurman, Cook County; L-R, row 2: Mrs. Mae Click (standing), Bee County, Mrs. Larry Tittle, Comanche County, Mrs. Jessie Kyle, Caldwell County, Mrs. Edna W. Trigg, Milam County (center, seated behind the banner), Mrs. Lee Baker, Wise County, Mrs. Ancel Harris (standing), Wichita County. Officials with the Texas Agricultural Extension Service and the USDA included: L-R, row 1: C.M. Evans, Supervisor of Collaborators, H.H. Williamson, Supervisor of Boys' Corn Clubs; L-R, row 3: O.H. Benson (standing), USDA. Taken in Waco, Texas, 1912. Credit: Cushing Memorial Library and Archives, Texas A&M University, College Station, Texas.

for developing programs to serve rural women at a college that refused to teach them. The University of Texas offered extension courses to women, and the TDA involved women in canning clubs, but women worried that these would cease to exist after the agreement. The TAEX hired its first woman full time in 1913, but she supervised girls' clubs only. The TDA hired two women full time by 1916 to work with institutes. Existing youth clubs and programs for rural women provided some leverage, but it was obvious that ultimate authority rested with white men.[30]

African Americans did not celebrate the consolidation of rural reform at Texas A&M either. By 1912, the USDA, with funds from the General Education Board, placed thirty-two black agents in nine southern states, excluding

Texas. Texas did not receive funding because it lay within the area infected by the boll weevil, and the GEB refused to pay for areas receiving government funds to counter infestation. Furthermore, some believed that Texans had enough financial resources to employ its own black agents. Texas ranked fifth in the nation in the number of black farmers, but Texas A&M did not see fit to use USDA funds to employ them even as land-grant colleges in other southern states, with private funding, did.[31]

African Americans lobbied the USDA for more positions for African Americans equal to those held by white agents. The National Association for the Advancement of Colored People argued that segregation in government employment would reduce the efficiency of both white and black agents in the service, and it would set a precedent that would have far-reaching consequences. In response, officials denied that the USDA had a segregation policy. Racism affected individual decisions, however, which affected policy. In 1913, Bradford Knapp, Seaman Knapp's son, and O. B. Martin, both USDA policy makers, believed that boys' and girls' clubs for black youth should incorporate "Negro" in the title to distinguish them from similar programs undertaken for white children. Martin feared that similarity would "cause trouble and conflict with the Canning Club work among the white girls." He suggested that black agents work with girls and their mothers and emphasize home improvement rather than home canning, as white girls and their mothers pursued. He suggested "Home Making Clubs" as more accurate and less controversial. They agreed that black children would earn "separate badges, of different design . . . they can not wear the same badges the white boys wear." Thus, at the time when Texas began to expand the service, national officials legitimized separate and distinctive offerings.[32]

During May 1914, southern legislators pushed the Smith-Lever Act through the U.S. Congress. The act created the Federal Extension Service and charged it with appropriating funds to state-based land-grant colleges to further extension work. This eliminated the use of private funding and northern influence in southern agriculture, which had furthered the employment of both white women and African Americans. The Smith-Lever Act also gave states the authority to distribute the public funds as they saw fit, without national intervention, thus allowing race segregation. By July 1914, the TAEX had drawn up plans, and Federal Extension Service administrators had approved them, that called for an "Agent in Home Demonstration Work," who would supervise girls' club work but also direct women home demonstration agents. This created the gender division of administration and program delivery that defined rural reform throughout the twentieth century.[33]

Texans waited more than a year after passage of the Smith-Lever Act, however, to expand offerings to rural blacks. Early in 1915, Clarence Ousley, TAEX director, wanted to increase the number of African American boys in corn clubs. Some staff wanted to isolate the agents to a small area around Prairie View A&M. Ousley, however, envisioned a larger workforce to cover a larger area. In August, TAEX employed three African Americans to serve black farm families. TAEX staffed it with qualified adults knowledgeable in modern scientific practices. The structure of the bureaucracy, with whites overseeing blacks at all levels, reinforced Jim Crow race relations. It also co-opted FIS programming, hiring Smith as the first Negro Division director, and drawing limited resources away from members of both FIS and TAEX clubs. White supervisors facilitated this by appropriating inadequate funds and expecting the African American staff to supplement their salaries with local support and to work with little to no office support even while producing measurable results among their black constituents. These factors made the black agents dependent on patronage from local commissioners courts to retain positions. Thus, the new federal program, enabled by a partnership between the national and state governments, reinforced grave inequities on the southern landscape.[34]

The creation of the Negro division included hiring a black woman, Mrs. M. E. V. Hunter, in a permanent position to manage programs for black women and girls. She began on August 1, 1915. Her employment preceded the creation of the first permanent position for a manager of white home demonstration agents at TAEX by eight months. Bernice Carter, who had worked as an assistant in girls club work since mid-September 1913, began as state home demonstration agent on April 1, 1916. Carter supervised Hunter in 1915, nonetheless, but Carter had little influence over larger TAEX administrative decisions. Between 1913 and 1916, male officials determined whom to hire as temporary female staff. TAEX director, Clarence Ousley reported in an October 1915 letter to Mrs. M. W. Sims that thirty-one women had been employed as county agents, and the budget allowed for expansion. He neglected to indicate that all female agent appointments were temporary—only Mrs. Hunter and Miss Carter were permanent. Despite employment in temporary positions, women assumed responsibility for expanded demonstrations, including poultry and egg marketing, dairying, gardening and canning, and home orchard management and nutrition. The TAEX published bulletins on homemade household conveniences and on poultry for them to distribute. Regardless, Ousley told Sims that the women hired exhibited shortcomings, and this had slowed integrating women into the service. Ousley claimed that few graduates with degrees in domestic science and household arts had knowledge of rural problems and solutions, and this made it difficult to staff available positions.[35]

A year later, Mr. S. B. Holman complained about women employees directly to Ousley. Holman expressed sexist opinions, blaming women for a disorganized home economics program that lacked direction. He observed that "this lack of spirit prevails more among the women members of the staff than among the men, probably because of their lack of logic and inability to understand the system." Ousley's letter to Holman, unlike his letter to Sims, was not diplomatic nor did it mask the tensions that had flared between progressive women seeking inclusion and the men who managed TAEX. Nor did Ousley's letter to Holman indicate the continued conflicts at the state and national level over the role of women in managing home demonstration work. Instead, Ousley's letter to Holman conveyed the deep-seeded sexism that, when combined with racism, allowed white men in authority to withhold opportunity, expend inadequate funds, expect impossible results, and yet still hold women and black employees accountable for failure.[36]

White women reformers and black men and women reformers influenced white decision-making. Both communicated with high-ranking officials and expected action. Both adapted to the stipulations white officials made and took advantage of opportunities that came along to further their own personal and career goals. But the opportunities that eventually became available to black men and women and white women reformers existed despite racially segregated and gender biased power structures created by men in authority. Consolidating rural reform in the hands of a few white Democrats at the TAEX undermined progressive reform initiatives and stymied discourse about alternative methods of responding to rural need. This limited rural reform to the model advocated by white Texas men, a model based in free-market capitalism with restrictions imposed by race and gender constructs and personal and class self-interest.

NOTES

1. For both Smith quotes see "Annual Address" of Hon. R. L. Smith, President, Farmers' Improvement Society of Texas, Delivered at Eagle Lake, Texas, October 8, 1902, at the 7th Annual Convocation, 7, 12–13, Farmers' Improvement Society of Texas, Smith-Cobb Family Papers, Baylor University, Waco, Texas (hereafter SCFP). For the first Knapp quote see "Our Colleges of Agriculture," typed manuscript (1907), 6; for the second, an excerpt from Knapp's last formal report, see Dr. Seaman A. Knapp, *Proceedings of the Fourth Annual Convention of the Southern Commercial Congress at the Session Arranged as a Memorial to the Late Dr. Seaman A. Knapp,* Held in Nashville, Tenn., April 9, 1912, Senate Doc. No. 537, 63rd Cong., 2nd sess. (Washington, D.C.: Government Printing Office, 1914), 9, both in Dr. Seaman A. Knapp papers, Southwest Collection/Special Collections Library, Texas Tech University, Lubbock, Texas.

2. *Proceedings, Second Meeting Texas State Farmers' Institute, 1912.* Texas Department of Agriculture Bulletin no. 27 (Sept.–Oct. 1912), 78–82. Mrs. R. L. Smith, *Play: Trial of Old King Credit* (Waco, Tex.: FIS, [c1919]), SCFP. Francis Isabella Isaacs, Smith's first wife, died Feb. 22, 1918, Marriage Record, Book I, 355, Colorado County Court House, Columbus, Tex.; "Robert Lloyd Smith," in *Who's Who in Colored America, 1930–31,* 3rd

ed. (New York: Garrett & Massie, 1932), 395. He married Ruby Loda Cobb on May 8, 1919 (Marriage License, SCFP). This makes it difficult to discern who wrote the undated play.

3. Studies that either focus on or incorporate rural Texas women and reform include Rebecca Sharpless, *Fertile Ground, Narrow Choices: Women on Texas Cotton Farms, 1900–1940* (Chapel Hill: University of North Carolina Press, 1999), Judith N. McArthur, *Creating the New Woman: The Rise of Southern Women's Progressive Culture in Texas, 1893–1918* (Urbana: University of Illinois Press, 1998), Marilyn Irvin Holt, *Linoleum, Better Babies and the Modern Farm Woman, 1890–1930* (Albuquerque: University of New Mexico Press, 1995). Bob Calvert wanted a history of home demonstration work in Texas. The last dissertation he chaired, Debra A. Reid, "Reaping a Greater Harvest: African Americans, Agrarian Reform, and the Texas Agricultural Extension Service" (PhD diss., Texas A&M University, 2000), expanded topically and temporally as *Reaping a Greater Harvest: African Americans, the Extension Service, and Rural Reform in Jim Crow Texas* (College Station: Texas A&M University Press, 2007), incorporated white women briefly. The history of home demonstration work in Texas remains unwritten.

4. Kathleen C. Hilton, "'Both in the Field, Each With a Plow': Race and Gender in USDA Policy, 1907–1929," in *Hidden Histories of Women in the New South,* eds. Virginia Bernhard, Betty Brandon, Elizabeth Fox-Genovese, Theda Perdue, and Elizabeth Hayes Turner (Columbia: University of Missouri Press, 1994), 117. For origins of segregation in Texas rural reform and an essay on sources, see Reid, *Reaping a Greater Harvest,* 1–21, 257–62. Carmen Harris summarizes the rich historiography of black extension work in "'The Extension Service is not an Integration Agency': The Idea of Race in the Cooperative Extension Service," *Agricultural History* 82, no. 2 (Spring 2008): 193–219.

5. Theodore Saloutos, *Farmer Movements in the South, 1865–1933* (Lincoln: University of Nebraska Press, 1960), 34, quote 38. Robert Arnold Calvert, "The Southern Grange: The Farmer's Search for Identity in the Gilded Age," (PhD diss. University of Texas at Austin, 1969), 4, 32, 44–46, 48–49, 52, 58, 312; Robert A. Calvert, "A. J. Rose and the Granger Concept of Reform," *Agricultural History* 51 (January 1977): 181–96.

6. Oral Interview, Walter A. Porter, conducted by Debra A. Reid, June 8, 1999. Tapes and transcription in author's possession (hereafter Porter interview). "Mortuary: Captain J. B. Porter," *Kaufman Herald,* October 19, 1917), http://www.txgenweb5.org/txkaufman/obituary/porterjb.htm (accessed March 22, 2007).

7. Letter, William A. Porter, Terrell, Texas, to Debra Reid, Bryan, Texas, May 8, 1999, in the author's possession. Porter interview. Porter and Terrell resident Horace Flatt concur on the tenant's name as McQuinney. Horace Flatt, phone conversation with Debra Reid, April 27, 1999, not recorded. William A. Porter's son, John Brooks Porter, recalled that the black family often shortened their name to Quinney but that the given name was McQuinney. See notes from unrecorded interview with John Brooks Porter, June 8, 1999, in the author's possession. "Death of Uncle Ben: Well Known Colored Man," *Kaufman Herald,* February 3, 1922), http://www.txgenweb5.org/txkaufman/obituary/quinneyb.htm (accessed March 22, 2007). McQuinney spellings vary. Kaufman County public records, transcribed and available via http://www.rootsweb.com/~txkaufma/ (accessed 23 March 2007) include McQuin-

ney, Quiney, Quinney, Quinnie, Quinny. Other public documents include even more spellings. John Quinnie, Population Schedule, 1900 Federal Census, Kaufman County, Enumeration District (ED) 73, Sheet 14. John and Sue Queney, Population Schedule, 1910 Federal Census, Kaufman County, ED 23, Sheet 2. Ben and Agnes McQueney appear on the same page. Albert Quinney listed Louisiana as his birthplace, Population Schedule, 1910 Federal Census, ED 34, Sheet 102. Tom Quincy, likely Quiney, given his wife's name and the constitution of the family, Population Schedule, 1910 Federal Census, Kaufman County, ED 32, Sheet 128. Bill Tipton, "The Porter Farm Today," *Acco Press,* February 1953, 8, identified Jack McQuinney as the tenant who farmed the demonstration plot.

8. Ben Quinney [McQuinney] ([1841]–1922); John Brooks Porter (1840–1917). John "Jack" McQuinney (1868–c.1944) 1900 Population Census, Kaufman County, sheet 14, line 67; Walter C. Porter (1868–1936). Porter Interview. John Quinnie, 1900 population census, Kaufman County, sheet 14, line 67. John and Sue Queney, 1910 population census, Kaufman County, sheet 2, household 20.

9. Henry Dethloff, *A Centennial History of Texas A&M University* (College Station: Texas A&M University Press, 1976), 1:3, 1:10–18, 1:310–15.

10. "Hon. Robert L. Smith," in *The National Encyclopedia of the Colored Race,* ed. Clement Richardson (Montgomery, Ala.: National Publishing, 1919), 1:383; "Robert Lloyd Smith," in *Who's Who in Colored America, 1928–1929,* 2nd ed. (New York: Who's Who in Colored America, n.d.), 341–42. Robert Carroll, "Robert Lloyd Smith and the Farmers' Improvement Society of Texas" (master's thesis, Baylor University, 1974), 16.

11. R. L. Smith, "An Uplifting Negro Cooperative Society," *The World's Work* 16 (July 1908): 10462–64; Carroll, "Smith and the FIS," 28, 33, 35–36, 37, 54, 57.

12. Reid, *Reaping a Greater Harvest,* 2–3. R. L. Smith refers to the Woman's Barnyard Auxiliary in "An Uplifting Negro Cooperative Society," 10464. Thad Sitton and James H. Conrad, *Freedom Colonies: Independent Black Texans in the Time of Jim Crow* (Austin: University of Texas Press, 2005), 18–42.

13. McArthur, *Creating the New Woman,* 36–39.

14. *The Farmers' Improvement Society . . . an Interesting Dialogue About its Objects and Methods* (Victoria: Farmers' Improvement Society of Texas, c.1900), 13, in SCFP. Texas A&M organized the Texas Agricultural Experiment Station in 1888 to investigate threats to Texas agriculture, teach students to mitigate the threats, and convey the information to noncollege students, thereby "solv[ing] problems which the private individual cannot afford, and is not prepared, to solve for himself." B. Youngblood, "Report of Director of Experiment Stations," in *Nineteenth Biennial Report of the Board of Directors of the Agricultural and Mechanical College of Texas, for the fiscal year ending August 31, 1913 and August 31, 1914* (Austin: A. C. Baldwin & Sons, 1915), 32–33. Douglas Helms, "Revision and Reversion: Changing Cultural Control Practices for the Cotton Boll Weevil," *Agricultural History* 54, no. 1, Agricultural History Symposium: Science and Technology in Agriculture (January 1980), 108–109. *Annual Address, FIS, 1902,* 16–17, in SCFP. *Constitution and By-Laws of the Farmers['] Improvement Society of Texas* (Waco: Farmers' Improvement Society of Texas, c.1909), 20, in SCFP.

15. *Annual Address, FIS, 1902,* 12, in SCFP. *Handbook of Texas Online,* s.v. "Farm and Ranch," http://www.tsha.utexas.edu/handbook/online/articles/FF/eefap.html (ac-

cessed March 26, 2007). For the quote "DOING better," etc., see *The Farmers' Improvement Society . . . an Interesting Dialogue About its Objects and Methods,* 14, in SCFP.

16. *Constitution and By-Laws of the FIS,* 20, in SCFP.

17. Reid, *Reaping a Greater Harvest,* 6, 13. Kone's father, a Confederate veteran, Samuel Reid Kone, owned twenty-two slaves in 1860. "S.R. Korns [*sic*] family," page 4, 1860 Federal Census, Hays County, Texas, http://www.usgwarchives.org/tx/hays/haystoc.htm (accessed March 3, 2007); "Slaves owned by S.R. Korns [*sic*]," page 10, 1860 Federal Slave Census, Hays County, Texas, http://www.usgwarchives.org/tx/hays/haystoc.htm (accessed March 3, 2007).

18. Reid, *Reaping a Greater Harvest,* 7–9. "Porter Demonstration Farm," *Terrell Times-Star,* February 5, 1904). Roy V. Scott, *The Reluctant Farmer: The Rise of Agricultural Extension to 1914* (Urbana: University of Illinois Press, 1970), 209–12.

19. Porter interview. "Porter Demonstration Farm," *Terrell Times-Star,* February 5, 1904. John E. Hutchinson, "The Texas Agricultural Extension Service: A Historical Overview," *Southwestern Agriculture: Pre-Columbian to Modern,* eds. Henry C. Dethloff and Irvin M. May Jr. (College Station: Texas A&M University Press, 1982), 128. Over time, McQuinney gained more recognition for his involvement in the project but never full credit for the work he performed. In 1929, a photograph taken by the USDA Federal Extension Service appeared in a commemorative publication. A copy of the photograph is in Texas Agricultural Extension Historical Files, 1914–1970, Cushing Memorial Library and Archives, Texas A&M University, College Station (hereafter TAEX Historical Files). The caption reads: "S-17943 Walter C. Porter, first farm demonstrator on his place, Terrell, Texas. The old negro worked the first demonstration tract of 100 acres back in 1903." It appeared in *Silver Anniversary Cooperative Demonstration Work, 1903–1928,* Proceedings of the Anniversary Meeting Held at Houston, Texas, February 5–7, 1929 (College Station: Extension Service, Agricultural and Mechanical College of Texas, 1929, 40, and is reprinted in Reid, *Reaping a Greater Harvest,* 8. In 1941, the photograph appeared again, but "the Negro" no longer received credit for working the field; rather, "the Negro worked for him on this farm." See Oscar B. Martin, *The Demonstration Work: Dr. Seaman A. Knapp's Contribution to Civilization* (San Antonio, Tex.: The Naylor Company, 1941), 33. Finally, in 1953, *Acco Press,* a publication that catered to cotton farmers and processors reprinted the photograph and identified Jack McQuinney by name. Yet, the caption still identified Porter as the "first farm demonstrator," thus devaluing McQuinney's contribution nonetheless. No longer was he a nameless helper who did the work, but "a Negro tenant," one of many, the article reported, that the Porter family cared for by providing modern housing and wages for labor in addition to a share of cotton grown. Bill Tipton, "The Porter Farm Today," *Acco Press* 31, no. 2, (February 1953), 8.

20. Reid, *Reaping a Greater Harvest,* 7, 9. Harris, "'The Extension Service is not an Integration Agency,'" 195.

21. Ibid., 12. *Constitution and By-Laws of the Juvenile Department of the Farmers Improvement Society, Adopted at the Twelfth Annual Convocation* (n.p., 1919), SCFP. The constitution was likely adopted in 1919, because Belle Smith was deceased at its publication, and Ruby Cobb was noted as her successor both as Smith's wife and as FIS Grand Preceptress. The Twelfth convocation likely referred to the twelfth annual meet-

ing of the Juvenile Department, not to the organization, which, by 1919, observed its twenty-fourth convocation.

22. W. F. Proctor, State Agent for East Texas, Farmers Cooperative Demonstration Work, Tyler, Texas, Report to the Bureau of Plant Industry, USDA, rec'd October 6, 1909, page 6, Extension Service Annual Reports, Texas (1909), Reel 1, T-890. Reports submitted by all agents are microfilmed and available as: Federal Extension Service, Annual Narrative and Statistical Reports of the Cooperative Extension Work Demonstration Programs. RG 33, National Archives and Records Administration Microfilm Series, (T-845–T-895). Reports submitted by agents in Texas between 1909 and 1945 are microfilmed as series T-890, and are housed in Payroll Services, Texas Agricultural Extension Service, College Station, Texas (hereafter, Annual Reports, TX (year), reel number, T-890). L. A. Nieburh, Agt., Brenham, Texas, to Mr. J. L. Quicksall, November 16, 1910, Annual Reports, TX (1910), Reel 1, T-890.

23. E. P. Elrod, Special Agent, Sherman, Texas, October 28, 1910, Annual Reports, TX (1910) Reel 1, T-890. Williamson to Ousley, April 23, 1915, box 4, TAEX Historical Files. [FIS] Trustees, D. N. McCoy, et al., Giddings, Texas [Lee County], "To all concerned," September 23, 1910, Annual Reports, TX (1910), reel 1, T-890, (underline in original).

24. *Constitution and By-Laws of the Juvenile Department of FIS,* quote 3, SCFP.

25. Crosby, "Building the Country Home," 33–35. Karen J. Ferguson, "Caught in 'No Man's Land': The Negro Cooperative Demonstration Service and the Ideology of Booker T. Washington, 1900–1916," *Agricultural History* 72, no. 1 (Winter 1998): 33–54.

26. *Report of the First Meeting, Texas State Farmers' Institute, 1911.* Texas Department of Agriculture Bulletin no. 21 (Sept.–Oct. 1911), 62, 63.

27. *Proceedings, Texas State Farmers' Institute, 1912,* 12. Edna W. Trigg, "Early Extension Work as I Remember It," in Kate Adele Hill, *Home Demonstration Work in Texas* (San Antonio, Tex.: Naylor, 1958), 16–19.

28. *Proceedings, Texas State Farmers' Institute, 1912,* 84–5. *Proceedings of the Third Meeting of the Texas State Farmers' Institute, 1913,* Texas Department of Agriculture Bulletin, no. 35 (January–February 1914), 58.

29. Dethloff, *History of Texas A&M,* 2:392–93. Larry D. Hill and Robert A. Calvert, "The University of Texas Extension Services and Progressivism," *Southwestern Historical Quarterly* 86 (1982), 238–39.

30. McArthur, *Creating the New Woman,* 48–53. Reid, *Reaping a Greater Harvest,* 16–17. "Appropriations, Department of Agriculture, For the Years Ending August 31, 1916, and August 31, 1917," *General Laws of the State of Texas, First Called Session, Thirty-Fourth Legislature,* 1915 (Austin: A. C. Baldwin & Sons, 1915), 158.

31. Jeannie Whayne, "'I Have Been through Fire': Black Agricultural Extension Agents and the Politics of Negotiation," in *African American Life in the Rural South, 1900–1950,* ed. R. Douglas Hurt (Columbia: University of Missouri Press, 2003), 152–88. States with more black farmers than Texas in 1910 included Mississippi, Georgia, Alabama, and South Carolina. *Negro Population, 1790–1815,* 588. Crosby, "Building the Country Home," 34–46; Earl W. Crosby, "The Roots of Black Agricultural Extension Work," *The Historian* 39, no. 2 (February 1977), 228–47; Earl W. Crosby, "Limited

Success Against Long Odds: The Black County Agent," *Agricultural History* 57, no. 3 (July 1983), 277–88; and Earl W. Crosby, "The Struggle for Existence: The Institutionalization of the Black County Agent System," *Agricultural History* 60, no. 2 (Spring 1986), 123–36. General Education Board, *The General Education Board: An Account of its Activities, 1902–1914* (New York: General Education Board, 1915), 26–7, 55. Reid, *Reaping a Greater Harvest,* 10–11.

32. Reid, *Reaping a Greater Harvest,* 17–18; Memoranda between O. B. Martin, Assistant in Charge of Demonstration Club Work, and Bradford Knapp, Special Agent in Charge, Office of Farmers' Cooperative Demonstration Work, Washington, D.C., December 1 and December 2, 1913, General Correspondence, 1908–1917, Extension Service, RG 33, National Archives and Records Administration, College Park, Maryland.

33. Wayne D. Rasmussen, *Taking the University to the People: Seventy-Five Years of Cooperative Extension* (Ames: Iowa State University Press, 1989), 24, 46–54, 56, 67–68. Dethloff, *History of Texas A&M,* 2:382–404. "Project No. 1, Extension Work in Agriculture and Home Economics in the State of Texas . . . June 22, 1914, approved July 17, 1914," box 8–11, TAEX Historical Files, 3.

34. Reid, *Reaping a Greater Harvest,* 18–21.

35. McArthur, *Creating the New Woman,* 48–51. Hill, *Home Demonstration Work in Texas,* 195. Bernice Carter, "A Brief Report on Canning Clubs and Home Demonstration Work in Texas as Given at Meeting, 1915," rec'd October 4, 1915, State Administration Reports, Annual Reports, TX (1915), Reel 1, T-890. Letter, Clarence Ousley, College Station, Texas, to Mrs. M. W. Sims, Bryan, Texas, October 19, 1915, box 8–41, TAEX Historical Files.

36. Letter, Mr. S. B. Holman to Mr. Ousley, September 22, 1916, box 8–41, TAEX Historical Files. Hilton, "Both in the Field, Each With a Plow," 114–33.

CHAPTER FOUR

Fighting on the Home Front

THE RHETORIC OF WOMAN SUFFRAGE IN WORLD WAR I

James Seymour

Nineteenth-century suffragists, including those in Texas, contended that women deserved the right to vote because of fairness. Since women paid taxes and were subject to the law, this line of reasoning went, then they should have a direct say in how those laws were created. Drawing on the ideas of John Locke, these women emphasized a fairness doctrine towards achieving the ballot that included ideas about natural rights of citizenship. Over time, suffragists added other arguments before World War I, specifically about what they considered to be women's higher moral standard, which would reform the corruption of the political process and enact needed changes such as prohibition.[1] Even though they branched out into other rhetorical areas, the fairness principles continued to be a mainstay of the rhetoric of woman suffrage until U.S. entry into World War I.

The women and men opposed to granting women the right the vote in Texas also echoed the rhetoric of national leaders in their debates over the suffrage question.[2] Most importantly, antisuffragists attacked the fairness doctrine directly. To them, women should be barred from voting because they were unable to serve in the military, to undergo posse comitatus service, or to serve on juries. The opponents of woman suffrage maintained that these responsibilities came with the privilege, not the right, of voting. Since women could not take part in them, they should not be accorded the privilege of the ballot, and they raised the specter of women voting for a war against men's wishes, in which the men then would have to fight. The antisuffrage position also utilized prevailing social beliefs in women's supposed inferiority to men, the unique role of home and family, and concerns over black women voting.[3] Overall, opponents of suffrage feared the consequences to existing social, familial, and political institutions if women had the ballot.

Fig. 4.1. Women registering to vote at the Travis County Courthouse in 1918. Credit: PICA 11669, Austin History Center, Austin Public Library.

On the eve of World War I, woman suffragists in Texas still largely followed the fairness doctrine in their argument. This line of thinking, essentially unchanged since the nineteenth century, was unable to counter the prevailing conservative social and political environment. For instance, the only organized suffrage efforts in Texas between 1905 and 1912 took place in Austin. Dr. Anna Howard Shaw visited and spoke about suffrage, prompting twenty-five women to organize a local suffrage association in 1908. Although the Austin women met into the 1910s, they never attempted to recruit women in other towns and never affiliated with the National American Woman Suffrage Association, limiting their effectiveness.[4]

Revealing the obstacles that woman suffragists faced, *The Texas Magazine* published an article by Mary Rider Lawrence in its August 1912 edition. While Lawrence asked several Texas businesswomen for their opinions on woman suffrage, the piece mostly covered the three opponents of suffrage, Miss Lydia Littman, Miss Henrietta Gordan, and Miss Leffler Corbett. Littman, Gordan, and Corbett employed standard arguments used by social conservatives against suffrage. Each sought to undermine a specific pro-suffrage argument with their reasoning.[5]

Reflecting her elite white status, Lydia Littman relied on the chivalry of men to protect women and welcomed the apparent moral superiority of women, which she feared voting would destroy. Littman began the attack by claiming "the business woman, more than others, learns to care little for the privilege of being allowed to vote," because "women in the business world learn quicker than others that they can safely leave political matters in the hands of the opposite sex." Littman reasoned a woman in Texas "knows that she wields a power indirectly, that she casts a vote indirectly, and the greatest of her conquests is that she can do these things without appearing among the masses at the polls on election days." She contended woman "is endowed by nature with a conscience keener than that of man" and the franchise would disrupt women's higher moral nature. Leffler concluded, "I dare say that there is no privilege that the Southern woman would not forego in order not to lose this respect and esteem of the men, and I might assign this as my greatest reason why the business woman, especially in the South, would shrink from the ballot."[6] If women voted, Littman concluded, southern men would abandon chivalry, as the women unsexed themselves by engaging in politics.

Henrietta Gordan echoed Littman's sentiments and then directly addressed the conditions in Colorado, where women had the vote. First, Gordan asserted that voting would "take woman out of her sphere in life," explained it would "weaken the characteristics of either sex," and pondered "what is to become of the home [under woman suffrage]?" Then Gordan contended, "The only unique product of suffrage in Colorado is the specie[s], part amazon, part masculinized female, who is the society boss." Rather than producing reforms, she insisted, "after the novelty of the thing had worn off," most Texas women would stop taking an active interest in politics and would vote according to their husband's or father's instructions. Gordan concluded that "the only result of suffrage is the unsexing of woman, making her masculine."[7]

Leffler Corbett also harkened to the chivalry of white men and attacked the types of women who she asserted wanted the ballot as being out of the mainstream. Corbett claimed that she had "never, under any circumstances, felt handicapped by the fact that I could not vote," and she explained, "I should shrink from the additional responsibility which mingling in politics would involve." She worried that the "ballot and its manifold responsibilities will entail hardships and handicaps and that women will ultimately lose more than they will gain thereby." Corbett insisted she had "always found men so considerate and chivalrous towards womenkind in general," and she worried about "whether they would have quite the same feelings towards us when meeting us as political opponents on election day." Speculating on the kinds of women who favored suffrage, Corbett saw the "ranks of the suffragists" as being filled with "wealthy women who are seeking a hobby" and "discontented housewives, who . . . have found life a disappointment." Corbett concluded Texas men had done a reasonably good job with politics and maintained, "I can see no defects with their administration of affairs that could possibly be improved by extending the suffrage to women."[8]

Lydia Littman, Henrietta Gordan, and Leffler Corbett put forth standard claims by social conservatives against suffrage. Each maintained that women's voting, far from helping them, would become a large burden, a trivial chore, or a desexing process. Reflecting their elite status, these women insisted they were content to allow chivalrous Texas gentlemen oversee their best interests in the government, and they feared losing this gallantry if they engaged in the masculine field of politics. Littman embraced what she considered to be women's superior moral nature, which voting would erode. Gordan worried about indifference at the polls after the first flush of voting, while Corbett fretted about maintaining chivalry and amicable relations between the sexes. For them, the proposed benefits of voting were far outweighed by the dire consequences it would have on social and gender relations.

Joseph Weldon Bailey emerged as a leading spokesman for socially conservative, states' rights Democrats in Texas and stood against progressive reforms, including woman suffrage. Bailey articulated, in a republished letter, two mainstay arguments against extending the franchise to women. He drew upon the nineteenth-century concern about women's nature, as he claimed, "the bad effect which a participation in angry controversy [politics] must necessarily exert upon a woman's gentleness and character would be sufficient to condemn it in my estimation." He maintained, "I have seen such decided changes wrought in the temper and habit of women by the mere advocacy of woman suffrage as to leave me in no doubt of what would happen if they are made a part of our political process."[9]

More importantly, Senator Bailey turned the fairness argument against the suffragists. He asserted, "no persons are entitled to exercise *all* of the privileges of citizenship unless they are able to perform *all* of the duties of citizenship." Bailey then defined the "three highest duties of citizenship" as "military service, posse comitatus service, and jury service . . . ," which, he argued "a woman, by her very nature, is incapable of performing." Expanding on this theme, he maintained that women "cannot fight in battles, and should not, therefore, be permitted to vote for a declaration of war," and women "cannot help the sheriff suppress a riot or arrest an outlaw, and should not, therefore, be permitted to make the laws under which men are required to undertake that dangerous service." Women's delicate sensibilities precluded them from hearing testimony in court trials, Bailey believed, and a Texan "would [not] be willing to send his mother, wife, daughter or sister into the jury room and have her locked up overnight with strange men deliberating on a case." He concluded, if "a woman who cannot perform those services shall yet have the right to make the laws under which men must perform them, [it] is to give her, not equal rights with man, but . . . in really [reality] to give her rights superior to man." Since women were incapable of fulfilling the responsibilities of citizenship, they should be barred from the privilege of voting. Any other position, Bailey insisted, would extend special rights to women and prove unfair to men.[10] Woman suffragists needed new reasons to overcome his challenge and the socially conservative women in *The Texas Magazine* article to generate support for their cause. The propaganda campaigns of World War I laid the foundation for that change.

In 1912, Eleanor Brackenridge and Annette Finnigan revived the woman suffrage organization in San Antonio and spread local chapters throughout the state. Without creating any new arguments in favor of woman suffrage, their groups focused on educating ordinary citizens about the reasons women needed the vote, still using the fairness idea. The University Interscholastic League (hereafter UIL) picked woman suffrage as a debate topic, resulting in the exposure of countless parents and students to pro-suffrage ideas. Woman suffrage received the endorsement of the influential Texas Federation of Women's Clubs, which helped make the idea respectable to many middle class women. Texas suffragists received permission to distribute information at the Texas State Fair in 1913. Members of the Dallas chapter of the Texas Equal Rights Association staffed yellow-and-white information tables at the Main Exposition Building, a busy central area where they were seen by many visitors. Fair officials designated October 23, 1913, as Suffrage Day and allowed suffrage leaders to give speeches.[11] These developments brought the pro-suffrage message directly to women, men, and children in their homes and schools. Further, their message reached people outside of major urban areas through the UIL and the State Fair.

Despite their educational advances, supporters of suffrage lacked new ideas to address the points of social conservatives. Although the groundswell of pro-suffrage support gained momentum among ordinary people, especially women, before 1914 the suffragists still needed to convince state political leaders to support their position. Lacking a compelling argument, Texas suffragists failed to overcome the political and social status quo. Conservative Texas politicians hesitated to embrace suffrage for a variety of reasons, stalling reform and rendering the educational movement ultimately ineffective in reaching concrete goals before the outbreak of World War I.

In 1914, Annette Finnigan embarked on a letter-writing campaign in order to uncover the status of woman suffrage among political leaders.[12] Targeting Democratic U.S. congressmen in Texas and their challengers in the primaries, Finnigan asked for their views on suffrage in order to gauge the chances of placing a constitutional amendment enfranchising women on the ballot. Some politicians refused to answer her query, while others returned vague or noncommittal replies. P. L. Parker, for instance, simply wrote "John 2:24 ['But Jesus did not commit himself unto them']" in the margin of Finnigan's letter and sent it back to her.[13] Most who responded to the survey expressed definite views about suffrage. In their responses, they displayed a cross section of positions on the issue, employed the most common prewar justifications both for and against it, and revealed the areas the suffragists had to overcome in order to achieve the vote.

A few of the politicians evidenced a cautious neutrality to suffrage, possibly reflecting an uncertainty of prevailing political trends. H. P. Taylor explained, "if I were sure that the majority of the ladies of Texas desired to have the ballot, I would most gladly vote for [it]." J. R. Astin wrote, "unless there is a public demand, then I . . . shall use my own best judgment and there is no such public demand in this case." Astin reasoned, "if my constituents or the people of Texas had expressed themselves in favor of submission of woman's suffrage as a Constitutional Amendment, then I would abide by their decision." Carlos Bee echoed their caution. Bee maintained, "I do not believe that at this time there is either a necessity or a demand for a change in the Constitution. When I am convinced that the men are unwilling to accord to women every relief they are entitled to, I will feel differently about it."[14] Woman suffragists had to convince neutral men like Taylor, Astin, and Bee that suffrage was both desired by the people of Texas and, most importantly, politically expedient.

Many respondents dismissed woman suffrage without explanation. The antisuffragists who elaborated on that position relied on standard claims about the lack of interest among Texas women in receiving the ballot or pointed to concerns about the negative consequences that women's voting would have on women's nature. James R. Wiley opposed suffrage because "the great mass of noble women of Texas are, as I believe, indifferent and care nothing for the right of the ballot." Dr. J. E. Clark based his antisuffrage view on what he considered women's morally pure nature. Clarke contended, "Politicks are too bad for a lady to mix in. It is bad enough for men. I am always willing to assist ladies in anything else." Religious justifications combined with Sen. Joseph Weldon Bailey's antisuffragism in J. R. Hairston's antisuffrage screed. Hairston explained, "I do not favor woman suffrage. Because I do not thinh [*sic*] it right for Women to have the supreme control of the State and nation. I do not beleive [*sic*] that God intended for Woman to have the controal [*sic*] of man."[15] Because Wiley, Clarke, and Hairston presented common obstacles, Texas women had to demonstrate they wanted and would use the ballot, and they had to circumvent conservative religious beliefs about gender roles.

A few politicians gave explicitly pro-suffrage replies. Wilbur J. Boring vowed, "I will not only vote in the Legislature to submit the amendment you desire, but I will do all in my power to help Texas women obtain the ballot." J. Rector of Eddy employed homespun views about "the sacred influence of the home [and] the training of the young . . . [which] make great men and great nations" in his support of woman suffrage. Rector declared, "I am a Southern man raised in the South, and language fails to express my appreciation of the virtue, moral worth and intellectual refinement of the Southern women, who stands without peer with her sex in the nations of the world; and I would be loath to place her in any position that would intimidate her usefullness [*sic*] in the sacred position she now holds in our hearts, but I have faith that in the exersize [*sic*] of thier [*sic*] suffrage that it would be on the side of right on all the great moral questions of the day."[16]

Rector argued that women's superior moral nature and their concern for the home and family would allow them to enact social reforms and to clean up political life. For him, woman suffrage represented a necessary reform of political life.

Racism suffused certain politicians' opinions about suffrage. Edward D. Ward pointed out the language of a proposed woman suffrage amendment would give all women the franchise. Ward maintained, "if an act could be passed that would only allow white women to vote and exclude the Negro women, I would favor it; but that would be in conflict with the 13th and 14th Amendments to the Constitution of the United States." As such, Ward asserted, he had to oppose suffrage because it would enfranchise African American women. Looking at the amendment, C. E. Farmer held a different view about the effects of woman suffrage on race relations. Farmer claimed, "Being a Southern gentlemen, a Jeffersonian Democrat, and believing our women are better and more intelligent than negroes and Mexicans, I will favor the submission of said question." B. B. Sturgeon, running for lieutenant governor, supported suffrage as well. Sturgeon professed, "I have never been able to understand why the laws of Texas prohibits [*sic*] the very best element of our people from casting their vote when, at the same time, it permits other elements [to vote] . . . [who do] not have at heart so keenly and so deeply the welfare of this government as the ones prohibited [from voting]."[17] The consequences of suffrage on race relations remained a powerful antisuffrage concern. By the end of World War I, woman suffragists in Texas, similar to Farmer and Sturgeon, manipulated racial and ethnic biases in their favor, advocating their enfranchisement to counter the votes of African Americans, Tejanos, and German Americans.

Annette Finnigan's letter-writing campaign revealed the status of woman suffrage among Texas politicians on the eve of the Great War. Many of them opposed suffrage and argued that women did not want the vote or that it would detract from their morally pure nature. Others expressed conservative religious convictions about gender roles or harkened back to Senator Bailey's criticism of suffrage. Finally, some focused on racist views that precluded their support for woman suffrage. In their letters, the politicians outlined the obstacles to suffrage that the women of Texas had to surmount. The educational efforts of the Texas suffragists had brought more people into the ranks of suffrage supporters and created a viable and enduring suffrage organization throughout the state. Now, Texas women had to concentrate their attention on overcoming antisuffrage rhetoric in the state and persuade politicians that they wanted and needed the ballot. The special circumstances during World War I enabled them to achieve their goal. Further, woman suffragists employed the racism and ethnic biases unleashed during World War I to reshape their arguments into a form acceptable to white Southern political leaders.

When the United States entered the Great War, the Texas Equal Suffrage Association harnessed the propaganda that the war generated to supply new rhetoric to support its political agenda. Texas women focused on two specific arguments to convince male voters and politicians alike to support national and state initiatives. First, woman suffragists pointed to their contributions during the war. As a total war, women's activities helped the United States defeat the Central powers and proved their value as citizens and dispelled the notion that women should be kept from voting because they could not serve in the military. Thus, women deserved the vote as compensation for their actions during the war. Second, women noted that German resident aliens were allowed to vote, playing on anti-German wartime hysteria, while southern white men who entered the military lost that right under the Texas Constitution. Suffragists demanded the vote to protect their men in uniform against the German voters at home. These twin arguments echoed throughout the suffrage battles of the war years in Texas.

Texas white women further demanded their right to vote while at the same time attacking the suffrage rights of others. Following in the vein of other white women in the South, Texas women marginalized the few African American women in Texas who showed interest in voting rights, keeping the Texas Equal Suffrage Association (hereafter TESA) an all-white group despite an effort by black women to join. Texas white suffragists further saw Mexican American women as another group who should remain without rights, lumping Tejanas with immigrant Mexican women as undesirable to their cause and to the state. Finally, and most explicitly, white suffragists viewed German women as part of the enemy in their midst during the Great War. This message became especially pronounced when the TESA harnessed wartime propaganda to their cause.[18]

From the beginning, the TESA dedicated its local suffrage organizations to wartime activities. Minnie Fisher Cunningham called for impressing the "sixteen [to] twenty thousand men and women [of the TESA], . . . from El Paso to Texarkana, from Amarillo to Brownsville" into war service to defeat Germany. To help alleviate food shortages among the Allies, she called for "a garden for every member" and advised women to "raise a garden yourself and urge every Suffragist to do so until your organization stands united in providing America and her allies with food to win the war." To finance the war, she recommended each suffragist purchase, every week, a twenty-five cent thrift stamp, noting it was "a small thing to ask, but there will be a great result if we will all do it." Cunningham told them to "place your entire organization with every facility at your command at the disposal of the County Chairman of the Woman's Liberty Loan Committee" to raise funds to defray costs of the war, as "the financing of this war is not a matter of choice. It is a sacred obligation to the men who have been asked to lay down their lives if need be." Cunningham herself oversaw two Liberty Loan campaigns.[19] Using these tactics, Texas suffragists simultaneously aided the United States in its battle to save democracy and created good will for their organization.

Texas suffrage leaders themselves performed a variety of work during the Great War. Minnie Fisher Cunningham, president, and Helen Moore, first vice president of the TESA volunteered for Red Cross nursing duty overseas. Although Cunningham never served, she became the state chairwoman of the Texas Woman's Anti-Vice Committee, which was organized to improve conditions around army camps and cantonments. Suffragists collected and rolled bandages and helped finance Red Cross hospitals in France that were staffed entirely by suffrage women. In her daily newspaper columns, Jane McCallum recorded, "In the work of food conservation, practically every woman in American has enlisted for the war." Evaluating their endeavors, McCallum announced, "the women of America have stood shoulder to shoulder with the men in the struggle for world's democracy. In raising the liberty loans, the Y.M.C.A. and the Y.W.C.A. funds and Red Cross millions, they not only gave their money but devoted their time and energy." Texas women committed themselves to winning the war, regarding their tasks as vital war measures. McCallum herself participated in a host of actions, such as working on the antivice crusade, collecting donations for the Red Cross, and selling war bonds.[20] These actions helped erode the idea that women should be excluded from the ballot because they were incapable of handling the obligations of citizenship through military service, which provided the lynchpin for Bailey's argument.

Based upon their actions, women viewed suffrage as a necessary piece of war legislation. Carrie Chapman Catt explained, "Woman are giving to this war . . . not just their wages and their incomes . . . [but] their services, their very life's blood—and that for a government which has so far refused them political acknowledgement." Texan Edith Graff explained, "Our women are doing all in their power to make the towns safe for the camps, to sell Liberty Bonds, to conserve food, and to help the government in other ways. But we believe the ballot would enable us to be even more useful" In December 1917, the National American Woman Suffrage Association (hereafter NAWSA) resolved to seek the vote through the passage of the Susan B. Anthony amendment in the U.S. Congress and outlined their rationale for seeking the ballot during the war. The suffragists maintained, "war is demanding from women unprecedented labor and sacrifice and women by millions are responding with utmost loyalty and devotion," thus "it is important to a country in war, even more than in peace, that all its loyal citizens should be equipped with the most up-to-date tools." The suffragists "pledge[d] our unswerving loyalty to our country, and the continuance of our aid in patriotic service, to help make the world safe for democracy, both at home and abroad." For members of the NAWSA, equal suffrage clearly would help win the war, and members of TESA agreed, ratifying the resolution at its state board meeting.[21]

In addition to the war service, Texas women seized on the anti-German and anti-immigrant bias created during the war. For Texas suffragists, German voters and their political allies prevented women from gaining the vote. As Cunningham explained, "I can point you to two men in the Texas delegation in Congress whose constituency is largely composed of alien enemies who are legal voters, who are not going to vote for Suffrage in Congress, and the reason they give is that their *constituents are opposed to it*! Do you think if those constituents *believed* women were pro-German that they would be *against* suffrage?" Cunningham highlighted the absurdity of native-born American women "having to appeal to alien enemies for American rights and privileges. This is one reason why we prefer the Federal Amendment at this time to a state campaign,—we escape this indignity. And true American men should be glad to relieve us of it."[22] Cunningham and other suffragists returned to this theme again during the ensuing efforts for the vote.

The Texas Equal Suffrage Association produced two different form letters, one for men and the other for women, as guides in writing congressmen to encourage support for the federal woman suffrage amendment. The men's letter focused on two arguments. In the first point, Texas men were told that the federal law was needed, "As a war measure" because "many of our public spirited and intelligent women are working for their full citizenship when they would prefer to give a greater measure of time to war service." Further, during this time of total war, women "have proven their readiness for the ballot by their patriotic fervor in forwarding the war plans of the nation." Contradicting arguments that women contributed little to the war, men should emphasize that women "have valorously helped make the towns safe for the camps, and the camps safe for the soldiers. They are supporting the Red Cross by work and money; they have sold and subscribed to Liberty Bonds, . . . They have given as freely as we men to the YMCA and the YWCA work and to the Comfort Funds of the Camps"[23] Women should have the franchise because they proved their citizenship through their war work.

In the next point, the men were advised to raise the issue of racial and ethnic concerns then prevalent among many white Democrats in Texas. The letter asserted, "In our state, . . . more than 40,000 Mexicans, many of whom do not speak English, yet vote on papers of first intention; and . . . the negroes, and the Southwest German[s]" all vote, while native-born white women were denied the franchise.[24] Native-born white women should be given the ballot in the interests of fairness since groups who they considered unpatriotic were allowed to vote. Woman suffrage, then, would strengthen the United States during the war and improve the overall quality of the electorate.

The form letter for women contained eight interrelated reasons to support a federal instead of a state constitutional amendment. Three reasons centered on racial and ethnic concerns for the Anthony amendment. Turning fears about black voters to their advantage, woman suffragists were told that "a State campaign forces us to appeal to negro men to raise us to their political status." Further, a "state campaign also forces us to appeal in Spanish to thousands of illiterate and alien Mexicans who in Texas vote on 'papers of first intention.'" Finally, a "state campaign also forces us to campaign amongst the ultraconservative German towns whose citizens are averse to giving women any recognition in government." A federal amendment extending the franchise to women would prevent white Texas women from appealing to African American, Mexican American, and German American voters, which a state referendum would entail. The letter for women concluded, "Our enfranchisement will enormously increase the white supremacy of Texas and give an impetus toward the best ideals of American Democracy." After the vote on the amendment, Cunningham announced suffragists, both men and women, had sent "bushels" of letters and telegrams to their congressmen.[25]

Texas women echoed these points when working for primary suffrage.[26] Hortense Ward favored combining women's service in the Great War with heightened concerns about ethnic origins in appeals. The TESA should "show how much the need of the women's vote in food matters." Further, women should "stress the fact about the German vote" when contemplating "the election of AMERICAN congressmen." Ward decried the absurdity of giving enemy aliens the franchise, while preventing native-born women from voting. She remembered "a man [who] claimed exemption from war duty as an *alien enemy,* but he votes for congressmen and all other officers next July—his papers were taken out in November 1917." She also pointed to "the other vote along the border where they are ready to ship across any amount of mexicans necessary to win."[27] In subsequent efforts, Texas suffragists echoed the twin themes of patriotic work and foreign participation to attract supporters.

Reflecting Hortense Ward's recommendations, Minnie Fisher Cunningham announced, "Our sons are being disfranchised as fast as they enter the armed forces . . . We want the right to vote so that while our sons are at the front fighting for democracy, we will be able to maintain good government at home." She repeated this theme in her instructions to local suffrage chapters when beginning a letter-writing campaign for primary suffrage. She asked, "Do you know that while our sons and brothers and husbands entering the Army and Navy are disfranchised, the alien enemy is enfranchised under the state constitution?" She continued, "Can we tolerate the idea of a pro-German legislature, governor or representation in Congress that will endanger the safety of our army? Shall the victory we win at France be thrown away at home?" Finally, she announced, "A thousand times NO, when by enfranchising the hundreds of thousands of loyal Texas women we can prevent it."[28] Woman suffrage would serve to strengthen Texas and the United States against its enemies, the German voters.

The Texas Equal Suffrage Association strongly encouraged the belief that women deserved primary suffrage because of their role in fighting the Central powers. It reminded voters of their "help in the sale of Thrift Stamps, of Liberty Bonds, . . . in all of the thousand and one lines of war work that is before us to do." Suffragists agreed that "it is proper that they should ask it, and essential that we should give it because we are American citizens and our country is at war." During the suffrage battle, "we believe the men of Texas will respond to our plea for help as we have responded to theirs." Under such reasoning, suffrage also became a reward for services undertaken to secure victory against Germany.[29]

Some TESA members wished to avoid a state constitutional referendum on woman suffrage, preferring to work towards ratification of the national amendment. During the second half of 1918, a movement developed independent of TESA to place a state amendment before the voters. The TESA strongly opposed this initiative and hoped to deflect a state election using patriotic appeals. As Cunningham explained, "our position on the State Amendment is this: We do not want that Amendment voted on until the Texas troops are back in civilian life. We think it most unfair, having asked for the submission of this question for many years, . . . that now, while a hundred and twenty five thousand straight American voters are absent from the electorate of Texas, we are in danger of having to wage a campaign . . . [when] every negro, Mexican and disloyal German may vote on our measure."[30] By citing the disfranchisement of soldiers, Texas women hoped to defer a state constitutional referendum until the federal act had passed or the soldiers had returned.

Despite their efforts, the voting amendment, which called for "the enfranchisement of Texas women and for the disfranchisement of aliens who have not perfected their citizenship papers" was decided on May 24, 1919. As Minnie Fisher Cunningham noted, "We have been very busy seeing to it that German is not taught [.] I wonder if it isn't just a little more important to see that German isn't *voted!*" The proposed amendment would remedy these political issues with a single vote. Before the election, Jessie Daniel Ames argued, "victory . . . will make Texas an All-American state."[31]

Despite initial misgivings, Texas suffragists responded to the referendum. They concentrated their appeals on patriotism and anti-German sentiments to generate support for the measure. Cunningham proclaimed, "In the winning or losing of the Second Amendment on your ballot, the State chooses between her women and the alien enemies within our gates as citizens." Texas women "have lived beside you, worked beside you, rejoiced, suffered, served and sorrowed beside you." Now, women wanted to vote beside men as well. She declared, "The door to citizenship is and has been open to the alien by the simple process of naturalization. The door to citizenship to loyal American women who by their service helped you win this war is closed unless your chivalry opens it for us with your vote on May 24th!" Hortense Ward contended, "We have paid too high a price for our democracy to allow anyone but a thoroughly Americanized American citizen to vote in our elections." She charged, "It is the mothers of Texas who are asking for suffrage . . . [who] put their entire time in war work."[32] By contrasting the patriotism of women with the alien enemies, Cunningham and Ward provided patriotic justifications for extending women the right to vote and eliminating the votes of noncitizens.

Despite Texas women's efforts, the state suffrage amendment lost by 25,000 votes. When the electorate rejected it, Texas suffragists primarily blamed the large numbers of resident aliens who voted. Jane McCallum noted in her diary for May 24 that it was a "sad day for Texas women, but just what we expected with so many of the State's best disfranchised by being in France, and all the Mexicans, Negroes, Republicans, I.W.W.s, Reds, socialists, and 'what-nots' including 'first paper' Huns allowed to vote while loyal American women were not." Cunningham claimed, "We have been defeated not in fair fight, but by fraudulent ballot and the massed vote of the deceived ignorant." The TESA produced a flier citing the "chief [reason] of all, the organized opposition of the foreign born and negro votes," which doomed the measure to failure. Later, Cunningham explained, "approximately 200,000 American men were out of the electorate in the United States Army . . . the marvel is that even our most optomistic [*sic*] friends expected us to win with that handicap." She concluded by reminding Texas Democrats that the state party platform endorsed woman suffrage by federal amendment, and she advised them to work towards that goal.[33]

On the first day of the 1919 legislative session, the Texas House endorsed national suffrage after three hours of debate, and the Texas Senate ratified it three days later. The measure went to Gov. Will Hobby, who signed it into law on July 1, 1919. As Minnie Fisher Cunningham, who led the suffrage forces in pushing for the measure, recalled, "Our men were wonderful. I've never seen such splendid team work, and they did every thing we asked or even suggested." Texas became the first southern state and the ninth state overall to ratify the Susan B. Anthony amendment and extend the full franchise to women.[34]

During World War I, women in Texas undertook a variety of actions designed to assist in the war effort. Texas white women demanded their own voting rights while denigrating or attacking the suffrage cause for others. Whether African American, German, or Tejanas, the Texas Equal Suffrage Association saw all of these other groups as potential liabilities or enemies to the cause. When woman suffrage became law in the state, these groups saw their rights restricted or abrogated completely. Texas white suffragists focused on their own actions during the Great War to justify extending the franchise to women like themselves because of their patriotic acts. Anti-German and anti-immigrant sentiment, inflamed by the United States government, became another tool against antisuffrage. By combining these two important rhetorical devices, women were able to provide the arguments necessary to convince male politicians, social conservatives, and male voters to support passage of the Susan B. Anthony amendment in ways that the nineteenth-century fairness doctrine could not. The rhetoric of the Great War provided woman suffragists this advantage in winning their own battle on the home front.

NOTES

1. See Aileen S. Kraditor, *The Ideas of the Woman Suffrage Movement, 1890–1920* (New York: Columbia University Press, 1965; reprint, New York: W. W. Norton, 1981), 44–64 (page references are to reprint edition); Karlyn Kohrs Campbell, *Man Cannot Speak For Her: A Critical Study of Early Feminist Rhetoric,* Vol. 1 (New York: Greenwood, 1989) 169; Scott, 165–66; Anne Firor Scott and Andrew M. Scott, *One Half the People: The Fight for Woman Suffrage* (Philadelphia: J. B. Lippincott, 1975) 25. Kraditor also postulated specific southern arguments for suffrage, such as maintaining white supremacy and fears that black men would pass laws that would adversely affect white women (164–65).

2. See Kraditor, 44–64; Campbell, 169; Scott, 165–66; Scott and Scott, 25.

3. See Kraditor, 15–41; Elna Green, "'Ideals of Government, of Home, and of Women': The Ideology of Southern White Antisuffragism," in *Hidden Histories of Women in the New South,* eds. Virginia Bernhard, Betty Brandon, Elizabeth Fox-Genovese, Theda Perdue, and Elizabeth Hayes Turner (Columbia: University of Missouri Press, 1994), 96–103; Anne Firor Scott, *The Southern Lady: From Pedestal to Politics, 1830–1930* (Chicago: University of Chicago Press, 1970), 167.

4. A. Elizabeth Taylor, "The Woman Suffrage Movement in Texas," *Journal of Southern History* 27 (May 1951): 202–203; Willie Dee Bowles, "The History of Woman Suffrage Movement in Texas" (master's thesis, University of Texas, Austin, 1939); Judith

Nichols McArthur, *Creating the New Woman: The Rise of Southern Women's Progressive Culture in Texas, 1893–1918* (Urbana: University of Illinois Press, 1998), 97.

5. Mary Rider Lawrence, "Woman's Suffrage in Texas: Some Opinions of Prominent Texas Women, For and Against," *The Texas Magazine* 6 (August 1912): 309–15. Littman served as assistant secretary of the Texas Bankers' Association. Gordan worked "with Tucker and Russell, Dallas" in an unstated capacity, while Corbett was a "noteteller, Austin National Bank." The antisuffragists had pages 309–15 and the suffragists had page 314–15.

6. Lawrence, 310, 311.

7. Ibid., 312, 313.

8. Ibid., 313–14.

9. The National American Woman Suffrage Association considered Bailey as the most powerful speaker for the antisuffrage side and worked to refute his views at Democratic conventions. Ida Husted Harper, *History of Woman Suffrage, Volume 5, 1900–1920* (New York: J. J. Little and Ives, 1922; reprint, New York: Arno and the New York Times, 1969), 589 (page numbers are to reprint edition). Joseph Weldon Bailey to Atkins Jefferson McLemore, April 17, 1913, Joseph W. Bailey Jr. Collection, Dallas Historical Society, Dallas (hereafter Bailey papers). McLemore was a friend and political protégée of Bailey's.

10. Bailey to McLemore, April 17, 1913, Bailey papers; Bailey probably expected his white southern readers to understand he meant African Americans when he talked about "strange men" in the jury rooms. Bailey declared women would have "abolished the distinction . . . between bad habits and crimes," leading to women becoming "reformers to suit the most fanatical." Bailey to McLemore, April 17, 1913, Bailey papers.

11. Mamie B. Vielock, "Texas Women Campaign For Suffrage" (master's thesis, St. Mary's University, San Antonio, 1949), 46; Johnowne Brackenridge Crutcher, "M. Eleanor Brackenridge, 1837–1924: A Third Generation Advocate of Education" (master's thesis, Trinity University in San Antonio, 1964), 20, 25–26, 88. *San Antonio Express,* February 19, 1912; quoted in Taylor, 203. *Dallas Morning News,* May 30, 1913. Edwin DuBois Shurter designed the Bulletin for debates distributed by the University Interscholastic League of Texas. It contained fifty "provocative questions" including a debate about women obtaining the franchise in Texas. Roy Benichek, *Educational Competition: The Story of the University Interscholastic League of Texas,* published for the University Interscholastic League (Austin: University of Texas Press, 1956), 213–14. Meagan Seaholm, "Earnest Women: The White Woman's Club Movement in Progressive Era Texas, 1880–1920" (PhD diss., Rice University, 1988), 346. The Texas Federation of Women's Clubs had 10,000 members by 1910, and 20,000 members, with 700 affiliated clubs, by 1917 (Seaholm, 346–47). Finnigan to Texas Women, December 16, 1918; second quote from Seaholm, 447, without attribution. For a full evaluation of the political actions of club women in Texas, consult Seaholm, chapters 4 and 5. *Dallas Morning News,* October 23, 1913; October 18, 1913; October 1, 1914; McArthur, 97–98.

12. Jane Y. McCallum, "Woman Suffrage in Texas," 3, unpublished manuscript, located in Jane Y. McCallum papers, Austin History Center (hereafter McCallum papers); Finnigan had been elected president of the Texas Equal Suffrage Association in the spring of 1914. *Dallas Morning News,* April 10, 1914.

13. Finnigan sent the letters at varying times in the summer of 1914. See letter, B. B. Sturgeon to Annette Finnigan, June 15, 1914; Carlos Bee to Annette Finnigan, July 17, 1914; J. Rector to Annette Finnigan, July 31, 1914, all McCallum papers. The suffrage association had decided, at the 1914 meeting, to concentrate on education rather than political action. Finnigan probably wanted to determine the viability of that stance. *Dallas Morning News,* April 9, 1914; April 10, 1914. P. L. Parker to Annette Finnigan, undated [Summer 1914], McCallum papers.

14. P. Taylor to Annette Finnigan, July 8, 1914; R. Astin to Annette Finnigan, July 31, 1914; Carlos Bee to Annette Finnigan, July 17, 1914, all McCallum papers.

15. Various letters to Annette Finnigan; James R. Wiley to Annette Finnigan, September 29, 1914; Dr. J. E. Clarke to Annette Finnigan, undated [Summer 1914]; J. R. Hairston to Annette Finnigan, August 18, 1914, all McCallum papers.

16. Wilbur J. Boring to Annette Finnigan, July 4, 1914; J. Rector to Annette Finnigan, July 31, 1914, all McCallum papers.

17. Edward D. Ward to Annette Finnigan, July 7, 1914; C. E. Farmer to Annette Finnigan, undated [Summer 1914]; B. B. Sturgeon to Annette Finnigan, June 15, 1914, all McCallum papers.

18. "Many Factors Contributed to the Apparent Defeat of Suffrage," undated [May, 1919], Minnie Fisher Cunningham Papers in the Houston Metropolitan Research Center, Houston Public Library (hereafter Cunningham papers); Letter, Minnie Fisher Cunningham to Mrs. E. Sampson, president of the Colored Women's Club, August 31, 1918, McCallum papers. Southern States Woman Suffrage Conference, *The Southern Problem* (New Orleans: c.1914), n.p.; McArthur, *Creating the New Woman,* 143–49.

19. McArthur, 120–42. See also Janet G. Humphrey, *A Texas Suffragist: Diaries and Writings of Jane Y. McCallum* (Austin: Ellen C. Temple, 1988) and *Citizens at Last: The Woman Suffrage Movement in Texas* (Austin: Ellen C. Temple, 1987). Minnie Fisher Cunningham to Atkins Jefferson McLemore, May 23, 1917, Atkins Jefferson McLemore papers, Barker Center for American History; University of Texas at Austin (hereafter McLemore papers). Minnie Fisher Cunningham to Texas Suffragists, February 19, 1918, McCallum papers. McArthur, 135.

20. Edith Hinkle League to Annie Thornton Perkins, April 2, 1918, Cunningham papers. Cunningham was a registered pharmacist. League to Perkins, May 20, 1918, Cunningham papers; Taylor, 206. Minnie Fisher Cunningham to Texas Suffragists, September 10, 1917, Cunningham papers. *Dallas Morning News,* January 15, 1918. Mrs. Bruce Reid, a member of the TESA and field secretary for Texas of the National Surgical Dressings Committee, specifically asked suffragists to roll bandages. *Austin American,* January 11, 1918. McArthur, 134.

21. *Austin American,* September 16, 1917. Edith Graff to Atkins Jefferson McLemore, November 27, 1917, McLemore papers. Loyalty Resolution, Cunningham papers. The conference ran December 12–15, 1917. Already in the Northeast, Elizabeth Herndon Potter, a vice president of the TESA, represented the TESA at the convention. Minnie Fisher Cunningham to Elizabeth Herndon Potter, December 3, 1917, Cunningham papers. Loyalty Resolution, Cunningham papers. The document stated the TESA passed the resolution on January 23, 1917, rather than 1918, which must be a transcription error.

22. McArthur, 137–39. McArthur focused more on the prohibition and anti-James

Ferguson sentiments in the state rather than the wartime exigencies. Minnie Fisher Cunningham to Dan Garrett, January 4, 1918, Cunningham papers. Emphasis in original. Cunningham to Garrett, January 4, 1918, Cunningham papers.

23. Drafts of two form letters, November, 1917, Cunningham papers; Draft of form letter, November 20, 1917, Cunningham papers. The other two reasons concerned the failure of the Texas legislature to give the voters a chance to vote on woman suffrage and the higher education levels of Texas women and their involvement in public schooling for their children.

24. Form letter, November 20, 1917, Cunningham papers.

25. Form letter, composed by Mrs. Elizabeth Herndon Potter, Smith County Equal Suffrage Association, undated [November, 1917], Cunningham papers. Minnie Fisher Cunningham to Elizabeth Herndon Potter, January 18, 1918, Cunningham papers.

26. Primary suffrage had been defeated in the regular session in 1917. Mrs. D. R. [Willie Dee] Bowles, "Points on the Work of the Texas Equal Suffrage Association," McCallum papers. The TESA decided against calling for it in the session dedicated to impeaching Ferguson, since it might detract from removing him or cost them votes. Minnie Fisher Cunningham to Hortense Ward, September 26, 1917, Cunningham papers.

27. Ward to Cunningham, January 10, 1918, Cunningham papers; emphasis in original.

28. *Dallas Morning News,* January 15, 1918. Minnie Fisher Cunningham to Texas Suffragists, February 19, 1918, Cunningham papers. Emphasis in original. A copy is also contained in the McCallum papers.

29. Undated memo, Cunningham papers. Implicitly, suffragists undermined Joseph Weldon Bailey's arguments against suffrage, which were based on women's exemption from military service. In total war, everyone participated in defeating the enemy.

30. Minnie Fisher Cunningham to Mr. W. L. Dean, November 21, 1918, Cunningham papers. Nannie Webb Curtis provided a notable exception and supported a state referendum.

31. The three other provisions called for state prohibition, land reform, and a pay increase for the governor. Memo, undated, Cunningham papers; *Dallas Morning News,* January 23, 1919. Minnie Fisher Cunningham to Dr. S. Brooks, April 2, [1919], Cunningham papers. Jessie Daniel Ames to unknown [Minnie Fisher Cunningham?], undated, Cunningham papers.

32. Press Statement released May 23, [1919], McCallum papers. *Dallas Morning News,* April 26, 1919. The paper reprinted her speech in Dallas.

33. *Dallas Morning News,* May 28, 1919; July 30, 1919. Humphrey, 134. Minnie Fisher Cunningham to Texas Suffragists, June 5, 1919, Cunningham papers. Harper, 602. Minnie Fisher Cunningham to J. C. McNealus, June 21, 1919, Cunningham papers. Cunningham sent a version of this letter to others, such as a Captain Sackett in the Texas House. Minnie Fisher Cunningham to Captain Sackett, June 20, 1919; form letter, June 21, 1919, Cunningham papers. She also intended for newspapers to reprint her letter.

34. *Dallas Morning News,* June 25, 1919; June 28, 1919; Cunningham to Catt, July 2, 1919, McCallum papers. The House voted 96 to 20 in favor, and the Senate voted 18 to 9 in favor of the amendment (Bowles, 107). Cunningham to Catt, July 2, 1919, McCallum papers. Taylor, 215.

CHAPTER FIVE

Contrasts in Neglect

PROGRESSIVE MUNICIPAL REFORM IN DALLAS AND SAN ANTONIO

Patricia E. Gower

After the Civil War, cities throughout Texas and the Southwest expanded rapidly. As populations grew, the demand for services rose dramatically. Municipal institutions often became overburdened and increasingly inadequate. Cities chose different ways to address the financial crises brought on by demand for services. Those involved in municipal government struggled to develop a more centralized form of city government where administration and political decisions rested in the hands of a small, select group. Those in control believed that they could protect their personal interests as well as the public interest better, by improving government. In Dallas, a predominately white, cohesive, and active business community centralized decisions relative to municipal policy and thus controlled access to services for minority and poor citizens for many years. In contrast, San Antonio's more diverse population and less cohesive business community did not reform machine politics in the city. While this allowed more niches for minority participation and increased access to services for some, persistent policies of low taxation led to the same denial of services that many Dallasites faced. Ultimately, those who secured services and better standards of living as a result did so because of their connections to those in power, while those who did not gain access became increasingly marginalized because of their race, ethnicity, or class.

Businessmen became some of the most aggressive advocates of urban political reform based in rational decision making, centralized administration, and nonpartisan politics. As a result, business ideology that placed emphasis on controlling costs over quality of life became an important element in the rationalization of urban administration. Businessmen's organizations advocated new types of city government that would operate at substantial savings and attract business-minded individuals into politics. Urban reformers believed that more centralized administration along with nonpartisan politics would eliminate the corruption inherent in the rough and tumble of urban politics. They identified universal suffrage and decentralized representation as the foundation of the boss system, and this led them to limit decision-making power to those who possessed an economic stake in the city. They believe that centralized administration, along with other tools, could overcome machine politics and shift power to representatives who identified with the business community. This privileged the interests of the business elite who controlled the finances of municipal government. They used their political leverage to protect their property interests and standards of living by channeling vital city services toward their own business and away from poor and minority areas.[1]

Patterns of discrimination became more evident in cities as businessmen began to call for a shift to citywide nonpartisan elections both to end ward-level constituencies and to increase the centralizing tendency in municipal government. As officials who owed their loyalties to a specific neighborhood lost elections as a result of changing voting regulations, the focus of civic government shifted to a citywide perspective. In the mind of structural reformers, this citywide focus helped bring badly needed services such as sewage and paved streets to the downtown business area first. Allocation of scarce resources and expensive services became contentious issues when politicians owed their election to specific wards not on the route of expanding services.[2]

Many believed that ward-based politics rewarded those who delivered services and patronage to their specific constituents with no thought for the needs of the city as a whole. Therefore, progressive reformers throughout the United States began to decry machine politics in the wards as the source of all corruption in urban government. In their eyes, political machines existed as evils that lurked like "a cesspool under nearly every city hall."[3]

Yet, inequity remained even as municipal governance abandoned ward politics and adopted business management models. Business organizations carried on energetic boostering enterprises to convince outsiders of the city's dynamic potential for growth and profit. To showcase the potential and desirability of their city over all competitors, most organizations stressed concentrating services and development in the downtown business area. Allocating tax money to downtown areas required that other areas wait for services such as sewage, water, and paved streets. Success in these efforts often hinged on support from the business community and exclusion of minority and poor neighborhoods from political power.[4]

The solution to all these issues emerged in the commission plan. In this form of municipal government, a board of commissioners replaced the traditional aldermanic system. Commissioners, elected at-large in nonpartisan elections, administered departments in the city administration. They also worked collectively as the city council with the mayor to set citywide policy.

Fig. 5.1. Paving Davilla Street, Granger, Texas, 1912. Credit: UTSA's Institute of Texan Cultures, No. 076-0322, Courtesy of Mrs. Stacy Labaj.

To many reformers, the commission form provided the structure needed to implement professional management without the perceived corruption and struggle over division of funds of ward-based politics.[5]

In both San Antonio and Dallas, New South philosophy often governed the debate surrounding these issues. New South civic leaders of Texas adhered to the strategy of economic growth coupled with fiscally conservative local government, low taxation, and a stable social system. This background shaped the efforts to extend services to citizens while still controlling costs. The demands for electricity, sewage, water service, and paved streets placed huge burdens on cities. These burdens could be lessened if the municipal government limited areas where services were delivered. Many New South cities such as Dallas had long shown a "pattern of elite leadership" in government in which the elite tried to control costs and taxation partly by limiting services to the poor areas. Other cities such as San Antonio limited services citywide. In all cases, limitations of services led to unhealthy and degraded living conditions for the residents of poor and minority areas that hovered on the edges of cities.[6]

In the growing cities, minorities were normally pushed to the margins in several ways. In the guise of restricted neighborhoods and expensive suburbs, informal residential segregation actually arrived in Texas much sooner than formal segregation. Informal and de facto segregation was more characteristic of most Texas cities for many years. In and around cities such as Dallas, African Americans lived both in freedmen's towns that formed at the dawn of emancipation and in scattered enclaves throughout white neighborhoods near their places of employment. Others clustered in isolated fringe areas, along rivers, railroad rights-of-way, and undeveloped land. In San Antonio, the sizeable Mexican American population lived on the west side of the San Antonio River while other ethnic groups built on the east side.[7]

Technologies such as streetcars, railroads, and automobiles fostered the growth of subdivisions and geographic expansion of cities, and as they expanded, more rigid patterns of segregation emerged. Middle- and upper-class professionals began to seek isolated and protected areas in which to live. Seclusion afforded them opportunities to increase their property values and protect their investments. Streetcar suburbs became a way to remove themselves racially as well as socially and economically from less affluent areas. Neighborhoods such as San Antonio's Olmos Park, Deer Park and Bellaire in Houston, and Dallas's Park Cities became exclusive retreats for middle- and upper-class businessmen and their families. Deed restrictions, which mandated who could buy the property, fixed housing prices, and outright segregation divided cities economically and racially.[8]

In many southern cities, issues of municipal control, annexation, and zoning involved more than simple boosterism or concerns over growth and planning. The extension of services, development of subdivisions, and placement of city limits intertwined closely with racial issues. A persistent aspect in southern city plans was the effort to create restricted neighborhoods and limit the annexation of minority populations outside the city limits. By annexing only prosperous subdivisions, business leaders could reduce costs, and poor and minority neighborhoods were forced to rely on county governments for services. While Jim Crow laws erected elaborate barriers to the presence of African Americans in public life, these other efforts influenced the quality of private living conditions much more directly.[9]

In 1901, Galveston implemented a commission government. Enthusiastic reviews indicated that the commission provided the business elite with the necessary tools in its struggle to control costs and in its political contests. Nonpartisan, at-large elections of commissioners diluted the voice of individual neighborhoods and enabled commissioners to focus services in downtown and middle-class areas. City government rested safely in the hands of the white business elite, which then funneled money without the problem of protests from areas that no longer had representation. These restrictions resulted in communities segregated not only by race but also by the presence of modern improvements.[10]

In Dallas, as in most rapidly expanding municipalities, various associations worked to publicize Dallas. They pressured its city council to feature improvements in the newspapers and to enlist real estate agents to promote their city. To carry on their promotion, commercial clubs also relied on the efforts of developers, railroads, and street railways to advertise Dallas through pamphlets and brochures. In this way, businessmen and politicians hoped to illustrate the dynamic growth patterns necessary to secure Dallas's dominance over all competitors.[11]

Dallas businessmen used all the tools available to them to continue the expansion and development of their city. Annexation added wealthy subdivisions such as Oak Cliff and also gave a needed boost in population. Developers also used the various tools in their efforts to control the expenditure of city money on the poor and minority population of Dallas. In particular, refusal to annex left most African Americans outside the city limits. As long as they continued to successfully relegate these groups to marginal positions both socially and politically, the ruling faction could reduce costs as well as maintain segregation and white supremacy. Exclusionary politics, such as the poll tax and at-large voting, also helped the city's elite shape the growth of Dallas and limit demands placed on city government.[12]

Traditionally, African Americans specifically clustered in areas that began as freedmen's towns on the outskirts of Dallas. Settlements such as Elm Thicket, Queen City, and neighborhoods like Deep Ellum featured tiny shacks built by the residents or substandard rental housing clustered along the river bottoms and on the north and south rim of the city. In these areas, African Americans suffered higher rates of tuberculosis, typhus, and other diseases than did white residents. Engaged in domestic service, many black Dallasites lived at least part time in the houses of their employers. By some estimates, up to 35 percent of the black population lived with employers. The health of this population increasingly became a source of concern because the population was more visible to white reformers; however, there was considerable reluctance to provide improved living conditions or health care.[13]

Despite the high rates of tuberculosis, venereal disease, and other diseases, changes in the treatment offered to blacks came slowly. Stephen Hay, as the first commission mayor, included in his report of advances made in his first administration that African Americans were now being treated for small pox, in segregated wards, at the Union Hospital. In most other ways, the health of the African American population in Dallas remained precarious and largely ignored by white reformers for many years.[14]

At best, African Americans appear infrequently in the city minutes or newspapers. It is always easy to ascertain if someone mentioned was black because the word "negro" always followed their name to assure that people knew the race of the person. One issue illustrates the contested nature of space in the growing city and the precarious position that blacks held in the effort to control space. The conflict took several years to resolve, but blacks ultimately lost. An old black settlement north of central Dallas grew up around a cemetery segregated for blacks. The property possessed little value in the eyes of early developers as squatters, small farmers, and laborers settled the area. Some of the squatters eventually bought their own bit of land from white landowners or became tenant farmers on the white-owned property. Others rented small ramshackle dwellings thrown up by white landowners. Protestants, Catholics, and Jews all bought land adjacent to the black cemetery, and these denominational cemeteries helped constrain black settlement to the north.[15]

As the middle-class population of Dallas moved inexorably north, establishing several subdivisions, white Dallasites sought to further limit and control the black population in the area. Strict segregation was out of the question due to the presence of black landowners and black servants living near employers. Instead, Dallas city government focused on the black cemetery. In 1902, the first effort began to close the cemetery. The city council heard a report that the cemetery for blacks was in very bad condition. A discussion centered on whether it should be closed, but at the time no decision was reached. The subject came up again as the last aldermanic council met. In September 1906, the council again heard that the cemetery was full and threatened the health of the surrounding area due to overcrowded conditions. The adjoining area included the Bowser and Lemmon subdivision, which was seeking annexation, and the growing white population exerted pressure on the council to act. They demanded and the council agreed that the city needed to close the cemetery and arrest anyone trying to bury a body there. The other cemeteries were not included in the council's decisions and remained available for burials.[16]

The new commission government in Dallas rarely addressed issues of concern to African American citizens, an indication of the lack of influence African Americans had on government business. In one of the few instances that any mention of the black population even appeared in the city minutes, the Colored Library Association received permission to use the City Auditorium in 1907, as long as they paid the utilities and the janitor to clean up after the meeting. In another instance, city commissioners began to seek an African American business to serve as undertaker for unclaimed African American bodies. The council wanted separate businesses to dispose of unclaimed white and black paupers to avoid any kind of mixing.[17]

In 1916, the city enacted an ordinance mandating racial segregation in residential areas. The ordinance, which passed unanimously, called for "preserving Peace, Preventing Conflict and Ill Feeling between the White and Colored People and for other Purposes, Prescribing a Penalty and Declaring an Emergency." After *Buchanan v. Warley* invalidated zoning for strictly racial purposes in 1917, the city continued using other tools. One of the easiest methods was the development of restricted neighborhoods. Often the restrictions made it impossible to sell to minorities, and this proved the most convenient way to control access for minorities in both Dallas and San Antonio.

As Dallas expanded geographically northward, and government-supported segregation expanded as well, blacks were increasingly forced out of their homes and neighborhoods and across the Trinity River into Oak Cliff and West Dallas.[18]

Only 14 percent of the black population owned their own property, and this meant that the other 86 percent who rented were extremely vulnerable to eviction and displacement. In 1910, of the 4,256 homes surveyed in African American areas, only 435 owned their houses outright. This allowed developers to use many means to relocate minorities. Besides development, Dallas city government also worked to move the black population out of areas ripe for development of expressways or other municipal works. Therefore, the black population was forced into smaller enclaves where overcrowding increased the health problems and decay.[19]

Reform-minded municipal officials used annexation to ensure racial control in Dallas and to enhance their own efforts to develop the city in keeping with white progressive ideals. Annexation added wealthy subdivisions such as Oak Cliff so boosters could prove to potential investors that Dallas would be a fiscally responsible decision and could yield returns on their investments. Annexation created distance between the poor areas and the vibrant downtown, and thus removed potential threats to white ideals about the public good. As long as white Dallasites relegated poor areas populated predominately by African Americans to marginal positions socially, politically, and geographically, the ruling faction could reduce costs thus reducing the expenses they bore for municipal services, and they could create and maintain segregation and white supremacy, which ensured that they could protect the public's interest as they saw fit.[20]

Annexation followed a specific path in relation to African Americans. Nonannexed areas fell outside the Dallas city limits. The residents, predominately African Americans, lost access to municipal services, which negatively affected their standard of living, and they could not influence political and economic decisions that undermined their authority over their own property investments. Dallas annexation policy, as a result, caused disproportionate damage in black areas and increased the poor health and decaying living conditions in many African American enclaves. Some black neighborhoods existed well within the city limits but others that grew up outside the city remained unannexed despite increasing proximity for several decades. This exclusionary method of annexation meant fewer demands for services on the city government. As white population growth forced blacks out of older areas in south and north Dallas neighborhoods, these unannexed areas in which the displaced settled became more crowded and less served by city government.[21]

The city could avoid the expense of extending services simply by refusing to annex minority areas. Particularly along the river bottoms, poor neighbor-

Fig. 5.2. Looking southeast on Germania Street (later Liberty Street) towards Swiss Avenue, Dallas, Texas, 1901. Credit: UTSA's Institute of Texan Cultures, No. 076-1065, Courtesy of Charlotte McGlamery.

hoods became polluted by raw sewage and often served as dumping grounds for garbage. In these areas, the small, overextended county government remained responsible for paving streets, installing electricity, and providing sewage. In many cases, these services remained unavailable for decades.[22]

Even in areas within city limits, the municipal requirement that mandated sharing of costs between the homeowner and the city for paving and improving streets meant that streets remained unpaved in poor areas. City commissioners usually attempted to defuse any criticism of the policies of neglect by pointing out that as soon as the residents of the areas came forward with their required share, paving could take place. Until the people in the neighborhoods paid their share of the costs, there was no way for even regular street cleaning to take place because streets remained unpaved.[23]

In most cities controlled by commission governments, minority and poor areas possessed little or no political leverage as a result of poll tax and at-large voting. These discriminatory practices likewise helped the elite in Dallas protect their property rights by shaping the city's growth and limiting demands placed on city government. At-large elections meant that individual wards lacked representatives to fight for them. In Dallas, the commission meetings featured few of the quarrels over service and resources that had been common under the aldermanic system. The silence on the issues of services for these marginal neighborhoods conveys the neglect and decay in them. In 1912, regular garbage collection began in white neighborhoods but not in African American ones. As Oak Cliff became progressively poorer, primitive conditions predominated in several areas. Particularly near the river bottoms, the black community still featured open latrines, shotgun shacks, and attendant health problems of tuberculosis, polio, and high infant mortality. In 1937, African Americans composed only 15 percent of the population of Dallas, which stood at over 260,000. In that same year, of the 117 deaths citywide from tuberculosis, forty-five (38.5%) came from the minority African American population. Other diseases associated with standard of living, including pellagra, affected African Americans in Dallas in a disproportionate way. Over two-thirds of the deaths from pellagra and fully half of the cases of venereal disease came from this small population. As late as 1927, inequity in living conditions prevailed, evidenced by a Civic Federation survey that documented at least one-quarter of the black population living in rental units totally unfit for human habitation.[24]

In the face of exclusion and neglect, African Americans in Dallas worked to forge a sense of community. Spurred by segregation and marginalization, blacks had to help each other and find ways around the resistance on the part of white Dallas residents to extend the benefits of full citizenship. Due to exclusion from white association, blacks were forced to form their own associations to address problems in African American neighborhoods. The Progressive Voters League conducted poll tax drives to gain a larger black vote in Dallas. Like their white middle-class counterparts, African American women formed the Colored Library Association to raise money and establish libraries in their neighborhoods for all black citizens. In other organizations and clubs, black men and women struggled to overcome the neglect faced by all black citizens that progressive ideology enabled the city government of Dallas to pursue.[25]

San Antonio's political and social context was much more complex than Dallas's. San Antonio began as a cluster of religious and military institutions during the Spanish Empire. In 1731, settlers from the Canary Islands arrived to stimulate the growth of a civilian settlement. They joined a small population of *mestizos,* blacks, and Indians already living in the area. After independence from Mexico in 1836, German and Irish immigrants moved into the city and joined with the elite formed from the descendants of the Canary Islanders. White Americans moved into San Antonio particularly after the war against Mexico that ended in 1848 and the Treaty of Guadalupe Hidalgo settled the Texas boundary issues. By 1850, San Antonio's population had risen to 3,488. After the Civil War, thirty different nationalities clustered in separate neighborhoods giving San Antonio a population more diverse than most other Texas cities.[26]

San Antonio's elite was dominated for some time by Germans who worked closely with Los Islenos and invested in agricultural and cattle enterprises. The business elite also cooperated with the military, which provided valuable ways to acquire capital from government spending. These external sources of income contributed to the economy of San Antonio without any concerted action from the commercial interests. As a result, the businessmen of San Antonio tended to focus on local rather than on external economic opportunities. Unlike Dallas business elite, San Antonio's commercial interests never saw the need to work closely together to carry out booster activities or attract business from other areas. By 1885, San Antonio possessed three major rail lines and the export of cattle and cotton coupled with the import of tourists led to prosperity and expansion without the need for stronger, unified action from the businessmen of San Antonio.[27]

The political arena that grew out of these elements was also outside the mainstream of Texas politics. Many Germans and Hispanics in San Antonio disapproved of secession and remained separate from Democratic Party politics. After the Civil War, Germans often cooperated with the Republicans and gained political power in San Antonio as a result of this alliance. African Americans also looked to the Republican Party for support against Democrats made up of ex-Confederates. Republicans grew increasingly uneasy about their party's identification with freed slaves and moved to minimize the influence of black or Hispanic voters, but African American and Mexican American voters were more unwelcome in the Democratic Party. As a result, Democrats could not assemble a coalition that could dominate the complex political situation in San Antonio. In response to the weaknesses of the two political parties, nonpartisan political machines formed to organize the different factions of the city.[28]

The first politician to successfully exploit the fluid setting of San Antonio to avoid party identification was James H. French. In 1875, French won the mayor's race on an Independent ticket. French worked with a group of men drawn from all areas of town. French went on to serve until 1887. In appreciation for their support, French rewarded his African American supporters with jobs as firemen and policemen in segregated units. The coalition avoided controlling gambling establishments or saloons clustered in poor neighborhoods or near military institutions in San Antonio. During this period, the goals for the elite focused on economy in city services. Improvements usually required the agreement of private citizens to assume the cost of a special assessment. These assessments were seldom agreed to and thus, San Antonio's growth was not accompanied by extensive municipal building, street paving, or lighting in most places in the city. Germans and southern white Democrats

Fig. 5.3. Businesses in 500 block of East Commerce Street, San Antonio, Texas, 1917. Credit: UTSA's Institute of Texan Cultures, No. 087-0118, Courtesy of Stanley H. Schmidt.

both agreed that the best government was the government that governed less. This orientation, while preserving low taxation valued by the city's elite, led to persistent neglect and exclusion of minority and poor citizens who could not afford special assessments.[29]

The mayor that succeeded French built a powerful machine that reflected the unique political context of San Antonio and allowed voting by minority groups while not violating the taboo of excess spending. Bryan Callaghan II came from a family composed of many strands of San Antonio history. His heritage drew on both the German and Tejano elite in San Antonio. He campaigned extensively in Hispanic areas of town and gathered support from organizations such as the San Pedro Political Club, which organized the Mexican American vote. Many viewed him in the traditional role of patron and repaid his patronage with support. Callaghan campaigned in Hispanic neighborhoods extensively. He also attracted black voters alienated by the Lily White Republicans. Both African Americans and Hispanics felt abandoned by established parties and turned to the nonpartisan candidate as their best option. From 1885 until 1912, with a few interludes of reform-centered politicians, his machine dominated San Antonio politics and provided many sources of patronage to his supporters. Minorities supported the machine and their support could be critical in close races where they could deliver important votes in wards where they were a majority or a substantial minority. However, while this support could lead to individual advancement, participation was not always accompanied by substantial rewards for the minority communities as a whole unless the votes were delivered as a bloc.[30]

Under Callaghan, funding of services increased on a limited basis. He used patronage to reward supporters with contracts—franchises for streetcar lines were granted, streets were paved, and fire hydrants installed in some areas. The sewage system, however, remained woefully inadequate, leading to several epidemics in the city. Many in the elite found his approach of low taxation and few services perfectly acceptable. The traditional reliance on external sources of income encouraged many businessmen to resist efforts to raise taxes so that the city could improve its services. In fact, some critics of Callaghan's organization blamed his administration for too much spending on infrastructure. In contrast, a few San Antonians complained that during his administration, the city did too little, particularly in the downtown area.[31]

Callaghan's major challenge came in the form of progressive ideology that moved into San Antonio in the 1890s. Newcomers to San Antonio were increasingly white, college educated, and Baptist. This new bloc of middle-class voters advocated efficiency, professionalism, and morality. Because many supported the growing demand for Prohibition, these progressives distrusted groups resistant to any control of the production and sale of alcohol, which had always served as profitable business in San Antonio. They also possessed the southern Protestant distrust of the Catholicism so prevalent in San Antonio. They attacked the support Callaghan's machine drew from neighborhoods that traditionally resisted calls for prohibition and began to call for at-large elections to remove the effect of ward-based politics. Like progressives in other areas, they advocated control by the white business element of municipal institutions as a way to ensure honesty and efficiency. They also supported the use of the poll tax to eliminate minority voters whom they viewed as corrupt and controlled by the machine.[32]

Beginning in 1893, progressive reformers criticized the nonpartisan Callaghan machine while calling for a nonpartisan organization to replace it. Progressive ideology firmly supported nonpartisan municipal elections as a way to avoid party politics and the attendant corruption. In San Antonio, however, the long history of nonpartisanship made it more difficult to differentiate a reform organization from other San Antonio nonpartisan machines. The new business leaders did not always agree with the older elite, who supported traditional networks of voters and supporters. Thus, reformers took power from Callaghan from 1893 to 1897, but Callaghan reclaimed the mayor's office in 1897.[33]

In 1899, Marshall Hicks, a progressive reformer, won the mayor's office. Under Hicks, San Antonio saw the creation of a nonpartisan school board, new financial disclosure rules, and the creation of separate fire and police commissions. In addition, the enactment of the poll tax in Texas eliminated poor and minority voters, who had long supported the machines. In San Antonio, however, the machine bosses still in place worked to retain voters, both black and Hispanic, to ensure loyalty. In 1905, Bryan Callaghan returned from political exile on the strength of those votes and remained in power until his death in 1912. His machine, however, now drew much more heavily on the working class and minority neighborhoods and less on the wealthier areas.[34]

By the time Callaghan died, progressive businessmen had been studying the Galveston, Houston, and Dallas experiments with commission government. In 1911, Thomas Conroy, a prominent real estate dealer, formed the Commission Government League. Many developers were dismayed at the lack of city spending for streets, water, and sewage services. Most of these services had to be built privately if they were to be built at all. The construction of over forty new subdivisions after 1907 with the costs for this development borne almost solely by the developers helped mobilize businessmen. But in San Antonio, the unusual political context once again made the issue of centralized municipal government divisive and polarizing. Some prominent local businessmen such as W. A. Wurzbach abandoned his previous support of Callaghan while others such as J. H. Kirkpatrick became Callaghan supporters. In February, Callaghan called for a special election, and record numbers of voters of all races turned out to vote. Perhaps aided by the special police dispatched by Callaghan to supervise the voting, commission government was defeated by 168 votes out of over 14,000. Once again, the machine politics of San Antonio triumphed over reform, supported by many who believed reform threatened their often tenuous participation in city politics and their authority over the public's interests.[35]

Later in the spring of 1911, Callaghan was reelected with the support of voters primarily in working class, Mexican American, and black areas. In July of the next year, however, Callaghan suddenly died. In 1913, Clinton Brown, a prominent local businessman, ran on the pledge to bring change to San Antonio. He did not specify the kind of change and managed to attract a diverse group of voters from all areas of the city. Once elected, he refused to push for commission government and focused on a wide range of needed improvements. Finally, Brown offered a very diluted form of commission government that retained the facade of progressive reform while maintaining a substantial amount of patronage available to the mayor. Once again, traditional power bases in San Antonio retained their hold on local politics despite the efforts of reformers.[36]

By the 1920s, San Antonio's political system remained in the hands of the machine politics that had controlled it for years. Some white business elite had tried to impose progressive reform models on San Antonio's government to make it more manageable and cost effective, but ethnic diversity and nonpartisan politics prevented the white elite from gaining control. In addition, many of the wealthier whites began to abandon older neighborhoods for racially homogenous subdivisions that remained outside the city limits. These neighborhoods also resisted annexation by incorporating so that San Antonio began to feature small municipal units that received their services from San Antonio at no cost to the municipalities, and it left the politics in San Antonio proper in the hands of machine politicians who did not miss the presence of those voters at all. San Antonio citizens absorbed the cost of these policies while receiving little in return for their support.[37]

By 1930, San Antonio's population was 40 percent Mexican American and Mexican national and 8 percent black. Many wealthier whites lived outside the city limits in racially and economically restricted subdivisions and did not participate in city elections. In this atmosphere, new bosses who organized minority voters could have substantial impact. One such boss, Charles Bellinger, attracted national attention for his ability to provide black voters and also claim substantial services for the African American East Side of town. Charles Bellinger negotiated for delivery of services and improvements and tolerance of his gambling operations, in return for the East Side vote. Bellinger negotiated with black preachers and could guarantee effective delivery of African American votes. In contrast, the Mexican American population lacked effective organization and political clout. While many Hispanic citizens voted, their votes were often purchased on an individual basis by the payment of their poll tax and an occasional piece of patronage.[38]

These unusual voting patterns created some unique results in San Antonio. The East Side of San Antonio, where most African Americans lived, featured paved streets, a sewage disposal system, a library, city parks, and an auditorium, all earned through the political manipulation of their votes. While more African Americans owned their houses than did Hispanic citizens, poverty and segregation characterized all minority neighborhoods. The West Side of town, where most Mexican Americans lived, featured one of the worst slums in the United States with unpaved roads crowded with tiny ramshackle homes. In the 1930s, many of the houses rented for as little as fifty cents a week, had dirt floors, and were without electricity, running water, or plumbing. Disease rates in these areas were alarmingly high, particularly rates of tuberculosis, and infant diarrhea.[39]

The plight of most black and Hispanic citizens of Texas failed to improve significantly under either machine politicians or progressive reformers. In Dallas, voter exclusion and at-large elections robbed many people of their voice in city politics. The absence of political power in poor and minority areas meant that the business and political elite could safely ignore them. In San Antonio, minorities voted in substantial numbers because machine politicians relied on their votes and paid poll taxes for many. The differences between the ways these votes were delivered, however, determined the level of services delivered in return. Black neighborhoods profited much more because their votes were delivered by bosses like Charles Bellinger while Mexican American votes were often purchased one on one. Additionally, a much larger proportion of African Americans paid their poll taxes and voted. Thus the African American East Side of town boasted several services, but blacks still suffered exclusion from suitable schools, employment, and health care. Still, the social costs of exclusionary and machine policies in both cities were immense. Progressive rhetoric held that reform in municipal government brought fairness and equity to all citizens. Texas reformers pushed the adoption of commission government as a way to improve city services for the whole city. But minority and poor neighborhoods in both cities suffered from a lack of services and poor health as a result of long-entrenched social attitudes and racism. White Texans often preached the progressive message of business elite control of municipal government as a way to end corruption and bring improvements to all. Minorities in Dallas and San Antonio knew better.[40]

NOTES

1. This paper began as a comparative study of municipal histories of Dallas and San Antonio. City minutes and other municipal sources provided vivid insight into the shaping of municipal priorities and policies. Documenting the impact of these policies on minority and poor citizens at the turn of the twentieth century, however, proved difficult. Historians can find evidence of the long neglect years later as minority citizens sought help in court to overcome the reluctance to provide services, but finding contemporary sources was difficult. Often only petitions to city councils and small notices in city newspapers illustrated the poverty of services as well as the reluctance of white elites to address the neglect in meaningful ways. Clinton Rogers Woodruff, *City Government by Commission* (New York: D. Appleton, 1914) *National Municipal League Series,* 3–5; James Weinstein, "Organized Business and the City Commission and Manager Movements," *Journal of Southern History* 28 (1962): 168, 170–73; Samuel P. Hays, "The Politics of Reform in Municipal Government in the Progressive Era," *Pacific Northwest Quarterly* 55 (1964), 167; Charles N. Glaab and A. Theodore Brown, *A History of Urban America,* 2nd ed. (New York: Macmillan, 1976), 180–81, 196.

2. Hayes, "The Politics of Reform," 161; Samuel P. Hays, "The Social Analysis of American Political History, 1880–1929," *Political Science Quarterly* 80 (1965), 383; Weinstein, "Organized Business and the City Commission and Manager Movements," 172–73, 176–77.

3. Arthur Meier Schlesinger Sr., *The Rise of the City, 1878–1898* (New York: Franklin Watt, 1975, first published, Macmillan, 1933) vol. 10, *A History of American Life,* 390; Michael Quigley Hooks, "The Struggle for Dominance: Urban Rivalry in North Texas, 1870–1910" (PhD diss., Texas Tech University, 1979), 60–61.

4. Jan Blodgett, *Land of Bright Promise: Advertising the Texas Panhandle and South Plains, 1870–1917* (Austin: University of Texas Press, 1988), 24–25; William L. McDonald, *Dallas Rediscovered: A Photographic Chronicle of Urban Expansion, 1870–1925,* introduction by A. C. Greene (Dallas: Dallas Historical Society, 1979), 29; Hooks, "The Struggle for Dominance," 60–61.

5. Bradley Robert Rice, *Progressive Cities: The Commission Government Movement in America, 1901–1920* (Austin: University of Texas Press, 1977) 3–6, 9–19; Martin J. Schiesl, *Politics of Efficiency: Municipal Administration and Reform in America, 1800–1920* (Berkeley: University of California Press, 1977), 21–25, 102, 135–36.

6. Harold L. Platt, *City Building in the New South: The Growth of Public Services in Houston, Texas, 1830–1910* (Philadelphia: Temple University Press, 1983), 211.

7. Philip Seib, *Dallas: Chasing the Urban Dream* (Dallas: Pressworks, 1986), 97; Sam Bass Warner Jr., *The Urban Wilderness: A History of the American City* (New York: Harper & Row, 1972), 101, 145; Howard Beeth and Cary D. Wintz, eds. (with introductions), *Black Dixie: Afro-Texas History and Culture in Houston* (College Station: Texas A&M University Press, 1992), 88; David G. McComb, *Houston: A History* (Austin: University of Texas Press, 1981), 108, 113; Patricia Lamkin, "A History of Blacks in San Angelo, 1869–1930" (master's thesis, Angelo State University, 1990), 74, 81; Robert Fisher, "Protecting Community and Property Values: Civic Clubs in Houston, 1909–70," in *Urban Texas: Politics and Development,* eds. Char Miller and Heywood T. Sanders (College Station; Texas A&M University Press, 1990), 131; McDonald, *Dallas Rediscovered,* 118.

8. Sam Bass Warner Jr., *Streetcar Suburbs: The Process of Growth in Boston, 1870–1900,* 2nd ed. (Cambridge, Mass.: Harvard University Press, 1978), 73; Warner, *The Urban Wilderness,* 101; Carolyn C. Gooden, "Dallas: Transformations of a Streetcar City" (master's thesis, University of Texas at Arlington, 1986), 51; McComb, *Houston, A History,* 98; Char Miller and Heywood T. Sanders, "Olmos Park and the Creation of a Suburban Bastion, 1927–39," in *Urban Texas,* 117; Cary D. Wintz, "The Emergence of a Black Neighborhood: Houston's Fourth Ward, 1865–1915," in *Urban Texas,* 104, 107; Fisher, "Protecting Community and Property Values," 129, 130; McDonald, *Dallas Rediscovered,* 147.

9. Edward Relph, *The Modern Urban Landscape* (Baltimore: Johns Hopkins University Press, 1987), 260–61; Warner, *City Building in the New South,* 209, 210–11; Joe R. Feagin, *Free Enterprise City: Houston in Political-Economic Perspective* (New Brunswick, N.J.: Rutgers University Press, 1988), 6; Schiesl, *The Politics of Efficiency,* 136; Fisher, "Protecting Community and Property Values," 131.

10. Dr. Robert Prince, *A History of Dallas From a Different Perspective* (Dallas: Nortex, 1993), 64, 68, 70; Schiesl, *Politics of Efficiency,* 4, 21, 196–97; Harold L. Platt, *The Electric City: Energy and the Growth of the Chicago Area, 1880–1930* (Chicago: University of Chicago Press, 1991), xvi; Platt, *City Building in the New South,* xix, 211; Feagin, *Free Enterprise City,* 25, 41, 55, 149, 269.

11. Robert Gary Peacock, "The Origins of Commission Government in Dallas, 1902–1907" (master's thesis, North Texas State University, 1975), 3, 24–25; Thomas Field, "Greater Dallas—What She Has Done, What She is Doing, What She Will Achieve!!" (n.p., c. 1906); Harold A. Stone, Don K. Price, and Kathryn H. Stone, *City Manager Government in Dallas* (Chicago: Public Administration Service, 1939), 8.

12. Platt, *City Building in the New South,* 201; Warner, *Streetcar Suburbs,* 32; Roy H. Williams and Kevin J. Shay, *Time Changes: An Alternative View of the History of Dallas* (Dallas: To Be, 1991), 42, 47–48.

13. Naomi Lede, "The Negro Voter in Dallas: A Study in Political Socialization"

(Dallas Center for Social Sciences Research, Bishop College, n.d.) n.p.; Jack Smith McCrary, "Neighboring Among Ethnic Groups in Dallas" (master's thesis, Southern Methodist University, 1949), 49–55; Patricia E. Hall, "The Origins of Modern Dallas" (PhD diss., University of Texas at Dallas, 1990), 39–41; Jim Schultze, *The Accommodation: The Politics of Race in an American City* (Secaucus, N.J.: Citadel Press, 1986), 9; Heloise M. Foreman, *Negro Life in Dallas* (Works Progress Administration Writers' Project, 1937), 3–4; McDonald, *Dallas Rediscovered,* 118, 123, 125.

14. Williams and Shay, *Time Changes,* 48; Foreman, *Negro Life,* 1–2; Prince, *History of Dallas From a Different Perspective,* 59, 76; William Siembieda and Peter Lupsha, "The Poverty of Public Services in the Sunbelt," in *The Rise of Sunbelt Cities,* eds. David C. Perry and Alfred J. Watkins (Beverly Hills, Calif.: Sage Publications, 1978), 172, 178; Jim Schultze, *The Accommodation: The Politics of Race in an American City* (Secaucus, N.J.: Citadel Press, 1986), 9–10; *Annual Reports of the City of Dallas, 1908–1909, 6.*

15. McDonald, *Dallas Rediscovered,* 175, 179, 181.

16. City Minutes, Dallas Municipal Archives, Dallas, Texas, vol. 28, 118; vol. 32, 259; McDonald, *Dallas Rediscovered,* 175.

17. City Minutes, vol. 1, 181; vol 5, 139, 236.

18. For 1916 quote, see City Minutes, vol. 12, 100, 398. For restrictions, see Schultze, *The Accomodation,* 9–10; for Dallas segregation, see Gooden, "Dallas: Transformation of a Streetcar City," 51.

19. *Negro Population: 1790–1915* (Washington D.C.: Department of the Census, 1918), 472; Schultze, *The Accommodation,* 9–10; Gooden, "Dallas: Transformation of a Streetcar City," 51.

20. Platt, *City Building in the New South,* 201; Warner, *Streetcar Suburbs,* 32;Williams and Shay, *Time Changes,* 42, 47–48.

21. Williams and Shay, *Time Changes,* 51; Seib, *Dallas: Chasing the Urban Dream,* 10, 92; Bill Minutaglio and Holly Williams, *The Hidden City: Oak Cliff, Texas* (Dallas: Elmwood Press and Old Oak Cliff Conservation League, 199), 178, 180; McDonald, *Dallas Rediscovered,* 117–18, 126.

22. Barry J. Kaplan, "Houston: The Gold Belt Buckle of the Sunbelt," *Sunbelt Cities: Politics and Growth Since World War II,* eds. Richard M. Bernard and Bradley R. Rice (Austin: University of Texas Press, 1983), 203; Martin V. Melosi, "Dallas–Fort Worth: Marketing the Metroplex," *Sunbelt Cities,* 175; Seib, *Dallas: Chasing the Urban Dream,* 10–11, 92.

23. Siembieda and Lupsha, "Poverty of Public Services," 174, 183; McComb, *Houston,* 203; Warner, *Streetcar Suburbs,* 32; Williams and Shay, *Time Changes,* 51.

24. Foreman, "Negro Life," 1–2; Minutaglio and Williams, *The Hidden City,* 178; Schultze, *The Accommodation,* 9–10; Williams and Shay, *Time Changes,* 51; Prince, *History of Dallas From a Different Perspective,* 76; Elmer Scott, *88 Eventful Years: Being the Intimate Story of Elmer Scott in Industry and the Humanities and of the Civic Federation of Dallas Over a Third of a Century* (Dallas: Civic Federation of Dallas, 1954), 43; Feagin, *Free Enterprise City,* 238–39.

25. For black resistance, see Maxine Holmes and Gerald D. Saxon, eds., *WPA Dallas Guide and History,* introduction by Gerald D. Saxon (Dallas: University of North Texas Press, 1992), 294; Prince, *History of Dallas from a Different Perspective,* 68; McDonald,

Dallas Rediscovered, 17, 118. For black organization formation, see City Minutes, vol. 2, 100; Elizabeth York Enstam, "They Called It Motherhood," *Hidden Histories of Women in the New South,* eds. Virginia Bernhard, Betty Brandon, Elizabeth Fox-Genovese, Theda Perdue, and Elizabeth Hayes Turner (Columbia: University of Missouri Press, 1994), 93–94.

26. Char Miller and David R. Johnson, "The Rise of Urban Texas," in *Urban Texas,* 12; Frank W. Jennings, *San Antonio: The Story of an Enchanted City,* 2nd ed. (Austin: Eakin, 2002), 8–9, 87–88.

27. David R. Johnson, "Frugal and Sparing: Interest Groups, Politics, and City Building in San Antonio, 1870–85," *Urban Texas,* 34–36; Kenneth Mason, *African Americans and Race Relations in San Antonio, Texas 1867–1937* (New York: Garland, 1998), 25–27; Julia Kirk Blackwelder, *Women of the Depression: Caste and Culture in San Antonio, 1929–1939,* 2nd ed. (College Station: Texas A&M University Press, 1998), 14, 16–17.

28. Mason, *African Americans and Race Relations,* 81, 85–88, 93–95; Johnson, "Frugal and Sparing," 37, 38, 47–48; Blackwelder, *Women of the Depression,* 16.

29. Johnson, "Frugal and Sparing," 48, 55; Mason, *African Americans and Race Relations,* 94.

30. John A. Booth and David R. Johnson, "Power and Progress in San Antonio Politics, 1836–1970," in *The Politics of San Antonio: Community, Progress & Power,* eds. David R. Johnson, John A. Booth, and Richard J. Harris (Lincoln: University of Nebraska Press, 1983), 8–11; Mason, *African Americans and Race Relations,* 109–10, 113; Jennings, *San Antonio,* 142; Blackwelder, *Women of the Depression,* 19

31. Booth and Johnson, "Power and Progress," 9.

32. San Antonio *Daily Express,* January 11, 1909; Booth and Johnson, "Power and Progress," 10–13; Mason, *African Americans and Race Relations,* 113, 216.

33. Booth and Johnson, "Power and Progress," 12–13; Mason, *African Americans and Race Relations,* 111.

34. J. Morgan Kousser, *The Shaping of Southern Politics: Suffrage Restrictions and the Establishment of the One-Party South, 1880–1910* (New Haven: Yale University Press, 1974), 251–53, 260; Amy Bridges, "Boss Tweed and V. O. Key in Texas," *Urban Texas,* 61–62; Booth and Johnson, "Power and Progress," 12; Mason, *African Americans and Race Relations,* 112.

35. Booth and Johnson, "Power and Progress," 12–15; Heywood T. Sanders, "Building a New Urban Infrastructure: The Creation of Postwar San Antonio," in *Urban Texas,* 156.

36. Tucker Gibson, "Mayoralty Politics in San Antonio, 1955–79," *The Politics of San Antonio,* 114–15; Booth and Johnson, "Power and Progress," 15–16; Sanders, "New Urban Infrastructure," 156–57; Mason, *African Americans and Race Relations,* 113.

37. Miller and Sanders, "Olmos Park and the Creations of a Suburban Bastion, 1927–39," in *Urban Texas,* 114, 117, 122, 124; Blackwelder, *Women of the Depression,* 19; Booth and Johnson, "Power and Progress," 16–18.

38. Audrey Granneberg, "Maury Maverick's San Antonio," *Survey Graphic: Magazine of Social Interpretation* 28, no. 7, July 1939: 421; Mason, *African Americans and Race*

Relations, 272–73; Blackwelder, *Women of the Depression,* 19; Sanders, "New Urban Infrastructure," 155–56.

39. Robert Brischetto, Charles L. Cotrell, and R. Michael Stevens, "Conflict and Change in the Political Culture of San Antonio in the 1970s," in *The Politics of San Antonio,* 76–77; Blackwelder, *Woman of the Depression,* 20; Mason, *African Americans and Race Relations,* 272; Granneberg, "Maury Maverick's San Antonio," 421.

40. Williams and Shay, *Time Changes,* 54, 55; Warner, *Streetcar Suburbs,* 32, 73; Platt, *City Building in the New South,* 200–201, 215; Marilynn Wood Hill, "A History of the Jewish Involvement in the Dallas Community" (master's thesis, Southern Methodist University, 1967), 51, 52–53; Mason, *African Americans and Race Relations,* 113; Booth and Johnson, "Conflict and Change," 76; Blackwelder, *Women of the Depression,* 18–19.

CHAPTER SIX

Religious Moderates and Race

THE TEXAS CHRISTIAN LIFE COMMISSION AND THE CALL FOR RACIAL RECONCILIATION, 1954–68

David K. Chrisman

The Baptist General Convention of Texas (hereafter BGCT) rose in numbers and strength in the twentieth century to become the state's largest Protestant denomination. The BGCT matched the growth of its parent Southern Baptist Convention (hereafter SBC), and the cultural differences of Texas Baptists never upset a denominational unity that spurred new churches, BGCT institutions, or mission programs that thrived in post–World War II conformity. Inherent in the BGCT's success was the perceived inalienable right to worship freely—a religious freedom grounded in the denomination's decentralized structure, conservative theology, and ardent defense of the separation of church and state. To Baptists, the Bible served as the final and only authority in theological belief for denominational executives, pastors, and church members. Through their freedom of interpreting Scripture, revered as the "priesthood of the believer," Texas Baptists pursued individual salvation as their primary means of social reformation. Likewise, Texas Baptists rested all structural authority on the local autonomy of their churches. The decentralized structure allowed congregational votes in local churches to check pastors or denominational leaders attempting to motivate churches against perceived social threats of injustices. This democratic claim of church autonomy supported Baptists as a "non-creedal" people with a heavy reliance on the separation of church and state that distinguished them from other Protestant bodies. Perhaps as most representative of a moral stewardship of the public's welfare in segregated Texas, a handful of Texas Baptist leaders applied their Bible-based theology to include the individual rights of black Texans in the spirit of integration.[1]

On May 17, 1954, the day the U.S. Supreme Court ordered public school desegregation in *Brown v. Board of Education,* Foy Valentine nervously concluded a workshop on race relations at First Baptist Church, Marshall, in deeply segregated East Texas. As a BGCT representative and director of its Christian Life Commission (hereafter Texas CLC), Valentine appeared in part due to an invitation by Arthur Rutledge, the church's pastor and the sitting chairman of the commission. Predicting the struggle to follow, the two Texas CLC members urged calm after the court's decision, appealed to the congregation's civic responsibility and evangelical spirit, and called for improved education to combat racism. Valentine charged Rutledge with building a better acceptance of the *Brown* decision, but this placed the Marshall pastor in a perplexing situation, and he ultimately failed at the task. Rutledge left the church in 1958, and by 1961, deacons blocked students from nearby Bishop College, Marshall's black Baptist school, and Wiley College from entering the sanctuary by locking arms at the church doors. When the congregation finally voted to accept blacks in their worship services in 1974, their vote came four years after the Marshall Independent School District fully integrated in compliance with a federal court order.[2]

The actions of First Baptist-Marshall suggest that race-conscious Baptist leaders like Valentine and Rutledge failed in overcoming their moral dilemma or in destroying the symbolic power of segregation on two fronts. Valentine appealed to the church's evangelical mission to improve race relations, but the *Brown v. Board of Education* decision to integrate schools with all deliberate speed "out moralized" segregated BGCT churches. Valentine embodied the denomination's spiritual dilemma. His convictions regarding the biblical mandates of justice and equality were handicapped by his denomination's racist and segregated culture. Any attempts to breach this divide were frustrated by popular interpretations of Baptist polity, theology, and commitment to separation of church and state. Their call for improved race relations never registered a sense of urgency among most white Baptists, while their paternalistic relationship with black Baptists never offered a practical support of true racial equality. Even though some BGCT leaders proved more progressive than their congregations by working in support of civil rights, their loyalty to the denomination's conservative theology and congregational structure forced them to develop a moderate strategy in calling for racial reformation.

The moderate strategy of Texas Baptists leaders grew out of Southwestern Seminary in the 1930s, where T. B. Maston, a professor of Christian ethics, singled out race relations as the most critical social concern for Baptists. Heavily influenced by Gunner Myrdal's manifesto for southern moderates, *An American Dilemma,* Maston taught a generation of students that the church served as one of many moral forces providing leadership in the gradual evolution of social advances. That "particular commitment" to racial justice attracted Valentine to the Fort Worth seminary in 1946, where he became Maston's protégé after spending the summer at Koinonia Farm, the interracial community experiment cofounded by Clarence Jordan in rural Americus,

Georgia. After completing his doctoral degree, Valentine's association with Maston created an opportunity in the BGCT when he accepted a part-time position as the first Interracial Coordinator of Student Work among Baptist students in Texas. The effort supported the extension mentality of the BGCT by combining its ministry to students, the Baptist Student Union, with the Home Mission Board's Ministry with Minorities. Valentine traveled to Butler College in Tyler, the Conroe Institute of Theology, and Bishop College in Marshall, where he assisted black students in pastoral training. The part-time position then turned into full-time in 1949, when the convention named him director of Baptist Student Work at Prairie View A&M College. Most of his work there, however, centered on his relationship with M. M. Pierson, a black pastor from Houston. Valentine's networking provided Pierson with denominational support and money to establish a Baptist Student Union (hereafter BSU) on campus, while Pierson gave Valentine access to black pastors in Houston and students on campus. Significantly, the application of the BSU fell to Pierson, who traveled to Prairie View once a week to conduct the "cooperative" effort at the segregated school.[3]

Momentum over the race issue ultimately led the BGCT to create the Texas CLC in 1951, tapping the denomination's director of its Ministry with Minorities, A. C. Miller, as director. The commission quickly emerged as a moderate social commentary within the conservative BGCT by 1953, selling itself to constituents as a voice "speaking to" and "not speaking for" Texas Baptists. The Texas CLC asked Baptists to apply scripture to "everyday life" situations on a range of subjects including political activism, economic concerns, war and peace, the separation of church and state, and family matters. Yet the Texas CLC devoted most of its early energy to race, providing pamphlets and holding annual workshops to educate white Texas Baptists with the hope of creating a spiritual tension that placed more responsibility on whites for the racial crisis. As the racial tension escalated across the nation during 1953, the Southern Baptist Convention (hereafter SBC) quickly adopted the nonfragmenting approach of the Texas CLC in organization and leadership by creating its own Christian Life Commission and naming Miller director of the denomination's effort (hereafter Southern Baptist CLC). BGCT executives then replaced Miller by appointing the young Valentine as director of the Texas CLC. With an objective of gradual racial reconciliation, this "Texas Connection" led the denomination's Christian life effort to usher in social integration among all segregated and increasingly alarmed Southern Baptists.[4]

The Texas CLC's moderate strategy of "speaking to" Baptist churches allowed the BGCT to run smoothly in May of 1954 when the Supreme Court handed down the *Brown* decision. As Valentine conducted his race relations workshop in Marshall, other Baptist leaders wrapped their carefully worded reactions around themes of responsible citizenship and spirituality. The moderate commentary reached rank-and-file Texas Baptists through the *Baptist Standard,* although it placed the paper's editor, David Gardner, in a difficult position. Having earlier strongly implied that "racial rabble rousers" and "ill-advised agitators" instigated the Court's decision, a month later Gardner's July 10 editorial respected the ruling as the "law of the land." He urged Texas Baptists "to keep calm, think clearly and act courageously" about the Court "whether we like it or not."[5] On the other hand, a watered down resolution prepared by A. C. Miller's Southern Baptist CLC was approved by the annual Southern Baptist Convention in St. Louis later in the year. The SBC's non-committal resolution "urged" all Baptists to work for reconciliation, recognize the court's decision as "adhering to the basic moral principles of our religion," and commended the court for deferring application of the decision.[6] The citizenship theme only seeped down to local associations and lacked a practical racial message. In rural settings such as the Burnet-Llano Baptist Association, prepared statements of the CLC asked members to study carefully the 1954 Race Relations resolution adopted by the SBC. It urged believers in the Hill Country to conduct themselves in "racial adjustments as Christians ought, giving a good accounting of themselves as servants of the Lord Jesus." Likewise, the Soda Lake Association in East Texas used the same statement in its Christian Life report by deemphasizing the race message and stressed that "family life in the churches" served as the "strongest bulwark against materialism, communism, secularism, or other evil forces which seek to destroy our faith." Through the church and the association, Christian citizens "should obey the laws of the land, cast the Christian ballot, pay taxes, and pray for those in authority."[7] After the SBC voted in Miami to begin a "Crusade for Christian Morality" in 1955, Valentine and the Texas CLC followed suit by expanding the new emphasis on Christian citizenship and implementing "a desperately needed revival of behavior" in areas of race relations, daily work, family life, citizenship, and moral issues.[8]

Long-standing and token BGCT cooperative and extensions programs undertaken by urban associations for black Baptists changed little after the *Brown* decision. The interracial Fellowship Bible Conference, sponsored by the Southeastern Baptist Association in Beaumont, met for the eighth consecutive year in 1954. The Austin Baptist Association (hereafter ABA) continued to provide vacation Bible schools for black and Latino youth. The ABA's report included "visits" between its Ministry with Minorities and the Negro Baptist Pastors Union. A year later the ABA failed to report on its Ministry with Minorities but cited a broader report on Miller's Southern Baptist CLC and its work in race relations. The Dallas Baptist Association worked jointly with a similar committee in the Dallas Negro Minister's Union to turn an early extension program into the Inter-Racial Baptist Fellowship Institute near downtown Dallas. In the BGCT's most cooperative venture in 1955, the Texas CLC joined efforts with the executive board and Department of Student Ministry to establish a BSU at Texas Southern University (hereafter TSU), the first BGCT-sponsored organization on the Houston campus. After renovating a house close to campus for the Baptist center, the board then named a young African American pastor, William A. "Bill" Lawson, to run it. The token employee addressed the executive board after his first year, joking that "he added some color to your program" and reporting the "happy problem" of not enough adequate space to reach interested students.[9] The interracial and paternalistic effort was a start in the right direction for many white Baptists, but their design in no way offered a path to social justice for black Baptists pursuing new found freedoms.

Apart from speaking to Baptists in the proper manner, Valentine used the Court's decision to admonish segregated BGCT churches during the commission's quarterly meeting in late June 1954. Texas Baptists and other Christians forced the federal government to act on a simple moral issue, arguing that "it's high time the churches assumed . . . spiritual leadership" and that Christians should heed the Bible and proper theology as the "ultimate solution" to racism and prejudice.[10] In an August article in the *Baptist Standard,* he attacked racist and overused lessons portraying blacks as "the Curse of Ham" and offered Scripture to disprove white exploitation of "colored help." Valentine's condescending tone lambasted "intentional misinterpretation of the Scripture" as completely ignorant of race relations, before he aptly concluded that "ye shall know the truth, and the truth shall set you free."[11] The language sounded similar to other religious advocates for racial justice and at least offered the potential of the Texas CLC to extend the bureaucratic power of the BGCT to a growing ecumenical movement demanding desegregation.

In contrast, the Texas Council of Churches (hereafter TCC) never concerned itself with inward denominational lessons on race and simply "spoke for" the urgency of the Court's decision. The council, headed by executive secretary Harold Kilpatrick, represented twelve Texas denominations and an estimated 1,250,000 constituents by 1954. Anticipating public reaction several weeks before the decision, the council gathered leading clergy from various denominations to address the Associated Press when the decision came down. William C. Martin, a Methodist bishop from Dallas, endorsed the justices by expressing the "positive brotherhood of man under the fatherhood of God." The Roman Catholic Archbishop of San Antonio, Robert E. Lucey, described the decision as "inevitable." San Antonio's rabbi of the Temple Beth-el, David Jacobson, pondered that "Thou shalt love thy neighbor" might really mean something. Others suggesting a unified religious voice in Texas by hitting the airwaves and newsprint included Everett H. Jones of the Episcopal Church and the Presbyterian J. Hoytt Boles. The only Baptist pastor active in the media blitz was Blake Smith, whose University Baptist Church in Austin had been ostracized from the BGCT for taking liberal positions on a range of issues, including unofficially integrating his church in 1950.[12] Valentine actively communicated with many members of the Texas Council of Churches, but his unwillingness to commit the Texas CLC to the public and political struggle over integration denied Texas Baptists any real opportunity in the larger context of the early civil rights movement.

Texas Baptists certainly had their opportunities in the political arena. The progressive Carlyle Marney nervously pastored his congregation at the First Baptist Church of Austin (hereafter FBC Austin), through the political tensions spurred by the decision. On any given Sunday during the summer of 1954, the conservative and segregationist governor of Texas, Allan Shivers, sat on the opposite side of the sanctuary from his liberal party challenger Ralph Yarborough. The two high-profile church members had faced each other once before in the hotly contested Democratic primary for governor in 1952, and they faced each other again in the 1954 primary runoff. Although Shivers eventually won the runoff and election and ultimately symbolized the political defense of segregation, racial tensions hardly affected the affluent Austin congregation.[13]

The lame-duck Shivers increasingly defended segregation to maintain his ultraconservative control of the state Democratic Executive Committee, despite a series of political defeats by 1955. Facing charges of corruption and scandal by that summer, Shivers mustered a last grasp for power by forming the Texas Advisory Commission on Segregation and packing it with radical segregationists. In February 1956, Shivers and the commission then pushed three segregationist referenda on the primary ballot. The referenda asked voters to take a position on interposition, consider stronger laws forbidding interracial marriage, and support exemptions from compulsory attendance at integrated schools. Throughout the entire election period, Shivers received support from segregationists quoting Scripture and citing religious principles. Letters to the governor viewed blacks as the "sons of Ham" and "smitten with a curse." Some referred the governor to the book of Genesis to argue that God "exercised discrimination by segregating his people." Supporting racial integration meant upsetting a racial order over 2,200 years old and "voluntarily transmitting this curse in a way the Lord did not intend."[14] Others defended the governor's Christian commitment outright. His close friend, Ross M. Sams of Waco, who served on the Baylor University board of trustees, wrote a letter to hundreds of "Friends in the Baptist Ministry." Sams sought to correct "wild, misleading, and absolutely false charges" hurled against the governor by first Ralph Yarborough supporters and later Price Daniel men. Avoiding the race issue, the letter showed that Shivers personified a good Baptist in office by closing down "big-time gambling . . . slot machines and punch boards." According to Sams, Shivers represented the consummate Christian citizen.[15]

With segregationist legislation pending in 1956, Valentine and his moderate message ran aground on the challenge of speaking to Texas Baptists in the midst of political and social defiance. Press coverage largely ignored a lukewarm resolution by the SBC supporting the second *Brown* decision in 1955, yet pounced on a segregationist speech in February given by the BGCT's most prominent pastor, W. A. Criswell. Pastor of the nation's largest Protestant church at First Baptist Church, Dallas, Criswell's sermon at the South Carolina Evangelism Conference veered off course by denouncing the Court's ruling as "a thing of idiocy and foolishness." Invited to address a joint assembly of the South Carolina legislature the next day and introduced to his political pulpit by Sen. Strom Thurmond, Criswell repeated his criticism of the Court and described those supporting integration as "a bunch of infidels, dying from the neck up."[16] Moderate Baptist leaders, seeking equal press coverage at the 1956 annual meeting of the SBC in Kansas City, disagreed over how to handle the embarrassing incident. Before the gathering, SBC president C. C. Warren asked convention speakers not to discuss race "in the face of grave issues." Herbert Howard, pastor of Park Cities Baptist Church in Dallas and a member of the Texas CLC, urged A. C. Miller and the Southern Baptist CLC to lead a floor debate on the race issue at the convention. Miller balked at Howard's request, arguing that such an action "would be nothing short of a calamity" and that "our people are simply not capable of discussing this matter objectively and without extreme emotion." Miller told the Dallas pastor that the Southern Baptist CLS held a responsibility to the whole convention, and that they must not voice their personal opinion regarding integration.[17]

In spite of Miller's effort to squelch the race issue in St. Louis, Baptist leaders indirectly introduced tension when they invited Billy Graham, a member of Criswell's church, as the keynote speaker. Graham broached the subject when he briefly urged racial understanding in the desegregation struggle. More significantly, T. B. Maston's convention speech on race dominated headlines in most secular and religious newspapers. In his eight-minute speech, "Southern Baptists and the Negro," he offered a cautious "guidance" for Southern Baptists in helping their communities adjust to desegregation. Maston, ever conciliatory, said that a difference of opinion "between us will never lead to a break in fellowship."[18] Later commenting on the Supreme Court's order for "all deliberate speed," the cautious Maston wrote that pushing "so-call[ed] integration too rapidly in some communities in the South might conceivably create problems just as serious as those it purports to solve." Maston believed that a careful gradualism represented true reformation, even though all Christians recognized that "our practices are far below the Christian ideal."[19]

With at least one prominent Texas Baptist pastor in Criswell publicly supporting a hard-line stand, Shivers opportunistically used events at Mansfield High School in August 1956 to play again on the public's fear over integration. Local problems started when a federal court found Mansfield's busing of black students to a segregated and poorly managed school in Fort Worth unlawful. When the court ordered Mansfield High to integrate on August 27, the first such case in Texas, a white mob of 300 responded by surrounding the high school and blocking black students from enrolling. The mob then used violence to intimidate city officials, pro-integration school board members, and the media. From Austin, Shivers referred to the mob as an "orderly protest" and defied the federal order by dispatching Texas Rangers. The Rangers officially "authorized" Mansfield's school board to transfer black students to Fort Worth as a matter of public order and safety.[20] Texas Baptists hesitated to take on the Mansfield incident directly. Jess Moody, the pastor at First Baptist-Mansfield and a BGCT executive, said nothing publicly about the incident. Three weeks before the crisis, the new editor of the *Baptist Standard,* E. S. James, admonished the National Association for the Advancement of Colored People (hereafter NAACP) over various initiatives and lectured the organization on "first class citizenship."[21] Almost three weeks after the Mansfield incident, however, Valentine was able to get the Texas CLC's carefully worded "Pledge in Time of Racial Tension" printed in the *Standard.* The moderate pledge asked individual Baptists "not to engage in nor to encourage any action involving or implying violence . . . Not to join with any group in actions which I would not carry out openly as in individual" and to "encourage by word and action moderation and patience at all times."[22] Valentine and the Texas CLC never criticized the governor directly until the race issue divided traditional BGCT relationships.

The Texas CLC's call for patience and moderation hardly affected local Baptist associations and congregations fractured by social integration. For example, violence began in September 1956 when angry whites picketed the integration of Lamar Technological College in Beaumont. Stirred by a newly created white citizen's council, white demonstrators blamed their agitation on the federal government, labor, and the NAACP. The violence soon spilled over to Baptist life when members of the school's BSU publicly supported enrolling African American students. The situation only grew worse for Beaumont churches within the Southeastern Baptist Association. At Calvary Baptist Church, pastor J. M. Sibley tried to keep his congregation together after a church member rammed a black man's car before assaulting the same man in public. Sibley's endorsement of the Lamar BSU led another member of Calvary to demand a deacons meeting for the purpose of firing the pastor and withdrawing the church from the SBC. After Sibley appealed to the Texas

CLC for help, Valentine responded, "it is a rather sad commentary that you are the only pastor in that area requesting literature," and he sent Sibley a copy of the Texas CLC's moderate "Pledge in Time of Racial Tension" released after the Mansfield incident.[23]

The racial tension at Lamar University and Calvary Baptist Church threatened Beaumont's long cooperative effort of the interracial Fellowship Bible Conference. The conference, initiated by A. C. Miller's Ministry with Minorities in 1947, had been held largely in African American churches until the white Highland Avenue Baptist Church hosted the fellowship in late 1955. Only eight blacks and one other white minister attended the conference in December 1956, hosted by the committee chair and pastor of South Park Baptist Church, Joseph Harbour. Harbour's deacons then voted not to invite the conference back the following year, citing the problems at Lamar and Calvary Baptist. One of Harbour's deacons later claimed that he was told by the pastor of Highland Avenue that the conference in 1955 resulted in the loss of forty families and that "the Negroes just took over our nurseries and restrooms."[24] Harbour then wrote black members of the conference to inform them about the canceled conference, and he invited Foy Valentine to come to Beaumont to "help with the situation." D. Manning Jackson, pastor of the African American Live Oak Baptist Church and member of the fellowship committee, angrily complained to Harbour, because Jackson's congregation spent over a year planning and advertising the aborted 1957 meeting. Jackson and other black ministers also thought it odd that Harbour appealed to Valentine. Blacks on the committee sought "to work it out with the white ministers and deacons of Beaumont," and they viewed a meeting with Valentine as unnecessary. Harbour then shot back a letter criticizing the "resentful, belligerent, and threatening tone" of Jackson. The insecure Harbour asked why black ministers condemned him for "not pulling your social chestnuts out of the fire" and "alienating yourselves from those . . . true friends through the ten years of fellowship." Harbour ultimately resigned as chairman of the committee, and the crises in Beaumont ended the interracial fellowship.[25]

When Valentine evaluated the "racial situation" in a speech at Southwestern Seminary in 1957, he described it as an "albatross about the neck of the nation." Valentine criticized still segregated urban school districts, blasted "respectable elements" involved in newly formed citizens councils in Texas, and demonstrated his disappointment with race-driven violence in Beaumont and Mansfield. Valentine then described the peculiar Baptist dilemma. He argued that although pastors "understood" race relations far better than their congregations due to "information provided by the CLC," they failed tragically in making their congregations apply Scripture to the race issue. At the same time, Valentine argued that pastors lagged behind their congregation because many refused to identify racial prejudice as a moral and spiritual problem and speak out against segregation. Valentine's frustration grew as Texas Baptists resisted his theological solution to the race problem.[26]

Valentine also lacked political fortitude in the structural context of the BGCT. Although Valentine finally attacked the race baiting of Shivers and his Texas Advisory Commission on Segregation in the same speech, the Texas CLC played only a minor role in defeating segregationist legislation in 1957. After voters approved the original segregationist referendum in November 1956, Valentine traveled to Austin to attend a special meeting of the ecumenical Texas Council of Churches (hereafter TCC). The council quickly elected Valentine chairman as the committee discussed strategies to pressure the legislature into defeating the segregationist agenda. When a majority of committee members wanted to release a series of ecumenical statements to newspapers opposing the "racist bills," Valentine once again described the media blitz as a mistake that "would crystallize opposition." He advocated lobbying legislators on a personal basis and refraining from "playing our actions up in any public way." Valentine then met with governor-elect Price Daniel before returning home to Dallas. The next day he wrote the TCC's executive director, Harold Kilpatrick, and resigned as chairman of the committee. While the TCC ultimately pressured the legislature to defeat most of the segregationist bills in 1957, the strength of the ecumenical movement suffered without the state's most visible Baptist advocate for improved race relations.[27]

Valentine's 1957 speech was certainly prophetic. By 1960, civil unrest in Texas threatened to match protests in other parts of the South. School desegregation in Texas became stagnant by 1961, with only 128 of 722 biracial districts integrated. Even after the passing of the federal Civil Rights Act of 1964, 90 percent of African American students in some large Texas cities attended predominantly black schools.[28] Boiling frustration of blacks seeking social equality accompanied the slow progress of desegregation. Although local newspapers agreed not to cover protests at the level seen in other parts of the South, the Texas civil rights movement fueled a white backlash and an already hostile political environment during the early 1960s. The strong anti–federal government sentiment, prevalent across the country, led many to be indifferent to, and in a few cases, to cheer, the assassination of President John F. Kennedy in Dallas in November 1963.

For African American Baptists who at times crossed paths with Texas Baptists, the Texas CLC's moderate strategy offered no immediate help in attacking legal segregation. Bill Lawson, a friend of Foy Valentine and the director of the BGCT-sponsored student union at TSU in Houston, indicates black Baptists' frustrations. A month after college students challenged segregation laws in Greensboro, North Carolina, thirteen Texas Southern students asked Lawson to help organize their own sit-in in Houston and instruct them in nonviolent tactics. After the stunned Lawson advised them not to demonstrate, the students told him they only sought his advice and not his permission.[29] The students then successfully protested a Houston Wiengarten store before the sit-in spread and forced negotiations with city officials. Lawson subsequently helped students draft a letter to consider a postponement settlement if city officials created a bi-racial committee to study the desegregation of Houston's public facilities.[30] By May, however, the foot-dragging of the mayor's biracial committee led Lawson to reconsider his moderate position of negotiation and gradualism. Accepting tactics of direct action, he suggested students conduct a general boycott of Houston businesses and offered his home to develop strategy and make picket signs. In June 1962, Lawson placed himself into a better position with Houston's black community when he left Texas Southern and accepted a call to pastor Wheeler Avenue Baptist Church, a "middle-class" congregation located near the campus. When TSU students planned a protest to take advantage of astronaut Gordon Cooper's nationally televised parade in May 1963, Lawson opened Wheeler Avenue as the base of operations. Fifteen minutes before the parade's scheduled start, a phone call to the church from white businessmen halted the mass protest by conceding segregationist practices. Many students believed the concession saved Houston from the largest civil rights protest in the entire South.[31]

Lawson dual aligned Wheeler Avenue with the BGCT and the black National Baptist Convention, and it was the first church in Houston with such a denominational arrangement. But the Texas CLC offered no tangible help in the continued struggle. For example, Lawson worked to bring Martin Luther King Jr. to TSU in 1964. Many of the state's denominations and religious institutions had solicited a visit from the busy civil rights activist, including the Austin Presbyterian Seminary, the Disciples of Christ, Rice University, and Southern Methodist University, which issued three invitations. Both the BGCT and Baylor University viewed King as too controversial in 1964, and never invited him to anything. Lawson appealed to King's longtime friend, Erma Jewell Hughes, to secure his appearance at TSU in May 1964.[32]

Students in Austin, San Antonio, Galveston, and Dallas also challenged local segregation laws during the same period. In Dallas, black students from Washington High School and Bishop College instigated stand-ins at the Palace and Majestic theaters on February 12, 1961. After fifty white students from Southern Methodist University later joined the stand-in, a general, though peaceful, confusion ensued. The *Dallas Morning News* blamed clergy and academics for the disorder and voiced its opposition to picketing as a "means of coercion."[33] The stand-ins also contributed to the Dallas residents' overall anxiety in 1961 after a federal court ordered Dallas schools to desegregate. A week after the stand-ins, T. B. Maston addressed the Dallas Pastors Conference at Cliff Temple Baptist Church. His moderate message, "The Role of

Fig. 6.1. William A. Lawson, speaking at a Missions Conference, 1964. Credit: Texas Baptist Historical Collection, Dallas, Texas.

a Pastor in a Community Facing Desegregation," urged ministers to "not let Dallas be another New Orleans or Little Rock" when desegregating its schools. Maston assured pastors that in communities already desegregated, "Negro pupils have not flooded previously all-white schools" and that where they enjoyed freedom of choice, "the vast majority of them continue to attend all-Negro or predominantly Negro schools." At the critical time of mounting protest in the city, Maston simply asked preachers to "show leadership in your church" and rely on the "citizenship appeal."[34]

Significantly, Maston's message hardly registered with BGCT churches as integration went from a national mandate to a local struggle. When several

African Americans attempted to enter K. Owen White's segregated First Baptist Church in Houston (hereafter FBC Houston) during the student protests in late 1962, ushers turned them away at the doors. White, who served as BGCT president in 1962 and was elected president of the SBC the following year, later described the incident as a mistake since he previously told ushers to seat "everyone who came to worship, regardless of race." Within a year, however, another young African American attempted to join White's congregation. Since FBC Houston based eligibility for membership on a consultation between the pastor and potential member, White decided that the African American was motivated by joining "the church where the president of the Southern Baptist Convention is pastor."[35] Once White denied the membership, the local chapter of the Congress of Racial Equality (hereafter CORE) threatened to picket the church, stage knee-ins, and "pack the pews." After the press broke the incident on Juneteenth, White clarified his position while vacationing in Canada. The pastor deeply regretted the incident rising at a time of "racial turmoil in other cities and tension in Houston," but he concluded that "there could be a wrong time to do a right thing."[36] Press coverage of the attempted church integration grew throughout the summer of 1963 as CORE members followed through with their protests. In August, the church denied two more African Americans applying for membership.[37] The incident led E. S. James, editor of the *Baptist Standard,* to comment on CORE's aggressive strategy. Although "Negroes have a right to seek membership in white churches . . . under ordinary circumstances," James announced, resorting to pickets and protests "wastes energy and hurts the cause they seek to promote." The condescending editor stated that integrating churches "will be done voluntarily or not at all." A reader of the *Standard* later asked James to clarify his position by pointing out that whites might also use ulterior motives in joining a church. James responded by recognizing "true motive" as impossible, but he confidently believed that "FBC Houston and White were justified" in denying membership "in this case."[38]

A fine line existed over membership motives between more conservative and ultimately fundamentalist churches in Texas, such as FBC Houston, and those with a more progressive reputation. After Carlyle Marney left FBC Austin in 1958, new pastor Madison Scott used his connections with Austin's Citizen Committee to invite local African Americans to worship as early as 1962. While some blacks regularly attended the church, none held memberships in the prestigious downtown congregation. This situation changed when a mild-mannered postal worker, Volma Overton, asked to join the congregation in the spring of 1963. Many church members believed Overton sought a political membership after his election the previous year as president of Austin's branch of the NAACP. Although evidence remains unclear as to the level of racial discord resulting from Overton's request, it split the congregation to a degree. Some members suggested it played a major role in Scott's resignation on May 26, 1963. Leadership in the budding racial crisis then fell to the chairman of deacons, Jack C. Goodman.[39] At a regular church business meeting in June, deacons read a clipping from the *Dallas Morning News* on the attempted integration of FBC Houston and agreed that White correctly used the motive defense to keep blacks out of his church "due to present circumstances." When another deacon asked what FBC Austin should do facing the same issue, a heated debate ensued before attendants passed a motion by a small margin stating that race "will not now nor in the future restrict the fellowship of this church to the white race."[40]

Goodman then met with Overton to judge the purity of the NAACP president's motives. The deacon later said he was "perfectly willing" to deny membership if he believed Overton sought it for political purposes. Nevertheless, the church adopted the motion in late June and Overton became the congregation's first black member.[41] Over time, the Austin congregation never questioned Overton's motive. Even though Overton resigned as president of Austin's NAACP in November 1963, he remained a key ingredient in the city's civil rights movement. Overton "marched on Washington" with King in August 1963; he led the controversial "read-in" of Austin's city council chamber in April 1964; he participated in Austin's school desegregation lawsuits; and he led the struggle for single-member districting in the city. Yet Overton also represented the quintessential Baptist layman. He served on FBC Austin's Social Ministries Committee and Mission Committee, taught Bible study and preschool and teenage Sunday schools, and visited local hospitals and nursing homes. A secret ballot elected Overton in 1967 as the first African American deacon in the church's history, and perhaps the first black deacon in any white BGCT congregation.[42] With the exception of a few urban congregations, however, most BGCT churches remained apathetic in committing to integration.

While the Texas CLC struggled during the early student protests, the response of mostly segregated BGCT churches frustrated some Texas Baptist moderates and pushed them toward political activism. Transition in the Texas CLC contributed to some of the struggle. When A. C. Miller announced his retirement from the Southern Baptist CLC in 1959, Valentine once again succeeded Miller when SBC executives named him in 1960 to direct the denominational body in Nashville, Tennessee. The timing of Valentine's move from the BGCT to the SBC suggests that Southern Baptist leaders were unwilling to risk the growth of the denomination over race where other Protestant bodies in the South faltered. Cultivating his moderate voice of only speaking to and educating Texas Baptists with biblical mandates, Valentine's nonfragmenting approach called for social justice within the confines of Baptist theology and structure at the very time the larger civil rights movement exploded in student protest. Jimmy R. Allen, another Maston student from Southwestern Seminary, took over the leadership of the Texas CLC and made it a political lobby and an outlet for his frustration with apathetic and segregated churches. Allen later described a Baptist hypocrisy by criticizing the often used "motive defense" of most Texas Baptist churches considering integration. To Allen, hypocrisy existed in the "attitudes of some of us who are eager to do battle about the rights of the Negro but are unwilling to accept him in any genuine sense within Christian fellowship." Yet a 1965 editorial by James in the *Standard* personified Baptist hypocrisy. Although James endorsed the right of blacks to join white churches, he described sit-ins and other forms of protest as "rather absurd and disgusting," and that "we will do well to excuse their mistake."[43]

Under Allen, the Texas CLC reached a turning point that coincided with the explosion of political and social activism prevalent in the Kennedy-Johnson years. Although the commission continued to point efforts toward white churches in the BGCT, it worked closer with the Texas Council of Churches and introduced formal political activism on most social issues, especially in race relations. Allen's Texas CLC worked to define responsible citizenship and clarify political participation for Baptists during the student protests. The theme at the Fourth Annual Texas CLC workshop at Baylor University in 1960 was Christian responsibility in a political world. And at the annual BGCT meeting in 1961, Allen told Texas Baptists that "the principal of church-state separation has never meant . . . that the Christian should not seek to influence policies of the state to reflect a higher morality."[44] The Texas CLC hosted over 400 pastors and laymen for their workshop at Southwestern Seminary in March 1962 and billed it as the first statewide conference for Southern Baptists devoted to "Christianity and Race Relations." Allen's opening remarks emphasized that the gathering only represented "further study of race relations," and that "no resolutions or recommendations would come out of it." He then gave way to an impressive, though mostly white, list of speakers dealing with various aspects of racial justice. Speakers included the Southern Baptist Brooks Hays, special assistant to John F. Kennedy in 1962, and Kyle Haselden, editor of the ecumenical and progressive *Christian Century.*

Allen also worked to enlist the *Baptist Standard* as a more progressive media outlet during the period of racial crises at FBC Houston and FBC Austin. With help from Valentine's SBC commission, Allen and James visited the White House in June 1963 after John F. Kennedy invited 250 church leaders to a racial justice conference hoping to gain support for his civil rights bill. James later used the *Standard* to describe the utter embarrassment he felt listening to the president and hearing the efforts of other denominations supporting "a peaceful and effective" desegregation. His June 26 editorial asked

Texas Baptists why Kennedy "had to ask for the help of ministers in finding a solution for a moral problem."[45] That same summer, James chose an ominous time to invite letters to the editor and devote a section in the paper to the "Pros and Cons of Race Relations." Many Texas Baptists viewed James and Allen, their trip to Washington, and the Texas CLC's defense of racial justice as an assault on their religious freedom and a violation the Baptist principle of separation of church and state. J. R. Reynolds of Dallas complained that "until the teachings of God's church strays from the teaching of the Bible, you do not have the right to inject problems of a political nature." R. D. Crews of Cypress complained that if "John F. Kennedy relates the Negro problem to a religious or 'moral' problem . . . alot of foolish people have fallen into a trap." Finally, Marvin Crain of Palestine wrote "just for the record: when tallying up the Kennedy-King-Warren Baptists, please include me out." James later brushed off complaints about the *Standard* not carrying pro-segregationist articles by claiming he never received any "constructive in its message."[46]

While the Texas CLC lost some support by 1963 from angry Baptists, they could also point to some minor political successes. Maston lobbied key members of Baylor University's board of trustees who were studying ways to integrate that university, the nation's largest Baptist institution.[47] An African American pastor, Marvin C. Griffin, moved to Ebenezer Baptist Church in Austin and prospered in his ministry by dual aligning his congregation. He continued the same mission programs and pulpit exchanges with white congregations in Austin that he started in Waco a decade before at New Hope Baptist Church. Griffin subsequently became the first African American selected as a member of the Texas CLC.[48] Yet race consciousness forced a more comprehensive political strategy of moderate Baptists in 1964 as the nation watched white-on-black violence in the streets of Birmingham, Jackson, and Selma. The Southern Baptist and Texas CLCs responded by digging deep to understand severe economic disparity and emphasized a more sophisticated explanation of social injustice.[49] In March, Valentine's SBC commission hosted 175 Baptists in its first Christian Citizenship seminar in Washington, D.C. The three-day session included Lyndon Johnson asking Baptists to mobilize support for his civil rights legislation and Allen encouraging ministers in political responsibility.[50] Valentine's CLC then organized two conferences on race relations at Ridgecrest, North Carolina, and at Glorieta, New Mexico. Similar to the Texas CLC's workshop on race two years before, the conferences brought in a range of speakers to address topics from "strategies for Southern Baptists in race relations" to "what the Negro wants now." Weston Ware, Allen's associate secretary of the Texas CLC, presented a paper at Glorieta that summarized the history of the civil rights movement from Montgomery in 1955 to Harlem in 1964. Ware, evaluating the strategy of nonviolent tactics from "a Christian perspective," concluded his address by sanctioning forms of protest as "aggressive love," recognizing the complexities of inner city poverty and race, and even supporting Martin Luther King Jr.'s criticism of the Supreme Court in the *Brown* decision granting "legal sanction to tokenism and . . . segregation."[51]

Momentum from the conferences and federal initiatives led moderate Baptist leaders to push the denomination harder for racial justice beginning in 1964. Valentine and his Southern Baptist CLC introduced the strongest race resolution in June at the annual Southern Baptist Convention at Atlantic City. The resolution expanded the usual indictment of racial discrimination and asked Baptists to seek specific cures for unfair housing practices, discriminatory employment, and the denial of voting rights. A "Baptist caucus" of messengers from Louisiana, Mississippi, and Alabama not only succeeded in toning down the "political" language of the resolution, but they successfully defeated a request by Valentine's Southern Baptist CLC for more funding from the denomination.[52] Yet the moderate strategy of Valentine and Allen garnered its most significant acceptance the next year when Southern Baptists met in Dallas for their 1965 annual meeting. In the aftermath of the passage of the Voting Rights Act of 1965 by Congress, Baptists delegates not only approved each of the Southern Baptist CLC's resolutions, including a peace resolution in response to the Vietnam conflict, but they also extended a vote of confidence for the commission as the "conscience of the convention." Messengers largely ignored a last ditch effort by segregationists to abolish the Southern Baptist CLC. Led by Carey Daniels, the executive vice president of the Dallas Citizens' Council and a local pastor, and ninety-two-year-old William Nevins, segregationists distributed leaflets and charged the commission with aiding communist agitation and supporting the "mongrelization" of the white race. The heightened emotion led to an embarrassing shouting match between Valentine and Daniels on the convention floor. Nevertheless, legislative accomplishments and the Dallas convention convinced some Baptist moderates that their efforts had paid off by late summer 1965.[53]

Undeterred by some Southern Baptists, Texas CLC leaders had already accelerated their strategy after Congress passed the Civil Rights Act of 1964. Allen used the Texas CLC's annual workshop in March 1965 to again rally Texas Baptists to political action. Moving the workshop to FBC Austin for the first time, Allen's conference featured representatives of each branch of state government, including Gov. John B. Connally. When the racial crisis once again dominated discussion, Allen openly addressed the limits of social activism by Baptists. He told his audience that Baptists could not eliminate their "barriers" of the priesthood of the believer and congregationalism for the sake of political action. Rather, responsible Baptists should penetrate those barriers, along with the barriers of political apathy and the uninformed vote. Allen cautioned Baptists, however, against forming a religious power block or a

Baptist lobby in the capital. Instead, Christian leaders should play the role of "catalysts—agents promoting others to act in the political arena."[54]

Despite the denominational and political accomplishments in 1965, race riots throughout urban America by late summer stunned secular and religious moderates. Younger black leaders in civil rights organizations grew tired of nonviolent tactics, purged white members, and demanded that all blacks take up arms in a show of solidarity. Against such a backdrop, conservative Baptists believers renewed their emphasis on theology and structure. They not only viewed the Texas CLC as increasingly supporting a purely leftist political position in race but also labeled Texas Baptist leaders as "liberals" calling for peaceful toleration in an increasingly lawless society. Leon Macon, editor of the *Alabama Baptist,* had already criticized Allen as a "social gospeler" and described both the Southern Baptist and Texas CLCs as the very power block that Allen warned against. Macon cited as evidence Valentine's citizenship seminar in Washington, D.C., the year before.[55] The events of late summer 1965 only widened the gap. On August 22, the weekend after Watts exploded in racial violence, Allen honored an earlier invitation and traveled to Los Angeles to preach to a large black congregation in the riot-torn area. Allen, later describing his observations in the *Standard,* concluded that violence and looting represented the "symbols of immediate white exploitation" and remained symptoms of a "class struggle with racial overtones." While condemning violence, Allen stressed that the incident "should not discredit the nonviolent efforts of black Christians to obtain justice and opportunity in our society." Closer to home, Allen asked Texas Baptists to use a Christian responsibility only "concerned with meeting the basic needs laid bare by this rioting." Allen argued that "poverty stricken people" in American ghettos "constitute one of the greatest challenges to Christian concern on the contemporary scene."[56]

Predictably, Allen's class interpretation of the Watts race riot in the *Standard* tore at the moderate approach to race and angered Texas Baptists of all stripes. "I feel as if my 14 year old daughter is being held by 2 hypocritical preachers," wrote Lloyd Burks of Rusk, Texas, "while a Negro rapes her and I am bound to a tree by hand cuffs." Another segregationist complained that with Valentine, Allen, and the CLC, "who needs enemies?" More significant was the criticism of other Baptist leaders. Leon Marsh, director of graduate studies at Southwestern Seminary, asked Allen why he should excuse the riot because of poverty. "We have a more fundamental problem here than race," Marsh asserted, "a problem that they have an obligation to get off their blessed assurance and go to work when the opportunity affords it." A Houston pastor, J. F. Selcraig, complained that he was "fed up with CLC's determination to make itself a platform for the political liberals both inside and outside the SBC."[57]

Unlike Valentine, who had directed the Texas CLC before him, Allen never placed the comfort of Baptists over the issue at hand. He steered the Texas CLC into a lobby organization directed at the state and federal legislatures. Much of the commission's political focus continued to center on class issues that exacerbated racism. "Dogging legislators" in Austin, Allen and the commission supported legislation outlawing racially discriminatory hiring practices, opposed bills providing segregated housing, and advocated bilingual education.[58] The Texas CLC's annual workshop at Southwestern Seminary in March included race themes for sessions on "Christianity and the Workaday World." Those attending the workshop received information packets on "collective bargaining" provided by the AFL-CIO and other materials from the National Association of Manufacturers. The Texas CLC held more seminars on "Baptists in the Political Process" and how to start effective action groups, including offering descriptive handouts on voter registration directed at a gambling referendum in 1968.[59]

The unity of the SBC, so successful because of the conservative theology and congregational structure of Baptists, wore down by the second half of the decade. Indeed, the moderate political strategy of Texas Baptists leaders cracked as early as 1964, when some believed the two CLCs blurred the Baptist theological mission. Jeff Cox, a BSU worker at Rice University, complained to Allen about the Texas CLC's request to make civil rights legislation and antipoverty efforts an essential part of Baptist evangelism. He believed the Texas CLC provided "so much irrelevant material" on politics that it made establishing evangelical programs too difficult.[60] Some churches in and out of Texas withdrew their support from the Southern Baptist CLC in 1965, arguing that Valentine was as guilty of conforming to "matters profoundly political" as society was in conforming to discrimination and segregation.[61] Although historians have not studied the reaction of local congregations to the Texas CLC's political strategy, the momentum of BGCT churches seemed to follow the same pattern. By 1967, baptisms in BGCT churches fell from previous years, Sunday school attendance dropped, and budgets no longer skyrocketed. The same year also represented the first time Baptist giving started a long and steady decline from previous decades.[62] Texas Baptist churches felt their spiritual dominance slipping away in a multicultural society.

Ironically, Texas Baptist leaders concerned about social fragmentation reached their summit of influence in the spring of 1968. Hosting its second Christian citizenship seminar in Washington, D.C., Valentine and the Southern Baptist CLC gathered Baptists with several prominent federal officials to consider a range of factors explaining racism and urban violence. The seminar concluded with Lyndon Johnson's Rose Garden address asking Baptist leaders to unite their churches in pursuing social justice. Later that spring at the Astrodome in Houston, Valentine read the most anticipated resolution

Fig. 6.2. Foy Valentine speaking at the 1968 Southern Baptist Convention. Credit: Southern Baptist Historical Library and Archives, Nashville, Tennessee.

of the annual Southern Baptist Convention. The resolution, "Our Statement Concerning the Crisis of the Nation," confessed the denomination's past failures in race relations and pledged all SBC agencies to fight discrimination. When messengers overwhelmingly approved the resolution, it symbolized that the nation's largest and most segregated Protestant denomination would actively support the civil rights movement. Texas Baptist leaders, utilizing a moderate political strategy in race, represented a type of social Christianity that seemingly changed the hearts of Southern Baptists.[63]

Yet continued violence across the country altered a potential watershed year for Texas Baptists advocating change. A week after the Southern Baptist CLC seminar in Washington, D.C., the assassination of Martin Luther King Jr. sparked more urban riots. Hours after Valentine read his race resolution to Baptists in Houston, another assassin's bullet murdered Robert F. Kennedy. Almost to spite themselves the next day, Baptist messengers then elected the denomination's most outspoken defender of segregation from a decade before, W. A. Criswell, as president of the SBC.[64] The opportunist Criswell later claimed his about-face in his racial views resulted from a deacon's meeting on the eve of his election where he was stirred by "Christ's loving presence." He then agreed to the language of the Texas CLC's resolution and ensured his election. Significantly, while Criswell never openly opposed the commission and gave Valentine credit "for being right on the race issue," he maintained an uneasy feeling about the commission's political activism.

The segregationist pastor easily criticized the social legislation supported by the Texas CLC as late as 1967. "I'd give 50 of them (African Americans) a job right now at my church's parking terrace," Criswell announced to the press, "but they don't want to work. They'd rather raise a ruckus over what they allege are their rights."[65]

As a price for their moderation, the Texas CLC won the BGCT's lukewarm support for racial justice due to their nonfragmenting strategy in the 1950s, but they started to lose their own churches by expanding that strategy in the 1960s. The Texas CLC's advocacy in race evolved into a legitimate political force but ultimately fragmented Baptists over proper understandings of their conservative theology and congregational structure, and what constituted the separation of church and state. While race was not the impetus for the later split between fundamentalist and moderate factions in the Southern Baptist Convention, the moderate strategy of race hardened those lines. In the larger context of the civil rights movement, race conscious Texas Baptists failed to overcome their moral dilemma or to destroy the symbolic power of segregation. Loyalty to theology and structure denied moderate Texas Baptists a serious social emphasis in race relations and needed support both to and from the ecumenical movement. The strategy left pursuit of racial reformation to the interpretation and autonomy of local churches, a strategy that enabled church members to "pick and choose" race as an important issue among others. Likewise, it never offered a serious alternative in supporting black Baptists at the heart of the struggle. Even now, the vast majority of churches aligned with the more moderate Baptist General Convention of Texas, or the conservative Southern Baptist Convention, remain largely segregated.

NOTES

1. Oral Memoirs of Foy Valentine, Interview 3, Institute for Oral History, Baylor University, Waco, Texas, 5, 7–8 (hereafter Valentine Memoirs); Foy Valentine, Dallas, Texas, interview by author, October 19, 1999, personal interview, tape recording; Cathy Soles, "The Integration of Marshall's Schools, 1999," 7, East Texas Baptist University, student paper in possession of author; and Jim Webb of Marshall, Texas, interview by author, April 23, 1999, personal interview, tape recording; and John W. Storey, *Texas Baptist Leadership and Social Christianity, 1900–1980* (College Station: Texas A&M University Press, 1986), 175. For overviews of the Marshall civil rights movement, see Donald Seals Jr., "The Wiley-Bishop Student Movement: A Case Study in the 1960 Civil Rights Sit-ins," *Southwestern Historical Quarterly* 106, no. 3 (January 2003): 419–40; and Gail K Beil, "Four Marshallites' Roles in the Passage of the Civil Rights Act of 1964," *Southwestern Historical Quarterly* 106, no. 1 (July 2002): 1–29.

2. Walter B. Shurden, *The Baptist Identity: Four Fragile Freedoms* (Macon, Ga.: Smyth & Helwys, 1993), 11, 13–14; and Grady Cothen, *What Happened to the Southern Baptist Convention? A Memoir of Controversy* (Macon, Ga.; Smyth & Helwys, 1993),

54–55; Oral Memoirs of E. S. James, Religion and Culture Project, Program for Oral History, Baylor University, 1973, 159–60; see also Lewis L. Gould, *Progressives and Prohibitionists: Texas Democrats in the Wilson Era* (Austin: University of Texas Press, 1973), 47–48; Harry Leon McBeth, *Texas Baptists: A Sesquicentennial History* (Dallas: Baptistway, 1998), 111–12; and Storey, 20.

3. Baptist General Convention of Texas, *Annual Proceedings,* 1951, 198, Baptist General Convention of Texas Building, Dallas, Texas (hereafter BGCT *Proceedings,* year); Valentine, personal interview; Valentine Memoirs, 7; James Dunn., "Through Graduates" in William M. Pinson Jr., ed., *An Approach to Christian Ethics: the Life, Contribution, and Thought of T. B. Maston* (Nashville: Broadman, 1979), 92–95; W. T. Moore, *His Heart is Black* (Nashville: The Home Mission Board of the Southern Baptist Convention, 1978), 56, 76; Thomas B. Maston, *Christianity and World Issues* (New York: Macmillan, 1957), 93–94, 96; Andrew M. Manis, *Southern Civil Religions in Conflict: Black and White Baptists and Civil Rights, 1947–1957* (Athens: University of Georgia Press, 1987), 15; and Storey, 13–14, 143, 153; and Mark Newman, *Getting Right With God: Southern Baptists and Desegregation, 1945–1995* (Tuscaloosa: University of Alabama Press, 2001), 70–71

4. For a more in-depth description of the origins of the Christian Life Commission, see Storey, 122–43; McBeth, 244–46; and Billy David Striklin, "An Interpretative History of the Christian Life Commission of the Baptist General Convention of Texas, 1950–1977" (PhD diss., Baylor University, 1981), 78–79.

5. *The Baptist Standard,* June 10, 1954; February 21, 1954; and November 13, 1952; also quoted in Storey, 177

6. Christian Life Commission Report of the Southern Baptist Convention, Meeting in St. Louis, 1954, Foy Valentine Papers, Texas Collection, Baylor University, Waco, Texas (hereafter Valentine Papers); see also Storey, 179–80.

7. "Report of the Christian Life Commission," Soda Lake Baptist Association, 105th Annual Session, 1954, Baptist General Convention of Texas, Regional Associational Minutes, Texas Collection, Baylor University, Waco, Texas (hereafter BGCT Regional Minutes); and Minutes of Burnet-Llano Baptist Association, 42nd Annual Session, October 7–8, 1954 (BGCT Regional Minutes).

8. Minutes of the Executive Board of the Baptist General Convention of Texas, June 5, 1956, 199–200, organized on CD-ROM by the Baptist General Convention of Texas, 1997, in possession of the author, original in the Texas Baptist Historical Collection, BGCT headquarters, Dallas, Texas. "Report of the Christian Life Commission," Soda Lake Baptist Association, 105th Annual Session, 1955, 16, BGCT Regional Minutes; and Storey, 172.

9. Quoted in BGCT Executive Board Minutes, June 5, 1956, 193–94; "Inter-racial Report" Minutes of Dallas Baptist Association, 50th Meeting, October 9, 1952 and 52nd Meeting, October 7–8, 1954, 53–54; and "Report of the Christian Life Commission," Minutes of the Austin Baptist Association, 63rd Annual Session, October 11, 1954, 23, BGCT Regional Minutes; Minutes of the Austin Baptist Association, 64th Annual Session, 1955, 19, BGCT Regional Minutes; and McBeth, 264.

10. Quoted in Storey, 178; see also BGCT *Proceedings,* 1954, 6.

11. *Baptist Standard,* August 12, 1954, 3.

12. Quoted in Ronnie Dugger, "Texas Christians Stem the Tide," *Christian Century* 74 (July 31, 1957): 912; and Telegram, sent to Gov. Allan Shivers and Ralph Yarborough from Blake Smith and Robert E. Ledbetter, July 11, 1954, copy in Archives, University Baptist Church, Austin, Texas.

13. Dugger, 912.

14. H. E. Deason of San Antonio to Allan Shivers, January 12, 1956, Blannie Reeves of Fort Worth to Allan Shivers, February 9, 1956; and Edward Henry Gunneson of Murfreesboro, Tennessee, January 20, 1956, all in Allan Shivers Papers, Lorenzo de Zavala State Archives and Library Building, Austin, Texas (hereafter Shivers Papers); and George Norris Green, *The Establishment in Texas Politics: The Primitive Years, 1938–1957* (Westport, Conn.: Greenwood, 1979), 187.

15. Campaign letter from Ross M. Sams of Waco, n.d., Shivers Papers.

16. *Dallas Morning News,* February 23, 1956, and February 24, 1956; Oral Memoirs of W. A. Criswell, Institute for Oral History, Baylor University, Waco, Texas, 266; Andrew M. Manis, "'Dying from Neck Up': Southern Baptist Resistance to the Civil Rights Movement," *Baptist History and Heritage: Baptists and the Civil Rights Movement* 34, no. 1 (Winter 1999): 33; and quoted in *Baptist Message,* (March 1, 1956): 1; and Storey, 183.

17. A. C. Miller of Nashville to Herbert R. Howard, April 13, 1956, Valentine Papers.

18. *Dallas Morning News,* June 1, 1956; Jones in Pinson, 63–64; and Storey, 133.

19. T. B. Maston, "On All Deliberate Speed," *Baptist Messenger,* July 12, 1956, copy in Thomas B. Maston Papers, accessed at Special Collection, A. Webb Roberts Library, Southwestern Baptist Theological Seminary, Fort Worth, Texas, now housed by Hardin Simmons University in Abilene, Texas (hereafter Maston Papers).

20. Green, 189; see also Robyn Duff Ladino, *Desegregating Texas Schools: Eisenhower, Shivers, and the Crisis at Mansfield High* (Austin: University of Texas Press, 1996), 93–122.

21. *The Baptist Standard,* August 11, 1956.

22. Ibid., September 15, 1956.

23. J. M. Sibley, Beaumont to Foy Valentine, October 15, 1956; Foy Valentine to J. M. Sibley, October 3, 1956; J. M. Sibley to Foy Valentine, October 22, 1956; and J. M. Sibley to Foy Valentine, July 3, 1957, Valentine Papers.

24. Joseph G. Harbour, Beaumont to Foy Valentine, October 23, 1956, and December 18, 1956, Foy Valentine to Joseph G. Harbour, December 21, 1956, Valentine Papers.

25. Joseph G. Harbour, Beaumont to Negro Baptist Pastor's Conference, January 16, 1957, and D. Manning Jackson, Beaumont to Joseph G. Harbour, January 8, 1957, Valentine Papers.

26. Foy Valentine, "An Evaluation of the Racial Situation in the South: Integration—Progress and Problems Among Southern Baptists," speech at Southwestern Baptist Theological Seminary, Fort Worth, Texas, 1957, Valentine Papers.

27. Ibid., and Foy Valentine to Harold Kilpatrick, December 5, 1956, Valentine Papers; see also Dugger, 912.

28. Alwyn Barr, *Black Texans: A History of African Americans in Texas, 1528–1995,* 2nd ed. (Norman: University of Oklahoma Press, 1996), 208; and Robert A. Calvert, "The

Civil Rights Movement in Texas," in *The Texas Heritage* 3rd ed., eds. Ben Procter and Archie P. McDonald (Wheeling: Harlan Davidson, 1998), 178.

29. Thomas R. Cole, *No Color Is My Kind: The Life of Eldrewey Stearns and the Integration of Houston* (Austin: University of Texas Press, 1997), 26–28, 38.

30. *Houston Post,* March 25, 1960; *Houston Chronicle,* March 26, 1960; and quoted in Cole, 43–45.

31. Cole, 53, 95; and Bill Lawson to Martin Luther King Jr., May 5, 1964, Martin Luther King Jr. Papers, Special Collections, Martin Luther King Jr., Center, Atlanta, Georgia (hereafter MLK Papers).

32. "Sunday Night at the Assembly," *The Christian: International Weekly of the Christian Churches* (Disciples of Christ) October 30, 1966, 8; Jack Swanzy, Houston, to King, November 7, 1962; Erma Jewell Hughes, Houston, to Dora McDonald, Atlanta, May 14, 1964; Martin Luther King Jr. to Bill Lawson, July 20, 1965; and Program, Thirtieth Annual Baccalaureate and Commencement Exercises, Erma Hughes Business College, May 17, 1964; and Program, The United Ministries of Texas Southern University Lecture Series, May 17, 1964, copies in MLK Papers.

33. *Dallas Morning News,* February 13, 1961, and February 14, 1961. See also Storey, 189.

34. *Dallas Morning News,* February 21, 1961; and *The Baptist Standard,* July 19, 1961.

35. *The Baptist Standard,* June 19, 1963.

36. Ibid., August 7, 1963; and *The Houston Chronicle,* April 14, 1975; and Storey, 192.

37. Victor Glass, "Emerging Factors in Race Relations in the United States," Exhibit B, Minutes of the 1963 Session of the Advisory Council of Southern Baptists For Work with Negroes, Maston Papers.

38. *The Baptist Standard,* August 7, 1963, September 4, 1963; and Storey, 192–93.

39. T. Michael Parrish, "Madison V. Scott, 1958–1963," *Into his Marvelous Light: 150 Year History of First Baptist Church, Austin, Texas* (Austin: First Baptist Church, 2001), 58–59; and Parrish, "William Ernest Denham, Jr., 1964–1975," 62; and Carolyn Jones, *Volma, My Journey: One Man's Impact on the Civil Rights Movement in Austin, Texas* (Austin: Eakin, 1998), xv, 51.

40. Minutes of business meeting for First Baptist Church, Austin, June 13, 1963, 2–4, in possession of Jack Goodman, Austin, Texas.

41. Jack C. Goodman of Austin, Texas, interview by author, September 17, 1999, First Baptist Church, Austin, Texas; and FBC Austin Minutes, June 26,1963.

42. Parrish, "Denham," 62; and Jones, xvi, 103–104.

43. *The Baptist Standard,* February 10, 1965, and March 24, 1965.

44. BGCT Proceedings, 1961, 82; Oral Memoirs of Jimmy Allen, Institute for Oral History, Texas Collection, Baylor University, Waco, Texas, 161; and Storey, 158–59.

45. *The Baptist Standard,* June 26, 1963; Letter from Jimmy Allen to John F. Kennedy, June 25, 1963, Valentine Papers.

46. It should be noted that James reprinted an equal number of supportive letters to the editor. *The Baptist Standard,* July 24, 1963, and April 22, 1964.

47. Thomas B. Maston to Wallace Bassett, June 23, 1963, Maston Papers.

48. Oral Memoirs of Marvin C. Griffin, Religion and Culture Project, Program for Oral History, Baylor University, Waco, Texas, 1982, 222–23.

49. Jimmy R. Allen of Big Canoe, Georgia, interview by author, January 9, 1998, Dallas, Texas.

50. Baptist Press release, March 26, 1964, 3, Valentine Papers.

51. Weston W. Ware, "A Christian Evaluation of the Nonviolent Movement," Christian Life Commission of Texas, Baptist General Convention of Texas, n.d., 79–80.

52. Letter from Robert H. Craft, Leawood, Kansas, to Foy Valentine, June 8, 1964; and Copy of "Southern Baptists Survey the World," *Christianity Today,* June 18, 1964, 42–43, Valentine Papers.

53. Weston Ware of Cedar Hill, Texas, interviewed by author, October 6, 1998, Dallas, Texas; Letter from W. S. Nevins of Lexington to Foy Valentine, June 9, 1965; and letter from Foy Valentine to Orba Lee Malone of El Paso, June 15, 1965, Valentine Papers.

54. *The Baptist Standard,* March 24, 1965.

55. *Alabama Baptist,* April 9, 1964, and April 23, 1964.

56. *The Baptist Standard,* September 8, 1965.

57. Letters from Lloyd Burks, Rusk to Foy Valentine, September 5, 1965; Leon Marsh, Fort Worth to Jimmy Allen, September 30, 1965; Tom H. Carothers, Palestine to Jimmy Allen, October 12, 1965, Valentine Papers.

58. Quoted in Storey, 158–59.

59. "Christianity and the Workaday World," Valentine Papers.

60. Letter from Jeff Cox, Houston to Jimmy Allen, May 13, 1964, Valentine papers.

61. Letter from Sage Avenue Baptist, Mobile, Alabama, June 15, 1965, Valentine papers.

62. *The Baptist Standard,* September 9, 1972; and McBeth, 285.

63. Storey, 196.

64. Ibid., 197.

65. W. A. Criswell, *Standing on the Promises* (Dallas: Word, 1990), 202, 211–12; and the *Fort Worth Star Telegram,* May 15, 1967, copy in Valentine Papers.

CHAPTER SEVEN

Elusive Unity

AFRICAN AMERICANS, MEXICAN AMERICANS, AND CIVIL RIGHTS IN HOUSTON

Brian D. Behnken

In March 1960, African Americans across Texas began sit-in demonstrations at segregated lunch counters, restaurants, and other public facilities. In Houston, local college students engineered these protests. They followed the example of four youths from Greensboro, North Carolina, who began sit-ins in February of that year and sparked a national movement. The *Houston Forward Times,* a black weekly newspaper, reported that protestors arrived at the lunch counters and "IN LESS than 30 minutes, 1) The white customers departed 2) The waitresses walked away . . . and a 'closed counter' sign was posted 3) Negroes then occupied all 30 of the counter's seats and THE SIT-IN STRIKES rampaging across the south for nearly 40 days had ARRIVED IN HOUSTON."[1]

African Americans hoped Mexican Americans would join their cause. After all, many Mexican Americans experienced discrimination in schools, in housing, at the ballot box, and, depending on skin color and local conditions, in public facilities. But Felix Tijerina, the national president of the League of United Latin American Citizens (LULAC) and a Houston restaurateur, made cooperation impossible. In a patronizing letter published in the *Houston Chronicle,* Tijerina disparaged the sit-ins and the activists. He claimed to sympathize with blacks because Mexican Americans had encountered prejudice and segregation in the past. But he argued that patient legal activism had eradicated this racism. Tijerina urged blacks to also show patience and contended that protests "cause much more harm than good. . . . The ladder must be climbed one step at a time." "I am convinced," he wrote, integration will not "be achieved with pressure, threats, demonstrations or picketing. And I, for one, will not agree to give in to such tactics." He also hinted that whites could respond to protests with economic reprisals. "The Negro has much more to lose than the white man," he stated. "For instance, and I pray it never

Fig. 7.1. Sit-in at the Weingarten's lunch counter, 1960. Credit: Houston Metropolitan Research Center, Houston Public Library, Houston, Texas.

happens, the employers could decide they could get along without Negro help in their businesses and homes. Such a decision would be a catastrophe for every Negro in Houston and in the South," Tijerina wrote.[2]

Throughout the civil rights era, unification largely eluded African Americans and Mexican Americans. Black protest activism disturbed many Mexican Americans, much as it did whites. Mexican American civic groups almost universally decried these demonstrations as dangerous and unwarranted. But segregation persisted for Mexican-origin people as well, which made some of Tijerina's assertions seem inaccurate and misguided. His response to African American/Mexican American unity foreshadowed the nature of race relations during the civil rights struggles in Houston. Indeed, Mexican Americans and blacks had a long history of antagonism in Texas. Throughout the twentieth century, Mexican Americans primarily fought for rights by positioning themselves as members of the white race. As Neil Foley, Thomas Guglielmo, Steven Wilson, Clare Sheridan, and Michael Phillips have noted, whiteness granted them the social and political protections of the white side of the Jim Crow system. But as whites, some Mexican Americans practiced anti-black racism, opposed the civil rights movement, and became a part of the group that blacks viewed as the implacable foe of their struggle. While some blacks regarded Mexican Americans as racially suspect foreigners who took jobs from native-born Americans, they usually did not treat Mexican-descent people in an overtly racist way. Instead, they simply ignored the Mexican American struggle for rights.[3]

Two episodes of protest activism indicate the dual Mexican American and African American struggles for civil rights in Houston. The black sit-in movement and the Mexican American response to it, as well as the Mexican American school boycott during the early 1970s and the black response to it, demonstrate that African Americans and Mexican Americans remained largely disunited in an urban environment during the modern civil rights movement. Racial animosities significantly reduced cooperation between these two groups. In pursuing inalienable rights—an all-inclusive term that encapsulates civil, social, and natural rights—mutual suspicions, personal enmities, and racism drove each group apart, despite their common problems.

Houston, the nation's fourth largest city, offers a good case study for comparing the civic activism of blacks and Mexican Americans, particularly because of the sizeable population of each group. African Americans constituted almost 25 percent of the city's total populace in the 1960s, while Mexican-origin people made up more than 10 percent and perhaps as much as 15 percent. The size and relative strength of each group contributed to African American/Mexican American disunity. There was no need for cooperative ventures as both groups had sufficient numbers to mount separate movements. In addition, blacks and Mexican Americans faced similar economic and living conditions, but class struggles created competition rather than unity. Finally, each group confronted a similar Jim Crow. Blacks and Mexican Americans both began to organize to combat discrimination in the early twentieth century, but these movements took off during the 1950s. Although both groups began their quest for civil rights at roughly the same time, they did not pursue shared goals. Instead, disunity prevailed.[4]

The sit-in movement that began in 1960 showed the vibrancy of the modern black freedom struggle in Houston. Sit-in protests commenced on March 4, 1960, when Texas Southern University (hereafter TSU) students filled the seats at a Weingarten's supermarket near the campus in Houston. TSU law student Eldrewey Stearns organized these demonstrations. Stearns and his cohort of TSU undergraduates created the Progressive Youth Association (hereafter PYA) to organize the sit-ins. The PYA anticipated the development of the Student Nonviolent Coordinating Committee, which black students founded in North Carolina roughly a month later. The PYA first targeted the lunch counters near TSU. They later set their sights on downtown department stores, theaters, and restaurants.[5]

The PYA activists led organized, professional, and nonviolent sit-ins. Students dressed in their Sunday best and carried instruction cards that explained how they should behave while sitting-in: "Don't leave your seat . . . don't block entrances to the store and aisles . . . don't speak to anyone without stating your purpose for being in this movement . . . do remember the teachings of Jesus Christ, Gandhi, and Martin Luther King." Within a week students began to use pickets along with sit-ins as forms of protest. Weingarten's staff closed their lunch counter, so students initiated a sit-in at the nearby Henke and Pillot supermarket. They also sat-in at a local drugstore and at Woolworths. The protests reached a fever pitch after barely three days.[6]

Then violence struck the black community. On the night of March 7, four white men kidnapped twenty-seven-year-old Felton Turner and took him to a wooded area of the city. There, they beat Turner, hung him by his feet from a tree, and gouged two rows of the letters "KKK" into his abdomen. The white men told Turner that the protests had received too much attention, even though he had not participated in the sit-ins. They also told him that "they had a job to do." Turner later recovered from this attack, but police never charged anyone with the crime. This incident reminded blacks that Texas could be as violent as Mississippi or Alabama. Instead of deterring the protests, the actions of these racists crystallized the resolve of the activists.[7]

The violence meted out against Felton Turner also forced Houston mayor Lewis Cutrer to act. Cutrer had run for mayor on a segregationist platform. Indeed, one of his campaign posters warned in bold type, "Will the Negroes Rule Our City?" and added, "here's hoping all the white people vote for Lewis Cutrer." Yet after only a few months in office, Mayor Cutrer had desegregated city swimming pools and the lunch counter at City Hall. He first responded to the sit-ins by contradictorily proclaiming that he would arrest the students for breaking the law while acknowledging that they had broken no laws. The mayor also decided to meet with Eldrewey Stearns and the other leaders of the PYA. He asked the students to end the protests to "assist in removing any cause that would result in violence." The students asked for desegregation. Neither side got what they wanted.[8]

It took Mayor Cutrer another week before he made any substantive response to the sit-in students. He began planning to form a biracial committee. Southern governments frequently used biracial committees to negotiate desegregation during the civil rights period and many cities successfully integrated using these committees. Houston did not follow this pattern. Instead, Cutrer used the idea of the biracial committee in an attempt to browbeat the activists into complying with his desires. Cutrer had simple goals—he wanted to stall the sit-ins. He held out the biracial committee as a carrot of hope for the black community, but he refused to appoint the committee until the students halted the protests. They refused, and the sit-ins continued.[9]

In late March, the students finally agreed to suspend protests to give the mayor time to act. Cutrer then formed a thirty-seven-member Citizens Relations Committee (hereafter CRC). The CRC quickly broke into two factions. Aloysius M. Wickliff, a prominent black attorney and president of the Harris County Council of Organizations, a local civic group, led one faction. He had supported the sit-ins from their inception and advocated immediate integration. Business leaders made up the other faction of the CRC. They supported segregation. The lone Mexican American appointed to the committee, LULAC President Felix Tijerina, joined the segregation faction.[10]

Tijerina continued to serve as a popular LULAC president. He also continued to make his views and opinions regarding blacks known to the general pubic. Tijerina's widely circulated letter opposing the sit-in movement stated that the Mexican American quest for rights had never "been of a nature to arouse further antagonisms," unlike the sit-ins. "Sit-downs," he wrote, "may be melodramatic and may focus attention on their desires but when they irritate . . . yes, even antagonize a large segment of the other population, they automatically setup larger and more difficult obstacles in the path of their progress." "There is also no law, fiat, or dictate that can assure social equality for white and black," Tijerina concluded, "because everyone has the right and the will to freely choose their friends and associates in business and social affairs." Cooperation from Tijerina, on the CRC or in the city more generally, proved impossible.[11]

Felix Tijerina's words carried great weight in the Mexican American community and on the mayor's CRC. His hostility toward the sit-ins held wide appeal, and one individual called his words "pearls of wisdom." As a restaurant owner, Tijerina seemed to fear, as did other businessmen, that admitting blacks could potentially drive away white customers who might not want to patronize integrated facilities. Beyond that, however, his opinions demonstrated the opposition of some Mexican American leaders to black civil rights. When A. M. Wickliff's pro-integration faction of the CRC voted to immediately integrate the city, Tijerina and the members of the pro-segregation faction decided that the time had come for the CRC to disband. The committee folded having achieved no goals.[12]

The failure of the biracial committee did not stop the students from protesting. Indeed, black Houstonians seemed presciently aware that the committee would accomplish nothing. The *Houston Informer,* the city's leading black weekly, never wrote a story about the CRC, which indicates the value blacks placed on the committee. Students in the PYA augmented protests after the committee disbanded. Along with sit-ins, they organized a boycott of downtown merchants over Mother's Day weekend in 1960 to show merchants the value of black patronage. The boycott proved hugely successful.[13]

Besides the sit-ins and boycotts, the students had learned that airing their grievances in local newspapers drew attention to their cause. As long as they could attract interest to themselves through the chronicling of the sit-ins, the

PYA would continue to exert pressure on the city. But Houston newspaper owners, wise to this ploy, agreed not to publish accounts of the sit-ins or other protests. After the biracial committee's failure, African American business leaders John Coleman, Mack Hannah, and Judson Robinson, as well as religious leaders such as Moses L. Price and William A. Lawson, met with white business leaders Bob Dundas (president of Foley's Department Store), Oveta Culp Hobby (of the *Houston Post*), and John T. Jones (of the *Houston Chronicle*) to try to reach some kind of settlement to end the sit-ins. Called together by Mayor Cutrer, the black business and religious leaders agreed with white leaders to a continued media blackout, while behind closed doors each side agreed quietly to desegregate the city.[14]

Media blackouts and behind-the-scenes negotiating tactics among white and black elites became the hallmark of Houston's civil rights movement. While the media blackout and the biracial committee weakened the movement, city leaders began the desegregation process. As restaurants integrated, several black customers chosen by black business and religious leaders patronized the newly integrated businesses. Backroom negotiations helped to achieve civil rights goals, but in the process they hindered the momentum of groups like the PYA. Without a voice in the press and a concrete goal to strive for, the PYA faltered. When the group resumed protests in 1961, the demonstrations proved incredibly weak. They succeeded in forcing Mayor Cutrer to integrate the newly built Astrodome. In 1962, the group joined with the Congress of Racial Equality to protest segregated bus stations. The PYA also planned a sit-down protest in 1963 to block a parade honoring astronaut Gordon Cooper, but they called off the demonstration after the mayor agreed to further accommodations. As a result, the group lost credibility in the city and folded shortly thereafter.[15]

Mexican Americans primarily had a negative response to black protest activism in the 1960s. For example, business owners such as Felix Tijerina did not follow the mandates of the negotiated desegregation in Houston, which remained entirely voluntary. Indeed, Tijerina did not integrate his restaurants until the passage of the Civil Rights Act of 1964, although he did so willingly once the federal government banned segregation.[16]

Many Mexican American leaders, including Felix Tijerina, publicly opposed black protest activism. He made his views clear shortly after the Houston sit-ins began. Similarly, in August of 1963, LULAC president Paul Andow reaffirmed the League's commitment to gradual progress and its opposition to black protests. He publicly denounced direct-action demonstrations to a crowd of 10,000 at the LULAC national convention. Andow needled those who used protests while simultaneously commending LULACers for their dignified activities. "We believe this dignity is now being threatened throughout the nation by some minority groups who are fomenting discord by demanding justice through mob violence [and] by undignified public demonstrations," he stated. Although civil rights activists adhered to nonviolent principles, Andow claimed that the protests were violent and "cast aspersions on our government in the eyes of the rest of the world." He discouraged LULACers, and Mexican Americans in general, from participating in protests with blacks. He also told them not to join "pseudo-civil rights organizations," referring to the National Association for the Advancement of Colored People (NAACP), because their "aims are more often political than humanitarian." He called any such unity "unhealthy alliances." These "unhealthy alliances," he contended, "will only drag us down and hurt our cause." Andow concluded by saying that "getting swallowed up in the craze of picket lines, marches, sit-ins and chain-ins will not solve the problem. Neither will joining forces with questionable civil rights groups."[17]

Paul Andow repeated these sentiments more vociferously at a meeting of LULAC's supreme council in 1963. In a national LULAC policy statement, he called the black civil rights movement's protest tactics "the present craze." He reminded LULACers that the League had long fought for rights without resorting to demonstrations. "We have not sought solutions to problems by marching to Washington, sit-in's or picketing," he stated, because "mass meetings and mass gatherings often times leads to mass hysteria." Andow told the assemblage that several unnamed groups had personally contacted him to form "a coalition." While he did not mention the NAACP by name, the Association had paid lip service to the concept of forming an alliance with LULAC in the late 1950s. The League had firmly rejected this idea, and Andow once again rebuffed any attempts at coalition building. "I caution you," he warned, "not to be a part of or align yourself with any pseudo political organization that professes to be the shining knight in a silver armor displaying the role of protector of human rights." His words seemed both angry and sarcastic. He closed by saying, "do not be led astray by promises of a glorious future."[18]

Tijerina, Andow, and other leaders perceived black gains as Mexican American losses. Thus, Mexican American leaders firmly communicated to African Americans that they could not look to groups like LULAC for aid and support. Like Felix Tijerina before him, Paul Andow made sure that association with groups such as the NAACP would not besmirch LULAC's image. The attention received by African American activists distracted from the conservative approach of LULAC. As political scientist Benjamin Marquez noted, LULAC also feared "the possibility that such displays of defiance and impatience for social change could be adopted by Mexican Americans." By rejecting the concept of direct-action demonstrations, LULAC undermined not only the potential for working with blacks but also with other Mexican Americans who disagreed with LULAC's conservative rhetoric. The League had an our-way-or-the-highway approach, one that ensured that unification between blacks and Mexican Americans would be impossible. Many Mexican Americans approved of their approach.[19]

Of course, not all Mexican Americans opposed or disliked the black civil rights movement. Henry B. Gonzalez, George Sánchez, and John J. Herrera, among others, supported black civil rights. Nevertheless, Mexican American white racial formation and the disparagement of the sit-ins damaged relations between African Americans and Mexican Americans. LULAC's reach increased in the early 1960s as the League grew to record numbers and the *LULAC News* had its greatest circulation to date. The group generated a discourse about race and rights, one that separated the black and Mexican American civil rights movements.[20]

Unity continued to elude both groups during the late 1960s and early 1970s when *Chicano* activists began to more forcefully protest school segregation in Houston. Not until 1970 did the Houston Independent School District (hereafter HISD) implement a new integration plan to comply with the 1954 *Brown v. Board of Education* decision. This plan integrated only African American and Mexican American schools, which blacks and *Chicanos* correctly viewed as discriminatory. *Chicanos* protested by boycotting HISD and forming separate Huelga Schools (strike schools). They also engineered several legal maneuvers aimed at integrating the schools. At almost every turn, the HISD effectively countered these activities.[21]

Chicanos dismissed the whiteness strategy in favor of a brownness strategy in their fight for integration. *Chicano* racial repositioning as brown people represented a crucial evolution in the Mexican American struggle. As an identifiable minority group, *Chicanos* could more easily utilize the equal protection granted by the Fourteenth Amendment. New groups such as the Mexican American Legal Defense and Education Fund (hereafter MALDEF) pushed the legal recognition of Mexican-origin people as a new minority to promote integration. But they had difficulty establishing brownness for school integration purposes in many urban environments.[22]

While Mexican American students and leaders began to advance *Chicano* brownness to promote integration, the HISD continued to classify Mexican Americans as white. This had significant ramifications when Houston initiated its new desegregation plan. Judge Ben C. Connally, who had overseen integration in Houston for more than a decade, pushed the board to adopt a fair desegregation plan in 1970. HISD responded by implementing a "pairing" plan that utilized buses to transfer students to different schools for integration purposes. "Pairing" worked by combining different grades from different schools. For example, at the grade school level, grades 1 and 3 from a majority black school would integrate with grades 2 and 4 from a white school. But the pairing plan combined predominately black and *Chicano* schools. Since HISD still classified Mexican Americans as white, by pairing *Chicano* schools and black schools the district achieved "integration." Clearly, pairing left white children unaffected by integration, the district's desired result. *Chicanos* would serve as symbolic "whites" for desegregation purposes—"pawns, puppets, and scapegoats" as one activist put it—thereby ensuring that white schools remained lily white. "By classifying us as Anglos, the HISD used the *Chicano* to show the federal courts that [schools] could be integrated," one *Chicano* editorialized. The whiteness strategy had come back to haunt Mexican Americans.[23]

These events greatly angered *Chicanos* who had begun to promote brownness. As the weekly newspaper *Papel Chicano* noted, "all 'integration' in Houston means is changing from one BAD school to another BAD school." Mexican Americans in Corpus Christi had won a local case, *Cisneros v. Corpus Christi ISD,* which officially recognized *Chicanos* as brown people in this district. In 1970, MALDEF sued Houston schools to establish a similar precedent. In *Ross v. Eckels,* MALDEF attorneys Mario Obledo and Abraham Ramírez contended that the district illegally segregated *Chicanos* and blacks. They further alleged that *Chicanos* constituted a distinct minority that the district needed to recognize as separate from whites. Judge Connally ruled against the plaintiffs. He disagreed with the findings in *Cisneros* and instead argued that Mexican Americans were white. Even more discouraging, Connally asserted that integrating *Chicanos* and blacks effectively desegregated schools. While MALDEF appealed, the Fifth Circuit Court of Appeals ultimately agreed with Connally. The pairing plan remained.[24]

These events triggered the most intense *Chicano* protests in Houston's history. Local leaders established the Mexican American Education Council (hereafter MAEC) as an umbrella organization to unite *Chicano* school integration protests. MAEC demanded that HISD halt the pairing plan and implement a fair desegregation program. When the school board refused, MAEC began a boycott of the Houston school system. On the first day of classes in 1970, an estimated 3,500 *Chicanos,* or approximately half of all Mexican-origin students, boycotted classes. Instead of going to HISD schools, these students attended Huelga or strike schools, which MAEC established in churches and community centers in Houston's barrios. In these schools, *Chicanos* received instruction in Mexican American history and culture, protest tactics, and bilingual education. The first Huelga Schools lasted for three weeks.[25]

The MAEC canceled the Huelga Schools after what became known as the HISD miniriot. At a meeting of the HISD school board in October 1970, *Chicanos* requested permission to speak. They hoped to convince the district to discard the pairing plan, but the board refused to hear them. An angry verbal exchange followed. When police officers attempted to silence the activists, a free-for-all ensued. After the fighting had ended, police arrested four-

Fig. 7.2. Mexican American protest at Houston Independent School District, August 28, 1970. Credit: Houston Metropolitan Research Center, Houston Public Library, Houston, Texas.

teen *Chicanos,* including several MAEC leaders. This miniriot most clearly showed *Chicano* anger over segregation. As a result, HISD agreed to appeal Judge Connally's busing plan and revise the pairing program.[26]

Despite the agreement, HISD issued a new pairing plan in early 1971 and refused to recognize *Chicanos* as brown people. Judge Connally quickly approved the new plan. MAEC responded by reactivating the Huelga School protests, even though MAEC had difficulty funding the schools. The strike schools limped along until April 1971 when MAEC secured a $65,000 grant from the U.S. Department of Housing, Education, and Welfare. This allowed the Huelga Schools to continue until the summer break.[27]

As the summer began and a new school year loomed, the MAEC planned to continue the Huelga Schools. Thousands of *Chicano* students had not set foot in an HISD school for nearly a year, and the situation did not appear likely to improve for the 1971–1972 school year. When Judge Connally handed down another decision favorable to the school board, MAEC and the MALDEF attorneys reacted angrily. Leonel Castillo, MAEC's director, and MALDEF's Abraham Ramírez both insisted that Connally should step down. Castillo lamented Connally's decision and stated that he was "sorry Judge Connally couldn't see the real world." Judge Connally reacted angrily to these comments. "Never in the 15 years since the initiation of this action have they (Mexican Americans) complained of this treatment (being claimed as white)," he asserted. "Content to be white for these many years," Judge Connally chastised Castillo, Ramírez, and the strikers, "now, when the shoe begins to pinch, the would-be-intervenors wish to be treated not as whites but as an 'identifiable ethnic group.' In short, they wish to be 'integrated' with whites, not blacks." Connally seemed to have hit the nail on the head. The judge asserted that Mexican Americans could not escape the burden of integration that all whites now had to shoulder. But Abraham Ramírez and Leonel Castillo responded with egalitarian words. Besides restating that *Chicanos* were brown, Castillo argued that MAEC wanted a "triethnic desegregation plan." He also noted that *Chicanos* did not attempt to "escape integrating with any group." Ramírez proved more succinct. "We do not want to be disintegrated with the blacks," he said, "as much as we want the whole community to be integrated, not just the blacks and Mexican-Americans." Despite these contentions, Connally refused to alter his decision and the Huelga Schools seemed destined to continue.[28]

For the 1971–1972 academic year, HISD once again implemented a pairing plan that duplicated the previous year's plan. The boycott began again when classes started in August of 1971. But this time the Huelga Schools proved a failure. According to historian Guadalupe San Miguel, group in-fighting and the lack of support from middle-class Mexican Americans doomed the boycott. Legal successes also contributed to the downfall of the Huelga Schools. After Judge Connally had ruled against the MALDEF lawyers in the *Ross* case, they appealed. In 1972, the Fifth Circuit Court of Appeals finally ruled in MALDEF's favor. The court asserted that, based on the *Cisneros* case, the district needed to consider *Chicanos* as an identifiable minority when creating an integration plan.[29]

While the Huelga Schools came to an end, they demonstrated Mexican American attempts to reidentify themselves as brown. Both whiteness and brownness ultimately failed to end racism, primarily because of white resistance. Like whiteness, brownness also had the potential to frustrate race relations with African Americans. Indeed, the Huelga Schools once again exposed animosities between African Americans and Mexican Americans. Many blacks openly supported the boycott. But others found something disingenuous in the *Chicano* response to the pairing plan. If *Chicanos* protested pairing, which integrated blacks and *Chicanos,* what did that say about Mexican American attitudes toward black people? While the NAACP backed the Huelga Schools, this support proved merely rhetorical. Some blacks believed that *Chicanos* simply did not want to go to school with African Americans. Others viewed the brownness strategy as a rhetorical device and as a mere tactic. Mexican Americans truly did not see themselves as a colored people, these African Americans argued. Rather, they simply used brownness strategically in the same way whiteness had served as a tactic. Blacks, therefore, did not boycott schools with *Chicanos.*[30]

Examples of Mexican American racism offended the black community and contributed to the black/brown divide. For example, *Chicano* parents expressed fear at sending their children to black schools because they stereotypically viewed the schools as unsafe. They also argued that blacks started fights with *Chicanos.* "Black students are always bossing us around, picking fights," one Huelga School student argued. "There's going to be trouble, fights," another intoned. Other students aired their own racist sentiments. One student stated that he would not attend his paired school because he wanted to avoid going to school with blacks. Another claimed that he would attend a Huelga School because at his paired school there were "too many blacks." One student stated explicitly that he boycotted classes because "the niggers always get what they want—*Chicanos* never do!" Another attended the Huelga Schools because "there are no colored people." These statements exacerbated racial tensions and undercut *Chicano* exclamations of ethnic difference and nonwhite status. Another student surmised that "the Blacks don't like to go to the Mexican-American [schools], and the Mexican-Americans don't like to go to the Black [schools], and the White people don't like to go to either one." Such sentiments prevented black and *Chicano* unity.[31]

The October 7, 1970, miniriot also demonstrated African American animosities toward Mexican Americans. The NAACP's Reverend D. Leon Everett had attended the meeting that resulted in the miniriot. Everett, the only black member on the school board, had sided with *Chicanos* and defended the Huelga Schools. He had also pushed HISD to recognize Mexican Americans as an identifiable minority group. But *Chicanos* had insulted Everett on two separate occasions, once at a triracial meeting at the University of Houston and once at the October 1970 HISD school board meeting. When the miniriot broke out, an unnamed *Chicano* yelled "we don't want to go to school with the Blacks because they are dirty!" The statement offended Reverend Everett. "Their position is quite clear to me," he argued, "on the one hand they say they want recognition as a minority group. On the other hand, there is every reason to believe they are anti-Black." When asked if he would continue to support the Huelga Schools, Everett replied, "as a Black man, I have my hands full. I will join any group of oppressed people . . . but when that group employs the same form of discrimination that I have been up against all these years, I will cut them loose." Clearly *Chicanos* had alienated an important ally.[32]

The MAEC had a great deal of difficulty altering the sentiments of *Chicanos* involved in the Huelga Schools. More importantly, the group had trouble repairing the bruised feelings of African Americans. As a result, black support of the Huelga Schools remained largely symbolic. As Reverend Everett and other blacks had surmised, and as some Mexican Americans had made clear, *Chicanos* simply did not want to go to school with blacks. Leonel Castillo and Abraham Ramírez certainly helped alleviate some of the tensions between blacks and *Chicanos* when they argued that MAEC and MALDEF wanted a fair, triethnic integration program. But the damage had been done. Most black civic organizations only rhetorically supported the school boycott after 1971. In an attempt to calm this situation, MAEC organized a meeting between leaders in the black and Mexican American communities. But meeting attendees from both groups largely talked past one another. *Chicanos* attempted to get blacks to see the racism inherent in the pairing plan. Blacks tried to get Mexican Americans to appreciate their long fight against segregation. *Chicanos* indicted black leaders for not bringing the Mexican American community into the integration process earlier. Blacks responded by accusing *Chicanos* of racism, both during the whiteness debate of years past and during the current brownness debate. *Chicanos* blamed black leaders for thinking that only African Americans fought for civil rights. Blacks responded by accusing *Chicanos* of being "Johnny or Poncho come lately." The meeting deteriorated into a shouting match with each side demanding that the other side recognize their sacrifices during the civil rights period. Unity remained elusive.[33]

Clearly, school issues generated great tensions among all ethnic groups in Houston. The pairing plan further inflamed these tensions. African Americans and Mexican Americans tried to work together, but as in previous generations, they failed. While the MAEC attempted to convince *Chicanos* of the benefits of integration, the Huelga Schools implied something entirely different. The boycott schools offered a new form of separate, segregated education. *Chicanos* established the Huelga Schools for *Chicanos.* By their very existence, these schools resisted integration. The "separatist" aspect of the Huelga Schools applied to both whites and African Americans. It assisted in the black/brown divide.[34]

African Americans and Mexican Americans both engaged in this separatist ideology. Indeed, many blacks had tired of integration by the late 1960s. White leaders and local governments had resisted school desegregation tooth and nail. Pairing, busing, and the hostilities these issues generated convinced many African Americans that they needed to scrap the concept of integration. And many did. Instead of promoting desegregated schools, black leaders began insisting that districts equally fund all schools. This resulted in animosities toward Mexican Americans. By promoting separatism, blacks rejected integration with whites and *Chicanos.* Mexican American separatist ideology mirrored black separatism. Local districts used *Chicanos* as pawns in the integration battles, and *Chicanos* understandably tired of this treatment and, in essence, self-segregated themselves in the Huelga Schools.[35]

But separatism thwarted attempts at unity because, quite simply, separation *separated* blacks and *Chicanos.* Mexican Americans and African Americans both communicated that they did not want to attend school with each other or with whites. In calling for separate schooling, black and Mexican American leaders largely dismissed the idea of working together. They rejected unity. A unified movement might have convinced local school districts to integrate all students, but this did not happen. Instead, each community looked out for its own interests.

In 1972, the Houston Council on Human Relations, a local civil rights organization, accurately summarized race relations between African Americans and Mexican Americans in its aptly titled *The Black/Mexican-American Project Report.* The report correctly noted that little information existed regarding relations between blacks and *Chicanos* because most Americans traditionally viewed "race" as a black/white issue. It primarily concentrated on housing, newspaper coverage, antipoverty programs, politics, and schools. It found that both groups "retain negative stereotypes and misconceptions of each other." The report also observed that social and economic inequalities contributed to interethnic tensions. *The Black/Mexican-American Project Report* generally blamed these tensions on whites because whites had prevented both groups from progressing economically and socially.[36]

Some of the most provocative findings in *The Black/Mexican-American Project Report* dealt with race and racism. For example, the report accurately noted that *Chicanos* preferred the company of whites whiles blacks preferred the company of *Chicanos,* that in schools blacks proved the least exclusionary of all three ethnic groups, that contrary to popular opinion at the time blacks were not more prone to fighting than other groups, and that all groups generally ignored race until racial tensions flared up. The study also found that 51 percent of blacks preferred attending black schools, 59 percent of *Chicanos* preferred attending predominately Mexican American schools, and 67 percent of whites preferred white schools. As a corollary, 44 percent of Mexican Americans stated they did not want to attend classes with blacks, while only 11 percent of blacks said they did not want to go to *Chicano* schools. The report noted quite clearly that "Blacks feel closer to Mexican-Americans than to Whites, but the Mexican-Americans do not reciprocate—they prefer to associate with Whites. As a result, Blacks are isolated from, and rejected by the other minority group in school."[37]

In many ways, this study mirrored a broader debate that took place in Houston and across the state. African Americans and Mexican Americans certainly seemed to understand the prejudicial attitudes that each had toward the other. But no one appeared to know what to do about these sentiments. Instead of confronting stereotypes and prejudices, both groups either blamed the other for their racism, talked past one another, or withdrew from the debate entirely by advocating separate schooling. This did not help to unite blacks and browns.

Both the sit-in movement and the Huelga School boycotts demonstrate the disunited nature of the African American and Mexican American civil rights movements. Few Mexican Americans participated with blacks during the sit-in protests in Houston. Instead, the Mexican American leadership in the state denigrated and demeaned the protests and protestors. This certainly did not help the black freedom struggle. While many Mexican-descent individuals may have sympathized with black activists, this did not translate into concrete action—they did not join blacks in the protests. And most black leaders did not ask Mexican Americans for assistance. African Americans seemed to believe that Mexican Americans, as a white people, stood with the enemy—racist whites. As several black interviewees have stated, Mexican Americans did not unite with blacks because "they thought they were white," a statement that speaks volumes about how African Americans regarded Mexican Americans and their attempts at white racial formation. In a similar vein, Houston minister and NAACP official C. Anderson Davis noted that "Mexican-Americans considered themselves white a long time . . . but they were not so proud to be allies with blacks." These statements indicate that African Americans knew how some *Chicanos* viewed blacks. It seems understandable, then, why blacks did not approach Mexican Americans about joining the sit-ins.[38]

The Huelga School protests generated a similar situation. Although *Chicanos* racially repositioned themselves during the *Chicano* era, the brownness strategy did not succeed any better than the whiteness strategy. Many African Americans found the whiteness strategy offensive and the brownness strategy insincere. Blacks responded to both strategies by ignoring them. This, of course, did not endear them to Mexican Americans. *Chicanos* did not want to attend paired schools with blacks. This, of course, did not endear them to African Americans. The end result seems obvious—no lasting unification occurred.

Race fractured the black and Mexican American communities throughout the civil rights period. Both groups, both movements followed separate paths. The quest for inalienable rights ultimately bogged down in competition between ethnic groups. African Americans and Mexican Americans each fought for their own group. Indeed, white Texans were hardly the sole opponents of African American and Mexican American rights as blacks and *Chicanos* frequently fought against each other. Mexican Americans resisted black advancement because they perceived African American rights as a threat to the rights of the Mexican-origin community. When *Chicanos* initiated a new movement, blacks responded in kind by only lamely supporting the Huelga Schools. When *Chicanos* aired their own prejudicial sentiments, blacks simply ignored the *Chicano* struggle. Blacks ultimately found the *Chicano* movement threatening because it could undermine the black quest for equality. The sit-in movement and the Mexican American response to it, and the Huelga School protests and the African American response to them, demonstrate the fractured nature of black/Mexican American relations in Houston. In each case, blacks and Mexican Americans failed to unite with each other. Racial differences proved impossible to overcome. Instead of working in unison, each group fought for itself. Any sense of unity proved elusive.

NOTES

1. "Local Portrait of a Sit-in," *Houston Forward Times,* March 12, 1960. For the sit-ins more generally, see, among many others, William H. Chafe, *Civilities and Civil Rights: Greensboro, North Carolina, and the Black Struggle for Freedom* (New York: Oxford University Press, 1981); John Dittmer, *Local People: The Struggle for Civil Rights in Mississippi* (Chicago: University of Illinois Press, 1994); Clayborne Carson, *In Struggle: SNCC and the Black Awakening of the 1960s* (Cambridge, Mass.: Harvard University Press, 1995); Charles M. Payne, *I've Got the Light of Freedom: The Organizing Tradition and the Mississippi Freedom Struggle* (Los Angeles: University of California Press, 1995); Adam Fairclough, *Race and Democracy: The Civil Rights Struggle in Louisiana* (Athens: University of Georgia Press, 1995); Glenn T. Eskew, *But for Birmingham: The Local and National Movements in the Civil Rights Struggle* (Chapel Hill: University of North Carolina Press, 1997). A note on terms: throughout this paper I utilize black and African American interchangeably to denote this community in Houston. Although people from many Latin American nations came to live in Houston, I have chosen to use Mexican-origin people, Mexican-descent people, Mexican American, and, where chronologically and politically appropriate, *Chicanos,* to describe this community.

2. For examples of the racism Mexican Americans experienced, see Pete Tijerina to Felix Tijerina, February 11, 1957, Paul Andow Collection, University of Texas, Benson Latin American Collection (hereinafter cited as BLAC); David Montejano, *Anglos and Mexicans in the Making of Texas, 1836–1986* (Austin: University of Texas Press, 1987), 262. Thomas Kreneck also makes light of this racism, noting that "discrimination because of skin color and their generalized 'fear of rebuff' prevented [Mexican Americans] from full participation in society." See Kreneck, *Mexican American Odyssey: Felix Tijerina, Entrepreneur and Civic Leader, 1905–1965* (College Station: Texas A&M University Press, 2001), 269. Similarly, in a 1962 letter to Gov. Price Daniel, teenager Ermelinda Holguin described segregation in the small Southwest Texas town of Imperial. She claimed that the staff at the Imperial Café had refused service to her and her friends because they "do not serve Spanish people." She begged Daniel for help and argued passionately that Mexican American youths should "have the same priviliges [*sic*] as an Anglo-American boy or girl." Ermelinda Holguin to Governor Daniel, April 15, 1962, Box 575, Folder "Civil Rights," Gov. Price Daniel Papers, Sam Houston Regional Library and Research Center, Texas State Library and Archives Commission. For the view that racism had already been eradicated, see George J. Garza to Honorable William Flores, April 15, 1955, William Flores Collection, BLAC; "It Can

Be Done!" *LULAC News,* May 1955. Tijerina's comments can be found in "Latin Leader Urges Negroes to be Patient," *Houston Chronicle,* 13 May 1960. See also the original and edited versions of this letter in Tijerina's archive, circa May 1960, Felix Tijerina Collection, Houston Public Library, Houston Metropolitan Research Center (hereinafter cited as HMRC).

3. Neil Foley, "Becoming Hispanic: Mexican Americans and the Faustian Bargain with Whiteness," *Reflexiones* (1997); Neil Foley, "Straddling the Color Line: The Legal Construction of Hispanic Identity in Texas," in *Not Just Black and White: Historical and Contemporary Perspectives on Immigration, Race, and Ethnicity in the United States,* eds. Nancy Foner and George Frederickson (New York: Russell Sage Foundation, 2005); Neil Foley, "Partly Colored or Other White: Mexican Americans and Their Problems with the Color Line," in *Beyond Black and White: Race, Ethnicity, and Gender in the U.S. South and Southwest,* eds. Stephanie Cole, Allison Parker, and Laura F. Edwards (College Station: Texas A&M University Press, 2003); Steven H. Wilson, "*Brown* Over 'Other White': Mexican Americans' Legal Arguments and Litigation Strategy in School Desegregation Lawsuits," *Law and History Review* 21, no. 1 (Spring 2003); Clare Sheridan, "'Another White Race': Mexican Americans and the Paradox of Whiteness in Jury Selection," *Law and History Review* 21, no. 1 (Spring 2003); Thomas A. Guglielmo, "Fighting for Caucasian Rights: Mexicans, Mexican Americans, and the Transnational Struggle for Civil Rights in World War II Texas," *Journal of American History* 92, no. 4 (March 2006); Michael Phillips, *White Metropolis: Race, Ethnicity, and Religion in Dallas, 1841–2001* (Austin: University of Texas Press, 2006).

4. Regarding demographics, where the black population was minuscule, in South Texas for example, cooperation with Mexican Americans proved somewhat less problematic. The same was true for Mexican-descent people in North and East Texas, where Mexican Americans were few in number. In these places, African Americans and Mexican Americans were often forced to cooperate because neither had the requisite strength to mount an independent movement. For a fuller discussion of events outside of Houston, see Brian D. Behnken, "Fighting Their Own Battles: Blacks, Mexican Americans, and the Struggle for Civil Rights in Texas," (PhD diss., University of California, Davis, 2007). For general histories of Houston, see David G. McComb, *Houston, A History* (Austin: University of Texas Press, 1981); Joe R. Feagin, *Free Enterprise City: Houston in Political-Economic Perspective* (New Brunswick, N.J.: Rutgers University Press, 1988); Marguerite Johnson, *Houston: The Unknown City, 1836–1946* (College Station: Texas A&M University Press, 1991); David G. McComb, *Houston: The Bayou City* (Austin: University of Texas Press, 1969). For histories on the Mexican American community in Houston, see Margarita B. Melville, "Mexicans," in *The Ethnic Groups of Houston,* ed. Fred R. von der Mehden (Houston: Rice University Studies, 1984); Guadalupe San Miguel Jr., *"Let All of Them Take Heed": Mexican-Americans and the Campaign for Educational Equality in Texas, 1910–1981* (Austin: University of Texas Press, 1987); Thomas H. Kreneck, *Del Pueblo: A Pictorial History of Houston's Hispanic Community* (Houston: Houston International University, 1989); Arnoldo De León, *Ethnicity in the Sunbelt: A History of Mexican-Americans in Houston* (College Station: Texas A&M University Press, 2001); Guadalupe San Miguel Jr., *Brown, Not White: School Integration and the Chicano Movement in Houston* (College Station: Texas A&M

University Press, 2001); Thomas H. Kreneck, *Mexican American Odyssey: Felix Tijerina, Entrepreneur and Civic Leader, 1905–1965* (College Station: Texas A&M University Press, 2001); Roberto R. Treviño, *The Church in the Barrio: Mexican Americans Ethno-Catholicism in Houston* (Chapel Hill: University of North Carolina Press, 2006). For examples of the black experience in Houston, see Robert D. Bullard, *Invisible Houston: The Black Experience in Boom and Bust* (College Station: Texas A&M University Press, 1987); Howard Beeth and Cary D. Wintz, eds., *Black Dixie: Afro-Texan History and Culture in Houston* (College Station: Texas A&M University Press, 1992); Alwyn Barr, *Black Texans: A History of African Americans in Texas, 1528–1995* (Norman: University of Oklahoma Press, 1996); Thomas Cole, *No Color is My Kind: The Life of Eldrewey Stearns and the Integration of Houston* (Austin: University of Texas Press, 1997); Merline Pitre, *In Struggle Against Jim Crow: Lulu B. White and the NAACP, 1900–1957* (College Station: Texas A&M University Press, 1999); Amilcar Shabazz, *Advancing Democracy: African Americans and the Struggle for Access and Equity in Higher Education in Texas* (Chapel Hill: University of North Carolina Press, 2004). Population statistics can be found in Beeth and Wintz, "Introduction," in *Black Dixie,* 89; De León, *Ethnicity in the Sunbelt,* 147. African American and Mexican American relations during the civil rights period remains a relatively understudied aspect of the scholarship on the civil rights movement, but for a good starting point see, Ramona Allaniz Houston, "African Americans, Mexican Americans, and Anglo Americans and the Desegregation of Texas, 1946–1957" (PhD diss., University of Texas, 2000); Mark Brilliant, "Color Lines: Civil Rights Struggles on America's 'Racial Frontier,' 1945–1975," (PhD diss., Stanford University, 2002); Laura Pulido, *Black, Brown, Yellow, and Left: Radical Activism in Los Angeles* (Los Angeles: University of California Press, 2006); Phillips, *White Metropolis;* Behnken, "Fighting Their Own Battles."

5. "TSU Students Fill Counter at Store," *Houston Post,* March 5, 1960. For a fuller account of the sit-in movement in Houston, see Cole, *No Color is My Kind;* F. Kenneth Jensen, "The Houston Sit-In Movement of 1960–61" in *Black Dixie,* eds. Beeth and Wintz.

6. "TSU Students Fill Counter at Store," *Houston Post,* March 5, 1960 (quotation). "Council of 60 Negro Groups Backs 'Strikes,'" *Houston Chronicle,* March 14, 1960. See also "TSU Student Group Widens its Sitdown," *Houston Post,* March 6, 1960; "Newest Student Sitdown Move Ended Peacefully," *Houston Post,* March 8, 1960; "Sitdown Students Move Campaign to 4th Store," *Houston Post,* March 9, 1960; "Sitdown Demonstration Spreads to 5th Store," *Houston Post,* March 10, 1960; "Usual Polite Manner Prevails . . . ," *Houston Informer,* March 19, 1960; "T.S.U. Students' 'Sit-ins,'" *Texas Observer,* March 11, 1960.

7. "T.S.U. Students' 'Sit-ins,'" *Texas Observer,* March 11, 1960; "Felton Turner: 'They said they had a job to do,'" *Houston Forward Times,* March 12, 1960 (quotation); "Torture Linked to Sit-Down," *Dallas Express,* March 12, 1960; "French Press Raps Human Branding in Houston, Tex," *Dallas Express,* March 19, 1960; Gloster B. Current to Francis L. Williams, March 9, 1960, NAACP Houston Branch Records (microfilm).

8. Lewis Cutrer Campaign Poster, Miscellaneous files, Box 26, Folder 10, HMRC (first quotation); "Mayor Cautions Students on Sitdown," *Houston Post,* March 16,

1960 (second quotation); "Mayor Ponders Biracial Talks," *Houston Chronicle,* March 17, 1960; "Usual Polite Manner Prevails . . ." *Houston Informer,* March 19, 1960.

9. On biracial committees, see Benjamin Muse, *Special Report, Memphis* (Southern Regional Council publication, 1964), 2, 7–8; Steven F. Lawson, "From Sit-in to Race Riot: Businessmen, Blacks, and the Pursuit of Moderation in Tampa, 1960–1967," in *Southern Businessmen and Desegregation,* eds. Elizabeth Jacoway and David R. Colburn (Baton Rouge: Louisiana State University Press, 1982), 262–67; Paul S. Lofton, "Calm and Exemplary: Desegregation in Columbia, South Carolina," in *Southern Businessmen and Desegregation,* eds. Jacoway and Colburn, 77–79. "Mayor Ponders Biracial Talks," *Houston Chronicle,* March 17, 1960.

10. "Mayor to Name Group to Study Biracial Problems," *Houston Chronicle,* March 29, 1960; "Six Accept Posts Here on Racial Group," *Houston Chronicle,* April 1, 1960; "Mayor Still Working on Biracial Panel," *Houston Chronicle,* April 4, 1960; "Houston Faces Integration," *Texas Observer,* April 1, 1960; Jensen, "The Houston Sit-In Movement of 1960–61," 217.

11. On Tijerina's popularity, see, for instance, the June 1959 edition of the *LULAC News,* which went so far as to reproduce Mount Rushmore with Tijerina's bust added to the monument, which appeared just below Thomas Jefferson. The caption under the illustration read "among the greatest." Mount Rushmore Image, *LULAC News,* June 1959. Signed copy of letter opposing sit-ins, circa May 1960, Felix Tijerina Collection, HMRC (quotations); "Latin Leader Urges Negroes to be Patient," *Houston Chronicle,* May 13, 1960.

12. Kreneck, *Mexican American Odyssey,* 262 (quotation); "Café Issue Splits Race Committee," *Houston Chronicle,* May 10, 1960. "Mayor's Bi-Racial Group to Disband . . . ," *Houston Post,* June 10, 1960.

13. Cole, *No Color Is My Kind,* 49; Jensen, "The Houston Sit-In Movement of 1960–61," 215.

14. What actually took place behind the closed doors remains somewhat mysterious, but these events are discussed in greater detail in Cole, *No Color Is My Kind,* 54–55; David Berman, director, *The Strange Demise of Jim Crow;* Jensen, "The Houston Sit-In Movement of 1960–61," 211–20; Martin Kuhlman, "The Civil Rights Movement in Texas: Desegregation of Public Accommodations, 1950–1964" (PhD diss., Texas Tech University, 1994), 142–53; Quentin R. Mease, *On Equal Footing: A Memoir* (Austin: Eakin, 2001), 92–103; Brian D. Behnken, "'Count on Me': Reverend M. L. Price of Texas, a Case Study in Civil Rights Leadership," *Journal of American Ethnic History* 25, no. 1 (Fall 2005): 73–74.

15. For examples of Sunbelt business integration, see Fisher, "The Urban Sunbelt in Comparative Perspective: Houston in Context," in *Essays on Sunbelt Cities and Recent Urban America,* eds. Robert B. Fairbanks and Kathleen Underwood, et al. (College Station: Texas A&M University Press, 1990), 33–54; Bruce J. Schulman, *From Cotton Belt to Sun Belt: Federal Policy, Economic Development, and the Transformation of the South, 1938–1980* (New York: Oxford University Press, 1991). On the success of the sit-ins, see "'Sit-Ins Resume' at Downtown Lunch Counters in Houston," *Houston Informer,* July 30, 1960; "Stearnes [*sic*] Says Students Were Served at Joske's—Pay Refused,"

Houston Informer, August 6, 1960; "Houston, a Backwater of the Revolt," *Texas Observer,* November 15, 1963; "Houston in Forefront of Rights Move in Texas," *Houston Chronicle,* July 3, 1964. On the weakness of the PYA after integration, see, Cole, *No Color Is My Kind,* 78–79; Mease, *On Equal Footing,* 84–87; Press Release, circa September 1961, NAACP Houston Branch Records (microfilm); Clarence A. Laws to Francis L. Williams, September 11, 1961, NAACP Houston Branch Records (microfilm). On the PYA and CORE, see "PYA Plans Theatre 'Stand-In,'" *Houston Informer,* February 11, 1961; "Coed Stand-In Attacked at Demonstration," *Houston Informer,* May 6, 1961; "'Freedom Riders' Sought Cup of Coffee Here," *Houston Forward Times,* August 19, 1961; "CORE Goes Into Action Here . . . ," *Houston Informer,* August 18, 1962; "CORE Sets Public Workshop . . . ," *Houston Informer,* August 25, 1962; "Public CORE Workshop Saturday," *Houston Forward Times,* August 25, 1962. On the PYA's demise, see, Cole, *No Color Is My Kind,* 95.

16. For the integration of Tijerina's restaurants, see, notice to employees from Felix Tijerina, July 3, 1964, Felix Tijerina Collection, HMRC.

17. "President's Message," *LULAC News,* August 1963; "LULAC Leader Assails Public Demonstrations," August 29, 1963, (probably *Houston Chronicle*) clippings files, LULAC Council #60 Collection, HMRC.

18. For the NAACP's weak attempts at unity, see for example, "The President's Address," 21st Annual Convention of the Texas State Conference of Branches NAACP, 1 November 1957, NAACP Texas State Conference papers (microfilm); "Some Criteria for Effective Inter-Group Branch Action," January 30, 1956, NAACP Texas State Conference papers (microfilm); "Interracial Unity Urged," *Dallas Express,* November 7, 1953. Paul Andow, "Civil Rights 'Quid Pro Quo,'" Statement of National Policy, Speech before National Supreme Council Meeting, August 25, 1963, William Flores Collection, BLAC (quotations). LULAC President William Bonilla made similar statements during his term in office in 1964. See, "Minorities and Their Future," *LULAC News,* November 1964.

19. Benjamin Márquez, *LULAC: The Evolution of a Mexican-American Political Organization* (Austin: University of Texas Press, 1993), 64.

20. For discussions of these leaders, see, Eugene Rodriguez Jr., *Henry B. Gonzalez: A Political Profile* (New York: Arno, 1976); Todd A. Sloane, *Gonzalez of Texas: A Congressman for the People* (Evanston, Ill.: John Gordon Burke, 1996); Jean Flynn, *Henry B. Gonzalez: Rebel with a Cause* (Austin: Eakin, 2004); Carlos K. Blanton, "George I. Sánchez, Ideology, and Whiteness in the Making of the Mexican American Civil Rights Movement, 1930–1960," *Journal of Southern History* 72, no. 3 (August 2006); Mario T. García, *Mexican Americans: Leadership, Ideology, and Identity, 1930–1960* (New Haven: Yale University Press, 1989); De León, *Ethnicity in the Sunbelt.* The growth of LULAC and the vitality of the *LULAC News* went hand in hand. The *LULAC News* often had financial trouble, but these problems dissipated in the 1960s. More Mexican Americans joined the League, which stabilized the *LULAC News,* which helped generate new members. See Márquez, *LULAC,* 7; Craig A. Kaplowitz, *LULAC, Mexican Americans, and National Policy* (College Station: Texas A&M University Press, 2005) chapter 3.

21. For a full account of these events, see, San Miguel, *Brown, Not White.*

22. "HISD Finds 90 Percent of Students in 101 Schools are of One Race," *Houston*

Chronicle, November 5, 1978; William Henry Kellar, *Make Haste Slowly: Moderates, Conservatives, and School Desegregation in Houston* (College Station: Texas A&M University Press, 1999); Luís Cano, "Illegal Discrimination and Segregation of *Chicano* Students in the Houston Independent School District," draft manuscript, n.d. (circa 1975), Luís Cano Collection, HMRC.

23. On the pairing plan, see "Geographic Plan Integration Goal is Not Yet Met," *Houston Chronicle,* September 2, 1970. In other cities in Texas, pairing became known as "lumping." Busing was another hot button issue that plagued many communities in the 1970s. "But We're Brown!" *Papel Chicano,* August 22–September 11, 1970 (first quotation); "Editorial: La Raza Fights Unfair Integration," *Papel Chicano,* August 22–September 11, 1970 (second quotation).

24. "But We're Brown!" *Papel Chicano,* August 22–September 11, 1970; "Massive Boycott of HISD Schools Brewing," *LULAC News,* August 1971; "Mixing Blacks and Raza, HISD 'Integration' Lies," *Papel Chicano,* August 8, 1970 (quotation). On the *Chicano* legal challenge to pairing, see "*Chicanos* Pose Special Problem, Board Says," *Houston Chronicle,* August 16, 1970; "League Files Suit," *Papel Chicano,* August 22–September 11, 1970; "The Reality of Being Brown, Corpus and Houston," *Papel Chicano,* September 26–October 9, 1970; *Ross v. Eckels,* 434 F. 2d 1140 (1970). *Ross v. Eckels* concluded that mixing Mexican Americans and blacks provided equal educational opportunities. See, also, Guadalupe San Miguel Jr., "Mexican American Organizations and the Changing Politics of School Desegregation," *Social Sciences Quarterly* 63, no. 4 (December 1982): 709–11.

25. "HUELGA SCHOOLS," MAEC flyer, n.d., Gregory Salazar papers, HMRC; "Freedom Schools Will Open During Boycott," *Houston Chronicle,* August 30, 1970; "Schools Open Calmly; 3,500 Latins Absent," *Houston Post,* September 1, 1970; "'Huelga' School Pupils Taught Word 'Boycott,'" *El Sol* (Houston), September 11, 1970; "Mexican-Americans Drop Part of Boycott," *Houston Post,* September 13, 1970; "Another First in Houston," *Papel Chicano,* September 26–October 9, 1970; "La Raza vs. the School Board," *Papel Chicano,* September 26–October 9, 1970; "MAEC Demands," *Papel Chicano,* September 26–October 9, 1970; "The Truth About the Boycott," MAEC flyer, n.d., Gregory Salazar papers, HMRC; "Reverendos Arturo M. Fernandez, Ruben M. Armendariz, Noe Montez, Antonio Maranon, Guillermo Chavez, Doroteo Alaniz, and Ismael Maldonado to the Houston City Council and the Houston Independent School District Board," September 21, 1970, Huelga Schools Collection, HMRC.

26. "Brown Power!" *Papel Chicano,* September 26–October 9, 1970; "Confusion at HISD," *Papel Chicano,* September 26–October 9, 1970; "Struggle Never Ends," *Papel Chicano,* September 26–October 9, 1970; "14 Arrested at HISD," *Papel Chicano,* September 26–October 9, 1970; "Los Nueve," *Papel Chicano,* October 10–October 23, 1970; "*Chicanos* Tell Houston School Board Not to Call Them 'White,'" *Muhammad Speaks,* n.d., in Gregory Salazar papers, HMRC; "Brown Power," *Dallas News,* December 23, 1970–January 12, 1971. Nine of those arrested were later indicted for damaging school property. For a full account of these events, see San Miguel, *Brown, Not White,* chapter 7. On MAEC's victory, see, "Boycott Ends-MAEC Wins," *Papel Chicano,* September 26–October 9, 1970; "¿Por Que La Huelga Escolar?" *Papel Chicano,* Septem-

ber 26–October 9, 1970; "Community Gains from School Boycott," *Papel Chicano,* October 10–October 23, 1970

27. "Hell No, No Vamos," *Papel Chicano,* February 3, 1971; "Pairing Brings Picketers," *Papel Chicanos,* February 20, 1971; "Adelante MAEC," *Papel Chicano,* February 20, 1971; "Huelga Schools Open," *Papel Chicano,* February 20, 1971; "Conservatives, Liberals, All the Same," *Papel Chicano,* February 20, 1971; "MAEC Funded for $65,000," *Papel Chicano,* February 20, 1971.

28. "Judge Raps *Chicanos* Over Pairing Protest," *Houston Chronicle,* May 26, 1971; "Pairing Plan Ruled Unacceptable," *Houston Chronicle,* May 26, 1971 (first quotation); "Houston Attorney Urges Appeal of Connally's School Ruling," *Houston Post,* May 26, 1971 (next four quotations—both papers used almost identical quotations from the judge and the attorneys); "Houston Attorney Urges Appeal of Connally's School Ruling," *Houston Post,* 26 May 1971 (fifth quotation); "Judges Differ in Integration," *El Sol* (Houston) June 4, 1971; "Judge Rules Against La Raza," *Papel Chicano,* June 12, 1971. *Chicanos* were generally incensed by Judge Connally's statements. For two examples, see Editorial (untitled), *Papel Chicanos,* June 12, 1971, 2; "The Supreme Duty," *Papel Chicano,* June 12, 1971.

29. "HISD Announces Racist Pairing Plan Again," *Papel Chicano,* July 15, 1971; "MAEC—What It's All About," *Papel Chicano,* July 15, 1971; "Justice—A Struggle But How Long La Raza?" *Papel Chicano,* July 29, 1971; "MAEC Declares Boycott Against HISD," *Papel Chicano,* August 12, 1971; "Boycott the Hell Out of Them!" *Papel Chicano,* August 12, 1971; "MAEC Rally" advertisement, *Papel Chicano,* August 12, 1971; "MAEC Calls for Boycott Support," *Papel Chicano,* August 12, 1971; "2,000 Attend MAEC School Boycott Rally," *El Sol* (Houston), August 20, 1971 "Raza Marches from Hidalgo to Eastwood Park for Justice in Education," *Papel Chicano,* October 14, 1971; "Huelga Schools Are Hope for La Raza Children," *Papel Chicano,* October 14, 1971; San Miguel, *Brown, Not White,* 175. In 1972, the Huelga Schools were transferred from the auspices of the Mexican American Education Council to the newly created *Centro-Escolar México-Americano* (CEMA, or the Mexican-American Central Schools). CEMA broadened the program and attempted to create, in essence, a *Chicano* school district. However, CEMA faltered only a short time later, and Huelga Schools came to an end. MAEC continued to operate until the late 1970s. See Unsigned letter, May 25, 1972, Huelga Schools of Houston Collection, HMRC; "MAEC advertisement," *La Vida Latina en Houston,* July 1975. *Keyes v. School District No. 1,* 413 U.S. 189 (1973) finally cemented Mexican American brownness in the canon of law.

30. For black support of the boycott, see "Your Black Brothers to Gregory Salazar," September 1, 1970, Gregory Salazar papers, HMRC. For African American views of *Chicanos* and brownness, see *The Black/Mexican-American Project Report,* a report of the Houston Council on Human Relations, (July 1972), 26–27; Carol B. Sherman, interview by author, Houston, Tex., July 20, 2000; Thelma Scott Bryant, interview by author, Houston, Tex., March 6, 2000.

31. "La Raza vs. the School Board," *Papel Chicano,* September 26–October 9, 1970 (first quotation); "Vatos' Views on School Zoning," *Papel Chicano,* August 8, 1970 (second and third quotations); "La Raza vs. the School Board," *Papel Chicano,* Septem-

ber 26–October 9, 1970 (fourth and fifth quotations); *The Black/Mexican-American Project Report,* 26–49, 47 (sixth quotation).

32. "Everett Split With Mexican-Americans," *Houston Forward Times,* September 19, 1970. See also "Desegregation Plan Still Goes," *Houston Informer,* February 14, 1970.

33. "Browns and Blacks Meet to Discuss Education," *Papel Chicano,* July 29, 1971.

34. "Conservatives, Liberals All the Same," *Papel Chicano,* February 20, 1971; "Should *Chicanos* Assimilate?" *Papel Chicano,* August 12, 1971.

35. For a discussion of this viewpoint, see, Richard Kluger, *Simple Justice: The History of Brown v. Board of Education and Black America's Struggle for Equality* (New York: Vintage Books, 1977); Peter Irons, Jim Crow's Children: The Broken Promise of the Brown Decision (New York: Viking Books, 2002); Jonathan Kozol, *The Shame of the Nation: The Restoration of Apartheid Schooling in America* (New York: Crown, 2005); Derrick Bell, *Silent Covenants: Brown v. Board of Education and the Unfulfilled Hopes for Racial Reform* (New York: Oxford University Press, 2005). Equalization represented a return to an earlier, late nineteenth/early twentieth-century tactic.

36. *The Black/Mexican-American Project Report,* 1; "The Black/Mexican-American Relations Project," *HCHR Newsletter,* November 1972, 2 (quotation).

37. *The Black/Mexican-American Project Report,* 35, 41.

38. Carol B. Sherman, interview by author, Houston, Tex., July 20, 2000; Thelma Scott Bryant, interview by author, Houston, Tex., March 6, 2000 (first quotation); Rev. C. Anderson Davis interview with Cheri Wolfe, December 15, 1993, Institute of Texan Cultures, San Antonio, 32 (second quotation).

CHAPTER EIGHT

Chicanismo and the Flexible Fourteenth Amendment

1960s Agitation and Litigation by Mexican American Youth in Texas

Steven Harmon Wilson

The experiences of *Chicano* high school students in Texas during the late 1960s serve as a microcosm to analyze the evolution—rather than the revolution—of the Mexican American civil rights struggle. It is useful in this case to remark that "immutable" is a synonym for inalienable, but also to remember that specific understandings of rights have changed over time. The history of inalienable rights is mostly a tale of gradual recognition of what in hindsight should have been patently obvious. Indeed, this is why the American Declaration of Independence can without irony claim that its stated truths are self-evident, although they seem to contradict millennia of custom. A profound shift in social and political attitudes culminated during the 1770s into a new definition of inalienable rights and gave rise to a new species of confrontational political activism. And so it was among young Mexican Americans in Texas nearly two hundred years later.

The shift of the 1960s was rooted not only in anger at the continuing racism of white, or "Anglo," society, but also in a new race consciousness that celebrated a worthy "brown" identity. Members of this generation called themselves *Chicanos* to demonstrate their pride in being *Mexicano,* indicating a shared indigenous or mestizo heritage. They took that name to counter white opinions and histories that disregarded Latino contributions to the origins, evolution, and culture of the Southwest. But the *Chicanos* also rejected the goals of their elders, the so-called "Mexican American Generation," which had so long sought accommodation and assimilation with whites. Although loosely defined, the *Chicano* movement was basically progressive, and even radical within the greater Latino community. *Chicanismo* was a direct repudiation of the sensibilities of the Mexican American middle class, which had become a stable pillar of the Democratic Party in Texas—a state party that, even under the relatively liberalizing influence of Lyndon B. Johnson, long retained a conservative orientation.[1]

Chicanos originally eschewed both the goals and the tactics of liberal politics. Instead of canvassing to win elections, or agreeing to exchange present votes for future patronage, they promoted mass protest, direct action, and self-reliance.[2] *Chicanos* at first had little use for the courts, an attitude that paradoxically had parallels within the "Mexican American Generation." Ultimately, however, some *Chicanos* recognized that working within the system rather than rejecting it outright could bring benefits. The courts once more beckoned when encouraging signals emanated from the White House, the Congress, and, especially, the U.S. Supreme Court, indicating that new legal tools were at hand. Mexican American civil rights still faced myriad legal obstacles, not just opposition and obstruction by recalcitrant officials, but also internecine disputes over community goals and priorities, ethnic labels and identities, and cultural and political commitments. Fortunately, the generational and ideological gaps among Latinos could be bridged by a fresh cohort of politically committed lawyers. Although generations collaborated in civil rights revival, *Chicano* youth led the way forward with their energy and idealism. These youthful activists deserve more recognition for having learned, and for having reminded their jaded elders, that the U.S. Constitution was flexible enough to serve both traditional and radical ends.

The history of Mexican American civil rights during the twentieth century traces many twists and turns because the participants in that history were forced to backtrack at significant points as they encountered resistance, reversals, and dead ends. For example, influential Mexican Americans in Texas and the rest of the Southwest long accepted the assumptions of the "Jim Crow" system of race-based segregation. It must have seemed that they had little choice in the matter. The division of U.S. society into a black-white binary was rooted in the constitutions of many states, the decisions of the U.S. Supreme Court, and the customs of a century. Jim Crow had the appearance of legal and social immutability, and Mexican Americans had learned to live within its structures and strictures. This led to their curious efforts to defend the seemingly "inalienable" rights of whites. People of Mexican origin suffered many humiliations and discrimination at the hands of white Texans. In defense, Mexican Americans relied on political, social, and religious organizations, business networks, and, when necessary, lawsuits, to establish and hold onto a precarious position within (but ever apart from) white-dominated society. This pragmatic approach is clearly evident in a string of legal challenges to segregated schools and other public institutions, in which Mexican American lawyers developed a strategy that seemed to defend Jim Crowism, so long as Hispanics were "white"—indeed, judges had considered them among "the other white races"—rather than "colored."[3]

African Americans, burdened with centuries of legal precedent that defined them as "colored," resisted and undermined the Jim Crow system. Their efforts enjoyed a stunning success when the U.S. Supreme Court dealt a fatal blow to Jim Crow and overturned racial segregation in the 1954 decision in *Brown v. Board of Education.* Mexican American lawyers did not recognize that this landmark in African American civil rights litigation should also have led them down a new constitutional path. Instead, Mexican Americans continued to defend their hard-earned position on the white side of the color line. They met with diminishing results in the post-*Brown* era, however, and Mexican American leaders all but abandoned the courtroom as expensive and unreliable. The legal results compared poorly with political achievements during the national ascendancy by Texas' Lyndon B. Johnson. Mexican Americans had good reason to celebrate in 1961, for example, when Johnson's allies Henry B. Gonzalez of San Antonio won election to the U.S. House of Representatives, and Reynaldo G. Garza of Brownsville was confirmed as the first Mexican American federal judge in U.S. history. In 1963, Mexican Americans briefly dominated the elected municipal government in Crystal City, Texas, after a hard-fought campaign conducted by unionists as well as leaders of the Political Association of Spanish Speaking Organizations, founded around 1960.[4]

Certainly, there were some social and political gains to celebrate in the 1960s. By the end of the decade, however, enthusiasm for assimilation and accommodation had begun to wane, and the Mexican American civil rights movement seemed adrift. Leaders in the Latino community began to complain that President Johnson took their support for granted. This was due in part to the unfulfilled promises of patronage and in part to the growing sense that the civil rights goals of African Americans had priority in the national consciousness. In an era of African American civil rights struggles, Mexican Americans had somehow become the "Minority Nobody Knows."[5]

Mexican Americans were still struggling with the artifacts of their "other white" strategy, which had yielded official confusion and community division regarding color, race, nationality, ethnicity, or some even clumsier construct. The landmark Civil Rights Act (hereafter CRA) of 1964, for example, authorized the Department of Health, Education, and Welfare (hereafter HEW) to issue goals and guidelines for school desegregation. Yet, despite the fact that the CRA extended to "national origin" minorities, and despite the fact that Mexican Americans continued to suffer from widespread discrimination, the HEW's Office of Civil Rights (hereafter OCR) diminished the value of the act for Mexican Americans through its interpretation of the act. When OCR first began to investigate alleged discrimination, it gathered statistics using only the black and white categories. Dr. Hector P. Garcia, the first Mexican American member of the U.S. Civil Rights Commission, and also the founder of the American G.I. Forum (hereafter AGIF), a Mexican American veterans' organization that also participated in several of the key legal battles of the 1950s rebuked OCR for failing to examine all complaints. Only then did HEW begin to collect separate data on Mexican Americans. In 1967, HEW began to release data on black, white, and "other" (examples included: "Indian American, Oriental, Eskimo, Mexican-American, Puerto Rican, Latin, Cuban, etc."). Later, the same agency published statistics on "Spanish Surnamed Americans," and it even issued a series of "Mexican-American Studies."[6]

But this categorical shift—to a newly official "other minority" status, as opposed to "other white" status—was resisted by those committed to the earlier strategy. In the October 1967 issue of the liberal-leaning *Texas Observer*, for example, Carlos Guerra, a Spanish-Surnamed and Mexican-descended student at Texas A&I (now Texas A&M University-Kingsville), wrote a column titled "Discourse by An Other," in which he challenged Washington's scheme to declare "the second largest minority group in the country non-White." Guerra's response suggests that, in addition to complaining about official statements that were effectively setting aside Mexican Americans as a distinct group, he was at the same time resistant to calls for "brown power" by *Chicano* activists, who were becoming active at Texas A&I. He was, in effect, arguing that the status of Mexican Americans as white is, was, and ought to be immutable. Guerra was on the wrong side of history: social, cultural, and political forces were seeking to change the terms of the discourse over racial and ethnic identity.[7]

The seeds of the *Chicano* movement in Texas and other southwestern states thrived among a generation energized by the well-publicized civil rights marches in the South, the emergence of Black Power in the North, and the antiwar activism growing on campuses across the nation. But until the migrant farm workers in California and Texas marched against unfair wages, dangerous conditions, and oppression by public officials who clearly took the side of growers, many Mexican Americans sensed that their own struggle towards social justice and legal equality had stalled. The agenda pursued by the United Farm Workers (hereafter UFW) resonated with Mexican American students who came of age during the 1960s. Both working-class *barrio*-bound youth and middle-class college-bound *Chicanos* counted César Chávez among their cultural heroes and role models.[8]

The emerging vanguard of the *Chicano* movement was not alone in admiring the dignity and discipline farm workers demonstrated through their long marches and strikes. Middle-class leaders also noticed that the farm workers' plight attracted a great deal of national media attention. In September 1966, after strikes, marches, and old-fashioned lobbying, the U.S. Congress had amended the Fair Labor Standards Act (hereafter FLSA), ending the decades-long blanket exemption of agricultural workers from the statute.

After a Texas state judge's injunction ended a UFW strike against low wages in the Rio Grande Valley, a U.S. Senate subcommittee visited the Valley in July 1967. The senators were considering recommendations to amend the FLSA further and took a great deal of testimony from participants on both sides of the controversy. The panel's investigation focused new attention on the patterns of discrimination by the white majority in Texas against Mexican Americans. The tone of the questions and the comments made by one of the subcommittee's youngest members, Sen. Edward M. Kennedy of Massachusetts, suggested that he favored the cause of the farm workers over that of the growers.[9]

The success of this ethnically tinged community activism, cross pollinated with civil rights consciousness, inspired students at St. Mary's University in San Antonio, A&I in Kingsville, and other majority Mexican American campuses, to embrace the politics of direct action. In 1967, students at St. Mary's founded the Mexican American Youth Organization (hereafter MAYO) and used it as a forum to fight more than just continued discrimination against Latinos. Like many other student-run organizations, MAYO protested the Vietnam conflict as evidence of the imperialism, violence, and racism they alleged was a major theme in U.S. history. And they condemned the "Mexican American Generation" for collaborating in the white's oppression of *La Raza* (the *Chicano* race). The activists called these liberal apologists for the status quo *vendidos* ("sellouts"). On occasion, a member of the "Mexican American Generation" responded to the challenge. Representative Gonzalez, for example, took to the floor of the House in 1969, denounced *Chicano* rhetoric as "hate," and defended the patriotism of Mexican Americans. Gonzalez rejected the term "Chicano," as well, describing himself as "an American of Spanish surname and of Mexican descent . . . what is commonly referred to as a Mexican American."[10]

Although to the firebrands, the middle class seemed collaborationist or, at best, complacent, the militant spirit of the times also began to animate members of the older generation. In spring 1966, fifty Mexican American leaders walked out of an Equal Employment Opportunity Commission conference because the planners were clearly preoccupied with African American issues and would not place Mexican Americans' concerns on the agenda. The early results of the exodus were gratifying: Johnson created an Inter-Agency Committee on Mexican-American Affairs, promised a White House conference to study ethnic discrimination in the Southwest, and appointed Mexican Americans to several government panels. It was then that the president had appointed Dr. Garcia to the U.S. Commission on Civil Rights.[11]

President Johnson's newest expression of *patron* politics did not mark a permanent change in his priorities. Soon, he was once more distracted by criticisms and protests from other quarters. Johnson delayed and ultimately abandoned plans for hosting the White House conference, and, instead, he authorized members of his cabinet to attend hearings of the new Inter-Agency Committee. James DeAnda, a longtime legal advisor to AGIF, testified at the hearing in El Paso during October 1967, and he stated that a major impediment to Mexican Americans' civil rights progress was that private resources could not sustain the high cost of frequent litigation. Noting that the 1964 CRA provided for the judicial award of plaintiffs' attorneys' fees in employment discrimination cases, DeAnda proposed similar federal government assistance in voting, jury, and school lawsuits.[12]

After several years of official dithering, some of DeAnda's recommendations were acted upon. In the meantime, Pete Tijerina, a lawyer in San Antonio, saw the same need and sought to increase the pot of private dollars available for lawsuits. He succeeded in obtaining a multimillion-dollar, multiyear grant from the Ford Foundation, and he used it to found the Mexican-American Legal Defense and Education Fund (originally MALD, but now MALDEF). When the Civil Rights Commission held its hearings in San Antonio during December 1968, Dr. Garcia invited Tijerina to describe his reasons for establishing MALDEF. Tijerina answered that his continuing experience in defending Mexican Americans before all-white juries, more than a decade after the Supreme Court had categorically condemned that situation in the 1954 decision, *Hernández v. Texas,* convinced him that a dedicated legal defense organization was necessary.[13]

The rising tide of these social, political, and even legal currents—an emerging militancy among campus leaders, a growing frustration among the political movers and shakers of the older generation, and a new willingness by lawyers to seek social justice through the courts—reached its high tide when Latino high school students were in their turn inspired to protest substandard facilities, conservative regulations of clothing and hair styles, and, as the war protests heated up, many other forms of personal and political expression. The issue that set them apart as budding *Chicano* activists rather than just one more cohort of disaffected youth, however, was that they began by rebelling specifically against the white-centered curriculum imposed on them. Students in San Antonio, El Paso, Houston, and smaller towns in Texas responded to local school boards' routine refusals to discuss their *Chicano*-inspired manifestos for reform through the act of "walking-out." Walkouts, often followed immediately by rallies and marches, seriously disrupted the targeted campuses. The clear influence of the farm workers' strikes was revealed by the frequent display of the UFW's thunderbird flag during the protests.[14]

MAYO leaders had only an advisory role in the high school walkouts until late in 1968, when the MAYO chapter at Pan American University played a more direct role in a confrontation at Hidalgo County's Edcouch-Elsa Independent School District. The Pan Am organizers had been instructing their younger protégés regarding *Chicano* politics and protest tactics for a few weeks when, in October 1968, two Edcouch-Elsa students were expelled for refusing to comply with the district's hairstyle rules. Other students, accompanied by MAYO mentors, met with the Edcouch-Elsa superintendent to demand that he reinstate the two students. The superintendent refused, and the student leaders resolved to walk out. The school board, consisting of three whites and two Mexican Americans—which was an indication that the issues at hand were generational, even class-based, as well as ethnic—met in early November to develop an official policy regarding the anticipated outbreak of student unrest. The board mailed notices to district parents, threatening to expel students who walked out, engaged in any other demonstrations, or joined organizations that disrupted schools. The board's notice blamed "outside agitators" for making the new disciplinary rules necessary.[15]

At the subsequent student rally, speakers announced two recommendations and made fifteen demands. The demands—for example, to include Latino cultural and historical perspectives in the curriculum and to end the long-standing rule forbidding the speaking of Spanish on school grounds—testified to the "Brown Power" ideology of *Chicanismo.* The Edcouch-Elsa ISD board refused to consider these demands, and more than 150 students walked out of the high school in mid-November. While many of the students demonstrated across the street, a committee of student leaders met with the principal, requesting an immediate meeting of the board. When the students pressed him on this issue, the principal summarily expelled them. When protests resumed the next day, teachers recorded the names of students they recognized, and these students were also expelled. Of the dozens of students of who had demonstrated on that second day of the walkout, the principal had the Hidalgo County sheriff arrest five. They were charged with loitering on school property.[16]

When the school board next met, four members upheld the mass expulsions but voted to schedule hearings where individual students could petition for readmission. The fifth board member, a Mexican American, abstained from the vote. Of the seventy-eight students who sought readmission during the first week of hearings, forty-seven were allowed to return to class on probation, and the remaining thirty-one were expelled for the balance of the semester. But ninety-four students did not request readmission.[17]

Instead, the expelled students took their school district to court, claiming that its policies violated their constitutional rights, specifically, the right to due process and equal protection of the laws under the Fourteenth Amendment. That response, and the form it took, was an indication that the *Chicano* movement was less concerned with separation from the mainstream than

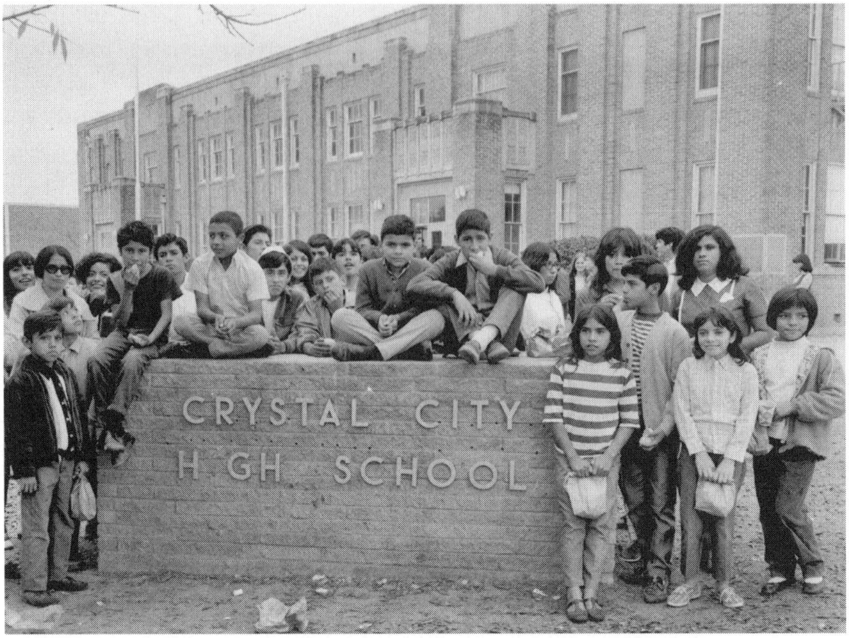

Fig. 8.1. Students posed around high school sign during boycott, Crystal City, Texas, 1969. Credit: San Antonio Light Collection, UTSA's Institute of Texan Cultures, No. L-4148-B, Courtesy of the Hearst Corporation.

the rhetoric proclaimed. Although the dual alienation of *Chicano* youth—from whites and from older Mexican Americans—was genuine, the often expressed desire for cultural separatism was never practical.[18]

Chicanos were not alone in seeking redress through litigation, even as they talked about revolution. Many U.S. Supreme Court decisions under Chief Justice Earl Warren concerned the Fourteenth Amendment, especially the seminal 1954 public school desegregation case *Brown v. Board of Education.* These emboldened the emergent or newly energized minority groups. One of the most significant of these decisions was *Monroe v. Pape* (1961). In *Monroe,* the Court gave new life to the Civil Rights Act of 1871—usually known as the Ku Klux Klan (KKK) Act—which had authorized private citizens to protect their rights by filing federal civil rights suits against state officials. Previously, between the 1870s and the 1930s, the Supreme Court had reluctantly overseen state officials' activities that affected state citizens and had used comity and respect for federalism to discourage lower courts from hearing relevant cases.[19]

The KKK Act became moribund as result of abstention doctrines that accommodated states' prerogatives. The justices briefly revived the 1871 statute in the 1939 case *Hague v. CIO,* when it affirmed a federal district judge's order enjoining officials in Jersey City, New Jersey, from enforcing an ordinance to prevent a labor rally in a public park. But the Court did not resurrect the full potential of the statute until it ruled in *Monroe* that a search by Chicago police had been undertaken as harassment and conducted in bad faith. Most significantly, officials who claimed merely to be doing their public duty could be held personally liable for a deprivation of private rights. This key decision came at a critical time in the history of the civil rights movement. It signaled the justices' unwillingness to allow what they subsequently called the "chilling effect" of the rules, regulations, and procedures that operated unduly to interfere with constitutionally protected rights of free speech or association, usually by forcing dissenting citizens to choose between safe passivity or risky participation in protest activities—whether public speaking, organizing, boycotting, or some form of civil disobedience—that put them at risk for arrest, fine, or some other sanction meted out by a hostile government official.[20]

This fresh reinterpretation of the states' responsibilities to enforce the federal Constitution encouraged African American activists to push harder for fundamental rights and reform in the post-*Brown* but still "Jim Crow" South. But the Court's rulings on the KKK Act, which is usually referred to as "Section 1983" (referencing its position in the codified federal statutes), did not limit the victory to such narrow categories as police harassment or racial discrimination against African Americans. Rather, these decisions expanded the range of state-initiated actions open to federal oversight and intervention. The result, in the words of the editors of a leading casebook on the federal courts, was "an impressive flood of litigation against state officers in the federal courts." In 1960, one year before *Monroe,* plaintiffs brought only 280 cases under Section 1983. By 1971, the number of complaints filed had risen to 4,609.[21]

The Edcouch-Elsa student activists were represented by a local attorney Bob Sanchez of McAllen and by volunteers from MALDEF. The legal team filed a section 1983 action on behalf of three of the five students who had been arrested for loitering, and two other students, naming the school district, superintendent, board members, and principal. The plaintiffs sought $50,000 in damages, based on the claim that the officials' prohibition of demonstrations and their methods of ending the walkout interfered with the students' exercise of their civil rights. Sanchez also complained that the blanket expulsions had deprived students of due process, in that they were sanctioned *prior* to their individual hearings. Thus, he also sought a temporary restraining order from U.S. district judge Reynaldo Garza of the Southern District of Texas.[22]

During his seven years on the federal bench, Judge Garza had not shown himself to be particularly sympathetic to the aims and claims of civil rights activists. He was a member of the "Mexican American Generation," had been active in Democratic politics, and was, like Representative Gonzalez, an old friend of embattled and soon-to-be-former President Lyndon Johnson. In fact, the conservative Garza's appointment to the federal court had been opposed by the liberal wing of the Democratic Party at the time of his nomination by President Kennedy. More to the point, and ominously for the plaintiffs, Garza had a decade earlier served as a commissioner of Brownsville and as a trustee of his own local school board. Yet, it was possible (perhaps) that Garza's personal experience would temper his conservatism: at the time of the suit, he had one son in college, who was preparing for applications to law school, and another son in the U.S. Army, who was already training for possible duty in Vietnam.[23]

An experienced jurist, Judge Garza mentioned none of these factors in court, but it seemed obvious from the first that he favored the plaintiffs' arguments. In short order, he issued the requested restraining order and ordered the board to admit all ninety-four suspended students pending the scheduled individual reviews. Garza then convened a hearing in Brownsville, during which the school district superintendent admitted that the district had no written criteria for deciding whether or not a particular student's expulsion was to be permanent. Instead, decisions rested on the student's attitude and actions during the walkout. Judge Garza, clearly incredulous at this admission, asked for amplification: "in other words, if they kowtowed to you and said you were a nice principal, they got back in?" The judge did not receive a satisfactory reply, and on December 19, 1968, he ruled that the arbitrary expulsion procedure and blanket ban on demonstrations were unconstitutional. He ordered the district to readmit the students and directed that all traces of the expulsions be expunged from the students' permanent files. But he assessed only a nominal damage award against the district.[24]

Almost all of the Edcouch-Elsa students returned to class. Beyond the satisfaction of seeing administrators scolded in public by a federal judge, raising the profile of the MAYO leaders, and perhaps encouraging larger walkouts in 1969, notably in Kingsville and Crystal City, the students actually gained little from the walkout or the lawsuit. But, as many of the efforts by 1960s activists were aimed at publicity and consciousness-raising, perhaps this was enough to be considered a successful protest. The role of MALDEF in this and other early legal actions is difficult to assess, but it appears that the new organization was moving cautiously and was not yet fully committed to a litigation revival. In protests subsequent to Edcouch-Elsa's, for example, MALDEF seemed mostly concerned with mediating negotiated settlements rather than filing lawsuits.[25]

One stark exception to this inclination toward settlement rather than litigation arose from the protest of the seventeen-year-old Lucinda Escalante. The controversy combined the *Chicano* rights movement in South Texas with a larger student protest of America's involvement in Vietnam, which had begun to build in the district beginning in the late 1960s. Escalante attended high school in La Feria, a border town between Brownsville and McAllen. She distributed leaflets in school corridors to announce a protest rally arranged by the MAYO-advised La Feria Youth Organization. MAYO had wanted to call attention to the number of *Chicanos* serving in Vietnam, which was high relative to their actual percentage of the U.S. and Texas populations. The principal suspended Escalante, and two students who had helped her pass out the leaflets, for three days, because they had distributed literature without permission. Escalante pointed out that no announced policy barred passing out leaflets and that other students distributed literature on school grounds, but the principal refused to reconsider.[26]

Escalante then visited La Feria's superintendent to request immediate reinstatement and a "timely" hearing on the suspension's legality. Two men accompanied her, Efrain Fernandez, the MAYO member who had given her the leaflets for distribution, and Roger Dunwell, who identified himself only as a "civil rights worker" but who had written the letter she presented to the superintendent. In it, Escalante suggested that the principal had violated her constitutional right to free speech and had denied her the right without due process. She referred the administrator to the recent U.S. Supreme Court decision in *Tinker v. Des Moines*. In *Tinker*, the Court had declared that students "do not shed their rights . . . at the schoolhouse door" and reversed the expulsions of three students who had protested the war by wearing black armbands to their school.[27]

Escalante had engaged in volunteer activities in the Rio Grande Valley, including poverty relief and voter registration, but she was now explicitly identifying her protest with the national struggle for students' rights. The La Feria superintendent refused to discuss her suspension. He denied that Fernandez and Dunwell had the authority to represent Escalante, who was a minor. Escalante later returned with a typed note signed by her father, but the superintendent still refused to intervene, arguing that it would be pointless, as only one day remained of the suspension.[28]

After the suspension expired, the La Feria school board denied Escalante's written request for a hearing. In December 1969, Brownsville lawyer Filemon B. Vela filed a section 1983 action in Judge Garza's court. He was joined in the suit by MALDEF cocounsel Tijerina and two other volunteer attorneys. The federal complaint, filed one year to the day after Garza enjoined the Edcouch-Elsa board, alleged that Escalante had been deprived of rights of speech and association guaranteed by the First Amendment and equal protection of the laws guaranteed by the Fourteenth Amendment. She had been singled out for punishment, the attorneys argued, because the principal disapproved of the message her leaflet contained not because of an infraction of his unwritten rule. They also contended that the board's deference to an unwritten rule in denying Escalante a hearing deprived her of due process. The attorneys requested that Judge Garza enjoin this rule, order the removal of any trace of the suspension from Escalante's record, and declare the official's actions unconstitutional. They also requested that he "award such other relief as is just and proper."[29]

Although the complaint did not employ the term "Chicano," as did many of the MALDEF-sponsored suits, the district's response to the suit indicates that the authorities believed that the MAYO militants were manipulating the impressionable Escalante in order to create a political issue that would advance the *Chicano* cause. Therefore, the district's lawyer, Orrin Johnson of Harlingen, seized on every opportunity to discredit MAYO and militant dissent in general. He disputed various points of fact in the complaint but also noted various errors in spelling. Johnson took special exception to the lawyers' use of "Mexican-American citizen" to describe Escalante. He noted that "according to her school record, Lucinda is a citizen of the United States and by law is not a hyphenated citizen of the United States." Finally, he claimed, the complaint had not correctly stated the issues in the case. According to Johnson, who posed them as questions, they were "(a) Must the corridors of the public schools—which belong to everyone—be used as the forum for distribution of unauthorized leaflets which cater to race prejudice and bigotry and which tend to demean or provoke other students purely on the basis of race or national origin?" And "(b) Does the right of free speech require that one always be allowed to use the corridors of a public school immediately before commencement of classes for leafleting designed to divide and excite the students on the basis of race or national origin and that also tends to disrupt order, discipline and neatness in the school?"[30]

Throughout his presentation, Johnson focused on the ethnic issues that Escalante allegedly sought to inflame. He explained that La Feria officials were angry that this student had brought "ethnically divisive" and provocative antiwar leaflets to school the day after a patriotic Veteran's Day assembly. His argument also relied, however, on a basic procedural question, which was "(c) May such unauthorized literature be so distributed at school without, first, obtaining the permission of the principal in contravention with the long-standing rules and practices of the school?"[31]

Few of the facts were disputed, and Judge Garza requested that the lawyers summarize their positions on the relevant case law. Vela argued that Supreme Court decisions, including *Board of Education v. Barnette,* the World War II-era "flag salute" case, and *Tinker* established that unless a student's speech or action "materially disrupted" the education of fellow students, it was protected by the First Amendment. He noted that, at La Feria, the principal had applied "his" rule regarding announcements inconsistently and had attempted to prevent specific subjects and opinions from being discussed in classrooms. This was the prior restraint that Garza had condemned in the Edcouch-Elsa district, Vela argued, and he must condemn it once again.[32]

Johnson disputed Vela's central argument that, since Escalante's activities were not disruptive, *Tinker* and other precedents applied. To the contrary, Johnson stated, leafleting had caused an "uneasy" feeling to pervade the school for the rest of the day. And he wrote: "if an individual wanted to incite the emotions of the students of La Feria High School just as the day's classes were to begin, she could not have picked a more volatile vehicle than an appeal to ethnic differences with the added force of the impact of the Viet Nam War." But Johnson implied that the impact of Escalante's leafleting on other students' learning environment was the secondary concern. The primary one, he noted, was the maintenance of the La Feria officials' ability to control the district's schools, free of the fear of students' lawsuits. Johnson appealed to Garza's sense of proportion and his judicial management sensitivities: "if there were a practical question to present to the [c]ourt, it would be this: How much time does a Federal Court have to spend on three-day suspensions of seventeen year old students who do not first attempt to work out their complaints about disciplinary actions through the administrative channels of the school?"[33]

Briefs from the attorneys merely restated their contentions: Vela and the MALDEF lawyers claimed Escalante's rights were denied; Johnson argued that she was a pawn in a ploy to disrupt the peace at La Feria high school. On August 1, 1970, Garza sustained the former position. He declared that "there was no evidence that the leaflets disrupted the activities of the school in any manner, and this made the suspension unconstitutional." The judge agreed with the school district that it could regulate the time, place, and manner of distributing literature on its campuses, as long as the rules were "reasonable and non-discriminatory," and content-neutral. Administrators might require that all materials be subjected to review prior to distribution, but the regulations were permissible only if they did not act as "a cloak for censorship and selective enforcement." The judge withheld the requested injunction against the principal's "so-called unwritten rule," however, and instead urged the La Feria district to develop regulations that met the conditions he outlined. Finally, noting that the three days Escalante had spent under suspension could not be replaced, Garza ordered the school district to expunge its files of any record of the "unconstitutional suspension."[34]

Judge Garza's support of the constitutional rights of Mexican American students in these cases does not indicate that he supported the goals of either *Chicano* militants or critics of U.S. policies. Yet, he seemed to accept the validity of the substance of the critiques from both quarters, perhaps because, as noted, his own sons were embodiments of the issues facing the nation. The judge never denied that is was an administrators' duty to keep control in schools, in order to provide an environment suitable for the education of the younger generation. But Garza's rulings in the Edcouch-Elsa and La Feria cases showed that he opposed arbitrary application of otherwise legitimate authority.[35]

In the late 1960s, MALDEF's participation in section 1983 lawsuits helped to reestablish litigation under the Fourteenth Amendment as a tool for vindicating Mexican American civil rights. These efforts indicated that the new organization could contend viably in constitutional disputes. However, MALDEF's early victories for students did not necessarily vindicate claims that Mexican Americans were a group held distinct from whites. Instead, as illustrated by the attorneys' strategies in the case, *Chicano* students in Texas were subject to, and were bound to object to, the same oppressive regulations as were white students. Nevertheless, ethnic identity seemed at the heart of the official responses to these student protest cases. Although Vela made few references to the ethnic aspects of Escalante's complaint, his opponent Johnson repeatedly referred to the taint of radical ethnic politics, especially MAYO's alleged efforts to turn Escalante's case into a *Chicano cause celebre.*[36]

Judge Garza's ruling was itself uninterested in Escalante's identity. Indeed, if he had decided the case the opposite way, the ruling would have had the same significance for *Chicanos as Chicanos,* that is, none at all. For it seems that Escalante's lawsuit did not actually represent just the struggle for *Chicano* civil rights. Instead, it was one among the many student controversies that Americans faced in the late 1960s. In the end, what was immutable was not the definitions of white, black, and brown, but the apparent need to struggle, over and over again, for civil rights that were—if only in hindsight—inalienable, because inalienable does not mean unbridgeable. The *Chicano* generation's contribution to civil rights history was not in achieving a separate sphere for themselves but in bringing about a meeting of the minds with the "Mexican American Generation." What the two generations shared in common—concern for social justice and desire to see progress on the civil rights front—outweighed their differences and allowed them to make common cause in the constitutional battles to come.[37]

NOTES

1. For a discussion of the generational issues that led to the rise of the *Chicano* challenge to the "Mexican American Generation," see Armando Gutiérrez and Herbert Hirsch, "The Militant Challenge to the American Ethos: 'Chicanos' and 'Mexican Americans,'" in *La Causa Politica: A Chicano Politics Reader,* ed. F. Chris Garcia (South Bend, Ind.: University of Notre Dame Press, 1974), 86–103. Also, see generally Mario

T. García, *Mexican Americans: Leadership, Ideology, and Identity, 1930–1960* (New Haven: Yale University Press, 1989), 13–22; and Carlos Munoz, *Youth, Identity, Power: The Chicano Movement* (New York: Verso, 1989).

2. See Juan Gómez Quiñones, *Chicano Politics: Reality and Promise, 1940–1990* (Albuquerque: University of New Mexico Press, 1990), 118–19; Ignacio M. Garcia, *Chicanismo: The Forging of a Militant Ethos Among Mexican-Americans* (Tucson: University of Arizona Press, 1997), 1–4; and Armando B. Rendón, *Chicano Manifesto: The History and Aspirations of the Second Largest Minority in America* (Berkeley, Calif.: Ollin and Associates, 1996; original, 1971), 200–202.

3. For the background of this approach, see Michael A. Olivas, ed., *"Colored Men and Hombres Aqui": Hernández v. Texas and the Emergence of Mexican American Lawyering* (Houston: Arte Publico, 2006). In part, the strategy involved choosing between "due process" and "equal protection" claims, both rooted in the language of the Fourteenth Amendment to the U.S. Constitution but implying different goals and results, see Steven H. Wilson, "*Brown* Over 'Other White': Mexican Americans' Legal Arguments and Litigation Strategy in Desegregation Litigation," *Law & History Review* 21, no. 1 (March 2003).

4. *Brown, et al. v. Board of Education of Topeka, Kansas,* 347 U.S. 483 (1954). See Julie Leininger Pycior, *LBJ & Mexican Americans: The Paradox of Power* (Austin: University of Texas Press, 1997), generally. Also Rodney E. Hero, *Latinos and the U.S. Political System: Two-Tiered Pluralism* (Philadelphia: Temple University Press, 1992). See Louise Ann Fisch, *All Rise: Reynaldo G. Garza, the First Mexican American Federal Judge* (College Station: Texas A&M University Press, 1996), 70–77, and generally. The claim of the title requires some clarification. Garza was not actually first, but he was the first federal judge to be widely *recognized* as a Mexican American. In 1947, President Truman appointed Harold R. Medina, the son of a Mexican father and a white mother, to the Southern District of New York. Medina was later promoted to the Second Circuit. Judge Medina dedicated a volume of his collected writings and speeches "to my father, Joaquin Adolfo Medina, born in the city of Merida, Yucatan, Mexico, on November 27, 1858." See Harold R. Medina, *The Anatomy of Freedom,* ed. C. Walter Barrett (New York: Henry Holy, 1959), v. But Medina was not regarded as Hispanic by white politicians, apparently was not raised as a Hispanic, and as a consequence, Medina's appointment is generally not regarded as being as politically significant as Garza's. The fact that an unrecognized or unremarked Hispanic sat on the federal bench underscores the fluidity of racial politics involving an ethnic identity claimed by Hispanics. See Fisch, *All Rise,* 177, note 1. Armando Navarro, *The Cristal Experiment: A Chicano Struggle for Community Control* (Madison: University of Wisconsin Press, 1998), 17–51, and generally for later political developments in the same city, in years after the *Chicano* movement emerged; Armando L. Trujillo, *Chicano Empowerment and Bilingual Education: Movimiento Politics in Crystal City, Texas* (New York: Garland, 1998).

5. Helen Rowan, "A Minority Nobody Knows," in *Mexican Americans in the United States: A Reader,* ed. John H. Burma (Cambridge, Mass.: Schenkman, 1978), 29.

6. 42 U.S.C. § 2000(a). See "Comment: The Courts, HEW, and Southern School Desegregation," *Yale Law Journal,* 77 (1967): 321. Also see Louis Fisher, "The Judge As Manager; Involvement of Judges in Public Welfare," *The Public Manager* 25 no. 3

(Fall 1996): 7–10; and: J. Harvie Wilkinson III, *From Brown to Bakke: The Supreme Court and School Integration: 1954–1978* (New York: Oxford University Press, 1979), 102–107. See Guadalupe Salinas, "Comment, Mexican-Americans and the Desegregation of Schools in the Southwest," *Houston Law Review* 8 (1971): 939. See Guadalupe San Miguel Jr., *"Let All of Them Take Heed": Mexican Americans and the Campaign for Educational Equality in Texas, 1910–1981* (Austin: University of Texas Press, 1987), 175–77. The "other" categories included "any racial or national origin group for which separate schools have in the past been maintained or which are recognized as significant 'minority groups' in the community." Noted in Jorge C. Rangel and Carlos M. Alcala, "Project Report, De Jure Segregation of Chicanos in Texas Schools," *Harvard Civil Rights-Civil Liberties Law Review* 7 (1972): 365–66, notes 352–69. Also see Testimony of Jerold D. Ward, December 11, 1968, in *U.S. Commission on Civil Rights, Hearing Held in San Antonio, Texas, 9–14 December 1968* (Washington, D.C.: U.S. Commission on Civil Rights, 1968), 331–39.

7. Carlos Guerra, "Discourse By An Other," *Texas Observer,* October 27, 1967, 14. For background on bureaucratic and internecine battles over racial and ethnic categories, see Steven H. Wilson, "Some Are Born White, Some Achieve Whiteness, and Some Have Whiteness Thrust Upon Them: Mexican Americans and the Politics of Racial Classification in the Federal Judicial Bureaucracy, Twenty-Five Years after *Hernández v. Texas,*" *UCLA Chicano-Latino Law Review* 25 (2005). This article is also available in Olivas, ed., *"Colored Men" and "Hombres Aquí,"* 123–42. Matt S. Meier and Feliciano Ribera, *Mexican Americans/American Mexicans: From Conquistadors to Chicanos* (New York: Hill and Wang, 1993; rev. ed. of *The Chicanos,* 1972), 211. David Montejano, *Anglos and Mexicans in the Making of Texas, 1836–1986* (Austin: University of Texas Press, 1987), 262–87. Walter Elwood Smith Jr., "Mexicano Resistance to Schooled Ethnicity: Ethnic Student Power in South Texas, 1930–1970" (PhD diss., University of Texas at Austin, 1978), 288–97; U.S. Commission on Civil Rights, Mexican-American Educational Study, Report I: *Ethnic Isolation of Mexican-Americans in the Public Schools of the Southwest* (Washington, D.C.: U.S. Commission on Civil Rights, 1970), 26.

8. The youth took the extraordinary marches organized by labor leader César Chávez to be demonstrations of *Chicanismo.* Despite Chávez's own denials that his movement had any ethnic particularity, most of the union's prospective members, especially in Texas, were Mexican-descended. Armando Navarro, *Mexican American Youth Organization: Avant-Garde of the Chicano Movement in Texas* (Austin: University of Texas Press, 1995), 22–36; Juan Gómez Quiñones, *Chicano Politics: Reality and Promise, 1940–1990* (Albuquerque: University of New Mexico Press, 1990), 101–105, 118–19. Also, see Ignacio M. Garcia, *Chicanismo: The Forging of a Militant Ethos Among Mexican-Americans* (Tucson: University of Arizona Press, 1997), 1–4.

9. 29 U.S.C. § 206(5). Subsection 5 was added by Pub.L. 89–601, § 302; 80 Stat. 830. "Little People's Day," *Texas Observer,* July 21, 1967, 5.

10. Navarro, *Mexican American Youth Organization,* 174, 198. Manuel G. Gonzalez, *Mexicanos: A History of Mexicans in the United States* (Bloomington: Indiana University Press, 1999), 219. Henry B. Gonzalez, from the *Congressional Record,* April 22, 1969, 91st Cong., 1st sess., "An Attack on Chicano Militants," in *A Documentary History of the*

Mexican Americans, eds. Wayne Moquin with Charles Van Doren (New York: Praeger, 1971), 358.

11. Manuel P. Servín, "The Post–World War II Mexican-American, 1945–1965: A Non-Achieving Minority," in *The Mexican-Americans: An Awakening Minority,* ed. Servín, 144. "Latin Leaders Walk Out on U.S.," *Texas Observer,* April 15, 1966, 5. Quiñones, *Chicano Politics,* 106–108. For the significance of this event, see Carl Allsup, *The American GI Forum: Origins and Evolution* (Austin: Center for Mexican American Studies/University of Texas Press, 1982), 160–61. For tensions and jealousies between Blacks and Mexican Americans in the mid-1960s, see Fred Barbaro, "Ethnic Resentment," in *Black/Brown/White Relations: Race Relations in the 1970s,* ed. Charles V. Willie (New Brunswick, N.J.: Transaction Books, 1977), 77–79. Guadalupe San Miguel Jr., *"Let All of Them Take Heed": Mexican Americans and the Campaign for Educational Equality in Texas, 1910–1981* (Austin: University of Texas Press, 1987), 164–69; and Guadalupe San Miguel Jr., "Mexican American Organizations and the Changing Politics of School Desegregation in Texas, 1945–1980," *Social Science Quarterly* 63 (1982): 708–709. Henry A. J. Ramos, *The American GI Forum: In Pursuit of the Dream, 1948–1983* (Houston: Arte Público, 1998). In 1969, Congress established the "Committee on Opportunities for Spanish Speaking People" to succeed the Inter-Agency Committee. Pub.L. 91–181, 83 Stat. 838 (1969).

12. In addition, DeAnda challenged the U.S. Justice Department to begin fighting discrimination against Mexican Americans with the vigor it finally was beginning to demonstrate in African Americans' cases. James DeAnda, "Civil Rights—Need For Executive Branch to Take Positive Steps to Rectify Discrimination in Jury Selection, Voting Eligibility and School Enrollment," in *The Mexican American: A New Focus on Opportunity,* Inter-Agency Committee on Mexican American Affairs (Washington, D.C.: U.S. Government Printing Office, 1967), 220–21. The El Paso meetings gave rise to another point of contention, when the Committee excluded the "militant" Mexican American leaders. Allsup, *The American GI Forum: Origins and Evolution,* 136–141; and Ramos, *The American GI Forum: In Pursuit of the Dream,* 99–106. Fees for counsel were provided in some employment discrimination cases under Title VII of the Civil Rights Act of 1964, 42 U.S.C. § 2000e-5(k).

13. Congress later enacted provisions similar to those DeAnda suggested. These statutes authorize and even encourage the award of attorney's fees to the prevailing parties in school desegregation cases. The case for court-ordered imposition of attorney's fees is particularly strong where the plaintiffs have incurred substantial expense due to the obstinate refusal of a school board to recognize and comply with its legal obligations. See "The Emergency School Aid Act of 1972," 20 U.S.C. § 1617. On October 19, 1976, Congress enacted the "Civil Rights Attorney's Fees Awards Act of 1976," 42 U.S.C. § 1988. This provided for prevailing plaintiffs to recover reasonable attorney's fees in § 1983 actions. The trial judge decides a "reasonable" fee. 42 U.S.C. § 1988(b), as amended by Pub.L. 104–317, Title III, § 309(b), 110 Stat. 3853 (119), describing "Attorney's fees." Also, see generally Alan Hirsch and Diane Sheehey, *Awarding Attorney's Fees in and Managing Fee Litigation* (Washington, D.C.: Federal Judicial Center, 1994). The U.S. attorney general waited until late 1969 to join in a Mexican American lawsuit.

Perez v. Sonora Independent School District, Civ. No. 6–224 (N.D. Tex, 1969). Noted in Gerald M. Birnberg, "Notes: *Brown v. Board of Education* Applies to Mexican-American Students and Any Other Readily Identifiable Ethnic-Minority Group or Class," *Texas Law Review* 49 (1971): 339, note 10. Tijerina sought funding from the Ford Foundation after discussing the need for such an organization with Jack Greenberg, the chief during the 1960s of the NAACP's litigation arm, the Legal Defense Fund (LDF or the "Inc. Fund"). Karen O'Connor and Lee Epstein, "A Legal Voice for the Chicano Community: The Activities of the Mexican American Legal Defense and Education Fund, 1968–82," in *The Mexican American Experience: An Interdisciplinary Anthology,* eds. Rodolfo O. De La Garza, Frank D. Bean, Charles M. Bonjean, Ricardo Romo, and Rodolfo Alvarez (Austin: University of Texas Press, 1985), 284–85. For the details of *Hernandez v. Texas,* 347 U.S. 475 (1954), which was nearly forgotten in the tumult of the *Brown* decision, see the introduction and various essays in *"Colored Men" and "Hombres Aquí,"* ed. Olivas.

14. Navarro, *Mexican American Youth Organization,* 115–18, 120–24; and Rendón, *Chicano Manifesto,* 174–94. Also Exhibits 12–16, in U.S. Commission on Civil Rights, *Hearing Held in San Antonio, Texas, 9–14 December 1968* (Washington, D.C.: U.S. Commission on Civil Rights, 1968), 881–92. California saw the same kind of student unrest. Dial Torgerson, "'Brown Power' Unity Seen Behind School Disorders," in *Mexican Americans in the United States,* ed. Burma, 279.

15. Navarro, *Mexican American Youth Organization,* 118–20. The "agitation" condemned by the school board proved critical to *Chicano* coordination. Miguel David Tirado, "Mexican American Community Political Organization: The Key to Chicano Political Power," in *La Causa Politica,* ed. F. Chris Garcia, 105–27.

16. For a "laundry list" of typical walkout demands, see Rendón, *Chicano Manifesto,* 177–79. For origins and ultimate abandonment in 1969 of "No Spanish" rules, see Thomas P. Carter, *Mexican Americans in School: A History of Educational Neglect* (New York: College Entrance Examination Board, 1970), 97–98; and Rangel and Alcala, "Project Report, De Jure Segregation of Chicanos in Texas Schools," 310, note 20. Navarro, *Mexican American Youth Organization,* 120–23.

17. Navarro, *Mexican American Youth Organization,* 120–23.

18. That separatist end was the announced goal of the most militant of the *Chicanos,* but most of the activists were willing to accept a symbolic homeland in the Southwest they called *Aztlán.* García, *Chicanismo,* 94–98. This kind of rhetoric led T. R. Fehrenbach, the author of a popular history of Texas published in 1968, to wonder whether South Texas was on the verge of becoming the Quebec of the United States. T. R. Fehrenbach, *Lone Star: A History of Texas and the Texans* (New York: Macmillan, 1968), 698–701.

19. 365 U.S. 167 (1961). Act of April 20, 1871 (ch. 22, sec. 1, 17 Stat. 13; formerly codified as R.S. Sect. 1979, then as 8 U.S.C. § 43; currently codified as amended at 42 U.S.C. §§ 1981–1983). This first section of the bill merely added civil and equitable remedies to the criminal penalties already established in the Civil Rights Act of 1866, and so it was the least controversial part of the 1871 act. This section was left intact, although it was narrowly interpreted, when the Supreme Court stripped the original act of much of its efficacy in the 1883 *Civil Rights Cases* by overturning provisions for

the freedmen's equal access to the nation's public accommodations, entertainment, and transportation, 109 U.S. 3 (1883). See William E. Nelson, *The Fourteenth Amendment: From Political Principle to Judicial Doctrine* (Cambridge, Mass.: Harvard University Press, 1988), 194–97; also Harold M. Hyman, *A More Perfect Union: The Impact of the Civil War and Reconstruction on the Constitution* (New York: Alfred A. Knopf, 1973), 529. For the Supreme Court's views on the legislative history of the Ku Klux Klan Act, see: *Monroe v. Pape,* 365 U.S. 167 (1961), 171; and: *Monell v. Department of Social Services,* 436 U.S. 658 (1978), 665. Phillip J. Cooper, *Hard Judicial Choices: Federal District Court Judges and State and Local Officials* (New York: Oxford University Press, 1988), 12–44, and generally.

20. 307 U.S. 496 (1939). Previously, federal courts had issued injunctions against labor organizers. The key to the *Monroe* ruling was that the equal protection section (§ 1983) required no proof of willful misconduct while the conspiracy section of the act (§ 1981) did. The officers, although not the city of Chicago itself, were made liable to pay civil damages. Note, "Developments in the Law: Section 1983 and Federalism," *Harvard Law Review* 90 (1977): 1169–72. See Matthew V. Hess, "Comment: Good Cop–Bad Cop: Reassessing the Legal Remedies for Police Misconduct," *Utah Law Review* (1993): 154. *Dombrowski v. Pfister,* 380 U.S. 479 (1965), at 487. The Court held that the "chilling effect" was substantial in those states with laws against organizing civil rights protests. The case "unleashed a torrent" of suits seeking protection from state prosecution. Frederick Schauer, "Fear, Risk, and the First Amendment: Unraveling the 'Chilling Effect,'" *Boston University Law Review* 58 (1978): 685. See Anthony G. Amsterdam, "Criminal Prosecutions Affecting Federally Guaranteed Civil Rights: Federal Removal and Habeas Corpus Jurisdiction to Abort State Court Trial," *University of Pennsylvania Law Review* 113 (1965): 828; and Frank L. Maraist, "Federal Injunctive Relief Against State Court Proceedings: The Significance of *Dombrowski,*" *Texas Law Review* 48 (1970): 535–607.

21. Stanley H. Friedelbaum, "The Warren Court and American Federalism—A Preliminary Appraisal," *University of Chicago Law Review* 28 (1960): 68, especially n. 80. Less than a decade after *Monroe,* some critics claimed that the expansion had already gone too far, because federal court jurisdiction in civil rights claims had grown to include situations that were arguably never intended to be subjects for equitable relief. At the least, critics suggested, some of the cases were better suited for state courts. Note, "Limiting the Section 1983 Action in the Wake of *Monroe v. Pape,*" *Harvard Law Review* 82 (1969): 1487. Others celebrated the trend and called for more of the same, claiming that only federal judges, by dint of experience, temperament, and tenure could adequately serve to right society's moral wrongs by conscientiously attending to individual's civil rights. Paul Chevigny, "Section 1983 Jurisdiction: A Reply," *Harvard Law Review* 83 (1970): 1357. The Court overruled parts of *Monroe,* but only to find that cities could be held liable for civil damages. *Monell v. Dept. of Social Services,* 436 U.S. 658 (1978). 42 U.S.C. § 1983, "Actions for Deprivations of Civil Rights Under Color of Law." The act provides that "Every person" who, "under any statute, ordinance, regulation, custom, or usage causes to be subjected, any citizen of the United States . . . to the deprivation of any rights, privileges, or immunities secured by the Constitution and laws, shall be liable to the party injured in an action at law, suit in equity, or

other proper proceeding for redress." Note, "The Federal Anti-Injunction Statute and Declaratory Judgments in Constitutional Litigation," *Harvard Law Review* 83 (1970): 1871–72. Between 1871, the year the Klan law was enacted, and 1939, the year the Court decided *Hague,* the federal courts reported nineteen cases filed under the equivalent of section 1983. Paul Bator, Paul Mishkin, Donald Shapiro, and Henry Wechsler, eds., *Hart and Wechsler's the Federal Courts and the Federal System,* 2nd ed. (Westbury, Conn.: Foundation Press, 1973), 950, n. 3. Also, see Karen M. Blum and Kathryn R. Urbonya, *Section 1983 Litigation* (Washington, D.C.: Federal Judicial Center, 1998), 1–6; and Eric H. Zagrans, "'Under Color of' What Law: A Reconstructed Model of Section 1983 Liability," *Virginia Law Review* 71 (1985): 499.

22. Navarro, *Mexican American Youth Organization,* 124.

23. For a sympathetic view of Garza's career, but one that also notes the divisions his appointment created within the Mexican American community in Texas, see Fisch, *All Rise,* 70–77; for his sons, 115–17. Pycior, *LBJ & Mexican Americans,* 116–24. The authors of two major histories of the Mexican American civil rights campaigns in Texas incorrectly identify the longstanding—albeit conservative—Democrat Garza as a Republican. This mistaken information might have become part the political lore of the state because Garza joined Governor Shivers in supporting Eisenhower against Stevenson. Allsup, *The American G.I. Forum,* 133; and, San Miguel Jr., *Let All of Them Take Heed,* 164–65. As critical legal scholar Richard Delgado assessed Garza's career, "Garza began—and even ended—with good social instincts and a love of justice." But it was "difficult for him to think of himself or his group in effective legal terms—as a people with a history of conquest and brutal treatment in need of redress." According to Delgado, he ruled "against [his] people . . . and other minorities." Richard Delgado, "Book Review: Rodrigo's Fifteenth Chronicle," 1187. N.B.: Delgado's article is a review of Fisch's biography of Garza.

24. Quoted in Navarro, *Mexican American Youth Organization,* 124. *Ramirez v. Edcouch-Elsa Independent School District,* unpublished, U.S. District Court for the Southern District of Texas (hereafter S.D. Tex.), 1969, Brownsville Division, Civ. No. 68-B-116. Note the students prevailed in December 1968, the same month the civil rights commissioners held hearings in San Antonio. San Miguel, *Let All of Them Take Heed,* 172–73; and Guadalupe San Miguel Jr., "'The Community is Beginning to Rumble': The Origins of Chicano Educational Protest in Houston, 1965–1970," *Houston Review* 13 (1991): 135–36.

25. Rangel and Alcala, "Project Report, De Jure Segregation of Chicanos in Texas Schools," 369. Navarro, *Mexican American Youth Organization,* 125–48.

26. Critics of the U.S. policy in Vietnam argued that the undeclared war was either unconstitutional or immoral and probably both. In any case, they believed that the government should end its military commitments in that country. Many protesters refused to register for the draft, burned their draft cards after registering, or simply resisted induction when they called. In each instance, these individuals risked incarceration in a federal prison. See, for example: *Schacht* v. *United States,* 398 U.S. 58 (1970); *Gee* v. *United States,* 319 F. Supp. 581 (S.D. Tex., 1970); and *Clay, AKA Ali* v. *United States;* 403 U.S. 698 (1971). The last case involved the appeal of boxer Muhammad Ali, born Cassius Clay, to overturn his conviction for refusal to submit to military induc-

tion in Houston. Judge Ingraham presided in the original trial in the Southern District of Texas. Failure to report for and to submit to induction into the U.S. Army was a violation of 50 App. U.S.C. § 462(a). As with many political and social controversies of a tumultuous era, the issues were translated into legal questions and spilled over into the nation's courtrooms. Whether the issue was the propriety of peaceful protest, civil disobedience, or even violent resistance to U.S. government policies, state and federal judges were called on to identify a bright line that separated the citizen's responsibility to follow the law from the right to dissent. For the generation of younger Americans asked to fight, the collective political goal of ending the war depended on an even more personal decision: whether to submit to induction into the military and risk death, or to resist the draft and risk prison. Certainly, this is an over simplification of the political and moral choices facing the generation of draft-age citizens. The implications of the ongoing involvement of U.S. troops were also issues among the even younger generation, still in high school but approaching draft age. Their efforts to protest the Vietnam War led to a landmark case before the Supreme Court, which asserted that even high school students did not "shed their constitutional rights to freedom of speech or expression at the schoolhouse gate." *Tinker v. Des Moines Independent Community School District,* 393 U.S. 503 (1969), 506 (hereafter *Tinker*). See John W. Johnson, *The Struggle for Student Rights: Tinker v. Des Moines and the 1960s* (Lawrence: University Press of Kansas, 1997). See also Allen J. Matusow, *The Unraveling of America: A History of Liberalism in the 1960s* (New York: Harper & Row, 1984), 394. Disproportionate rates of Hispanic enlistment or draft into the service was an issue that MAYO raised frequently in the late 1960s. The mimeographed leaflets announced the time, place, and reason of the rally on one side in Spanish, and it listed the relevant draft statistics in English on the reverse side. The information seems to be based on an article by Prof. Ralph Guzman of the University of California at Santa Cruz, which Rep. Edward R. Roybal of California entered into the *Congressional Record.* See: "Mexican-American Casualties in Vietnam," from the *Congressional Record,* 91st Cong., 1st sess., October 8, 1969, 91st Cong., 1st sess.; Representative Roybal's entry has been reprinted in Moquin and Van Doren, *A Documentary History of the Mexican Americans,* 371–73. The two other students, Ortiz and Trevino, were also suspended for leafleting, but they do not play a large part in the subsequent case, because they declined to join Escalante's lawsuit. One effect of their brief participation in the protest is that their refusal to join the suit convinced Judge Garza to deny Escalante's request to expand the suit into a class action. See *Escalante v. La Feria Independent School District,* unpublished (S.D. Tex., 1970) (hereafter cited as *Escalante v. La Feria ISD*); Civil Action (Civ. A.) No. 69-B-163, S.D. Tex., Brownsville Division, National Archives and Records Administration-Southwest Region (hereafter NARA-SWA), RG 21, Box 491, Folder for Case No. 69-B-163. See Memorandum and Order, 1 August 1970, 1–4.

27. She did not mention the possibility that she had been singled out by a white principal because she was a *Chicana.* See Escalante's letter, dated November 14, 1969, labeled "Defendants Exhibit No. 2," in *Escalante v. La Feria ISD,* NARA-SWA, RG 21, Box 492, Folder for Case No. 69-B-163.

28. In *Tinker,* announced February 24, 1969, the justices supported the students' claim that they were citizens under the Constitution and therefore entitled by the

Fourteenth Amendment to equal protection under the law. See Johnson, *The Struggle for Student Rights,* ix–x, and generally. *Escalante v. La Feria ISD,* NARA-SWA, RG 21, Box 492, Folder for Case No. 69-B-163. See Escalante's deposition, filed May 20, 1970, 9–10, 15–16, 40–41. The date of the deposition session is not provided, but must have been February 5, 1970: during the proceedings, Escalante referred to her eighteenth birthday "two days ago," and gives her birthday as February 3; see deposition, 4.

29. The declaratory judgment was available under the Declaratory Judgment Act, 28 U.S.C. § 2201. *Escalante v. La Feria ISD,* NARA-SWA, RG 21, Box 491, Folder for Case No. 69-B-163. See Complaint, December 19, 1969, 1–4; Defendant's Motion to Dismiss, January 26, 1970.

30. Ibid. Also see Complaint, December 19, 1969, 1; Defendant's Original Answer, January 26, 1970, 1–2.

31. Ibid. Also see Complaint, December 19, 1969, 1; Defendant's Original Answer, January 26, 1970, 3–9.

32. See *West Virginia State Board of Education v. Barnette,* 319 U.S. 624 (1943). *Escalante v. La Feria ISD,* NARA-SWA, RG 21, Box 491, Folder for Case No. 69-B-163. See Trial Brief, filed May 15, 1970, 3–10.

33. Ibid. Also see Defendant's Trial Memorandum, filed June 20, 1970, 7, 17–18. The school district sought to have the case dismissed because Escalante had not exhausted her administrative options before filing the federal case. Garza admitted that recent Fifth Circuit decisions suggested that he should have sent Escalante to negotiate further with the La Feria board of education. However, he decided that this would have been futile; the two other students suspended with Escalante, Ortiz and Trevino, used the administrative channels, but their suspensions remained in full effect. On this ground, Garza denied the district's motion to dismiss the case. See Ibid. Memorandum and Order, August 1, 1970, 5.

34. Ibid. Memorandum and Order, August 1, 1970, 6.

35. The basic fairness of these rulings indicate why the liberal Mexican American leaders, who in 1961 had opposed Garza's appointment to the federal district bench, later lobbied for Garza when President Johnson was considering candidates to fill the Supreme Court seat left vacant by retiring Associate Justice Tom C. Clark. Clark's seat eventually went to Thurgood Marshall. Fisch, *All Rise,* 115–17.

36. Navarro, *Mexican American Youth Organization,* 157–58. In its early years, MALDEF also accepted minor claims of the "legal aid" variety, concerning minor disputes, which did not actually require legal counsel. O'Connor and Epstein suggest that, despite some victories, MALDEF was not an effective constitutional litigator until at least 1973; moreover, even then, it lost more often than it won. O'Connor and Epstein, "A Legal Voice for the Chicano Community," 285.

37. For background on these disputes, see Steven Harmon Wilson, *The Rise of Judicial Management in the U.S. District Court, Southern District of Texas, 1955–2000* (Athens: University of Georgia Press, 2003).

Contributors

ALWYN BARR is professor of history at Texas Tech University and a former chair of the history department. He has written five books including *Black Texans: A History of African Americans in Texas, 1528–1995* (2nd ed., 1996) and *African Texans* (2004). He edited, with Robert A. Calvert, *Black Leaders: Texans for Their Times* (1981) and wrote the introduction to *Black Cowboys of Texas*, edited by Sara R. Massey (2000) as well as several articles on African American history in professional journals. He served as president of the Texas State Historical Association and remains a TSHA fellow, and has also served on the Humanities Texas board. His future writing plans include the expansion into a book of his essay on African American conventions.

BRIAN D. BEHNKEN is visiting assistant professor of history at Texas A&M University. He received his PhD from the University of California–Davis. His dissertation, "Fighting Their Own Battles: Blacks, Mexican Americans, and the Struggle for Civil Rights in Texas," explores the African American and Hispanic civil rights movements within a comparative framework. He is the author of "'Count On Me': Reverend M. L. Price of Texas, a Case Study in Civil Rights Leadership" (*Journal of American Ethnic History*, Fall 2005) and "'The Dallas Way': Protest, Response, and the Civil Rights Experience in Big D and Beyond" (*Southwestern Historical Quarterly*, July 2007), which won the H. Bailey Carroll Award from the Texas State Historical Association.

DAVID K. CHRISMAN is associate professor of history at the University of Mary Hardin–Baylor in Belton, Texas, and serves as chair of the Department of History and Political Science. He taught previously at East Texas Baptist University. Chrisman received his BA and MA from Baylor University, before completing the PhD at Texas A&M University in 2001. His publications have appeared in *The Journal of Southern History, The Register of the Kentucky Historical Society, The Journal of Texas Baptist History,* and *The Journal for the American Studies Association of Texas.* His dissertation, "The Price of Moderation: Texas Baptists and Racial Integration, 1948–1968," explores the strategy of the Baptist General Convention of Texas and its measured support of the civil rights movement in Texas. He is currently editing his dissertation for publication.

PATRICIA E. GOWER is professor of history at University of the Incarnate Word in San Antonio, Texas. She has held the position of chair of the Department of History there since 1997. She received her MA in history from Angelo State University in 1990 and her PhD in history from Texas A&M University in 1996. Her article "Blacks in San Angelo: Relations Between Fort Concho and The City, 1875–1889," *West Texas Historical Association Year Book* (1990) was reprinted in *Slavery to Integration: Black Americans in West Texas,* edited by Bruce A. Glasrud and Paul H. Carlson with Tai D. Kreidler (2008). Gower has also contributed to *El Campanario, The Fort Concho Report, The East Texas Historical Journal, Legacies: Journal of the Dallas Historical Society,* and *The Journal of South Texas.* Along with Tim Draves, she received a Humanities Texas grant to establish an online *Journal of Life and Culture in San Antonio* in 1997 and currently serves as executive editor of the journal that welcomes submissions on all aspects of life in San Antonio, Texas, http://www.uiw.edu/sanantonio/.

GEORGE N. GREEN, after receiving his PhD from Florida State University, joined the history faculty at the University of Texas at Arlington in 1966. He has served as professor of history at UTA since 1981. He is the author of *The Establishment in Texas Politics,* in print since 1979, two urban biographies, *Hurst, Euless & Bedford* (1995) and *The History of North Richland Hills* (1998), over thirty scholarly articles, and various popular essays and booklets. He is writing a history of the labor movement in Texas. He established the Texas Labor and Political Archives at UTA in 1967. He is a fellow of the Texas State Historical Association and served as president of the TSHA during 2003–2004.

DEBRA A. REID is associate professor of history at Eastern Illinois University and visiting associate professor in the College of Agriculture, Consumer and Environmental Sciences at the University of Illinois, and she received her MA from Baylor University in 1996 and her PhD from Texas A&M University in 2000. Her dissertation, the last that Robert A. Calvert chaired, received the Gilbert C. Fite Award from the Agricultural History Society. The book that resulted, *Reaping a Greater Harvest: African Americans, the*

Extension Service and Rural Reform in Jim Crow Texas (2007), won the T. R. Fehrenbach Award from the Texas Historical Commission. Her articles on women, gender, and rural minority history have appeared in *Agricultural History,* the *Bulletin* of the Association for Living History, Farm and Agricultural Museums (ALHFAM), the *Midwest Open Air Museums Magazine, History News,* the *Journal of Urban History,* and in two anthologies, *The Countryside in the Age of the Modern State* (2001) and *Interpreting Historic House Museums* (2002).

JAMES SEYMOUR has been professor of history at Lone Star College–Cy-Fair in Cypress, Texas, since 2003 and has served as the chair of the Department of History since 2005. He received his MA and his PhD from Texas A&M University. His dissertation, "War within a War," explored the effects of World War I on prohibition and woman suffrage in Texas. In 2008, he received the Faculty Excellence Award from Lone Star College–Cy-Fair, which was awarded at the conference of the National Institute for Staff & Organizational Development. He also was named to *Who's Who in America* in 2008. His publications include "Evils More Deadly than the Carnage of the Battlefield: The Fight for Prohibition in McLennan County" in the *East Texas Historical Journal* (January 2002) and "'Arise at Once': The Drive for Prohibition in San Antonio during the First World War" in the *Journal of Life and Culture in San Antonio,* http://www.uiw.edu/sanantonio/seymour.html.

STEVEN HARMON WILSON is associate dean of liberal arts at Tulsa Community College's metro campus. From 2003 to 2006, he was associate professor of history at Prairie View A&M University in Texas. Wilson received his MA and PhD in history from Rice University, where he focused on U.S. legal and constitutional history. He previously earned a BS in Electrical Engineering at Rice, and, before becoming a historian, worked at the National Security Agency and the National Aeronautics and Space Administration. Wilson is the author of *The Rise of Judicial Management in the U.S. District Court, Southern District of Texas, 1955–2000* (2003), "Some Are Born White, Some Achieve Whiteness, and Some Have Whiteness Thrust Upon Them: Mexican Americans and the Politics of Racial Classification in the Federal Judicial Bureaucracy, Twenty-Five Years after *Hernández v. Texas*" (in *"Colored Men" and "Hombres Aquí": Hernández v. Texas and the Emergence of Mexican American Lawyering,* edited by Michael A. Olivas (2006), and "*Brown* Over 'Other White': Mexican Americans' Legal Arguments and Litigation Strategy in Desegregation Litigation" (*Law & History Review,* March 2003).

Index